SURVIVING
EXECUTION

About the author

Ian Woods has worked for Sky News since 1995, including spells as Sports Editor, United States Correspondent, and Australia Correspondent. He is currently a Senior Correspondent reporting both domestic and international news. *Surviving Execution* is his first book.

SURVIVING EXECUTION

IAN WOODS

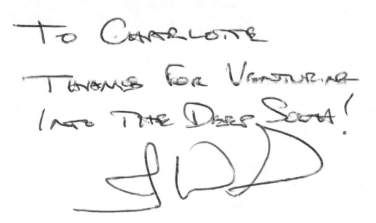

To CHARLOTTE

THANKS FOR VENTURING

INTO THE DEEP SOUTH!

Atlantic Books
London

First published in Great Britain in 2017 by Atlantic Books,
an imprint of Atlantic Books Ltd.

1 2 3 4 5 6 7 8 9

A CIP catalogue record for this book is available from the British
Library.

Paperback ISBN: 978-1-78649-1-862
Trade paperback ISBN: 978-1-78649-1-848
E-book ISBN: 978-1-78649-1-855

Printed in Italy by Grafica Veneta

Atlantic Books
An Imprint of Atlantic Books Ltd
Ormond House
26–27 Boswell Street
London
WC1N 3JZ

www.atlantic-books.co.uk

For my son, Oscar

CONTENTS

WHO'S WHO

Oklahoma 2015–16

Richard Glossip: death-row inmate

Justin Sneed: convicted killer

Kim Van Atta: friend of Glossip

Don Knight: Glossip's attorney

Sister Helen Prejean: anti-death-penalty campaigner

Anita Trammell: warden, Oklahoma State Penitentiary

Mary Fallin: Governor of Oklahoma

Alex Weintz: Governor's spokesman

Scott Pruitt: Oklahoma Attorney General

David Prater: District Attorney, Oklahoma County

Robert Patton: Director, Oklahoma Department of
   Corrections

Terri Watkins: Communications Director, Department of
   Corrections

Phil Cross: Fox 25 reporter

Ralph Shortey: Oklahoma state senator

Mark Henricksen: Glossip attorney

Kathleen Lord: Glossip attorney

Dale Baich: death-penalty attorney

Bud Welch: father of Oklahoma bombing victim

Randall Workman: former prison warden

Donna Van Treese: widow of murder victim

Billie Jo Boyiddle: Glossip's niece

Christina Glossip-Hodge: daughter

Ericka Glossip-Hodge: daughter

Crystal Martinez: friend of Glossip
Susan Sarandon: actress and campaigner
Kim Bellware: reporter, *Huffington Post*
Cary Aspinwall: reporter, *The Frontier*
Ziva Branstetter: reporter, *The Frontier*
Graham Lee Brewer: reporter, *The Oklahoman*
Marc Dreyer: Pardon and Parole Board chairman
Robert Dunham: Death Penalty Information Center

Oklahoma 1997–8
Barry Van Treese: motel owner and murder victim
D-Anna Wood: Glossip's girlfriend
Cliff Everhart: part-time security man at motel
Billye Hooper: motel receptionist
Bob Bemo: detective, Oklahoma City Police
Bill Cook: detective, Oklahoma City Police
Tim Brown: patrol officer, Oklahoma City Police
Fern Smith: Assistant District Attorney
Wayne Fournerat: defence attorney
Richard Freeman: judge
David McKenzie: attorney

Oklahoma 2004
Lynn Burch: Glossip's attorney
Connie Smothermon: Assistant District Attorney
Silas Lyman: Glossip's attorney
Wayne Woodyard: Glossip's attorney
Twyla Mason Gray: judge
Kenneth Van Treese: brother of murder victim

Prologue

30 September 2015

The banging on doors began just before 3 p.m., the time the condemned man was due to die. More than forty inmates on death row joined the noisy protest as they imagined one of their own being strapped to the gurney, an intravenous tube ready to carry the deadly chemicals into his vein. The din echoed around Unit H of Oklahoma State Penitentiary and into Cell LL adjacent to the death chamber.

Richard Glossip was sitting on his solid concrete bunk, naked apart from his boxer shorts, with a thin blanket around his shoulders to keep him warm. He'd been like this for more than an hour, waiting to be taken on what should have been a short walk to his death.

He ought to have been dead by now. Or at least being prepped for death. His fellow inmates thought he was taking his final breaths, and believed they were giving him a fitting send-off. But the banging subsided and Richard Glossip was still alive.

He wanted to know what was happening, but he also longed to be taken outside. Glossip had spent fifty straight days in the isolation cells close to the death chamber. All that time he had been deprived of privacy. The light was kept on twenty-four hours a day, so that a guard could watch his every move. It was deemed necessary in case the prisoner tried to harm himself, or, worse, take his own life before the state had the chance to kill him.

Even for a man who had spent the last eighteen years behind bars, the isolation cell was a particular form of torture. All luxuries had been taken away when he was moved here, depriving him of the music he loved to listen to on his MP3 player. He'd already been here longer than the prison authorities had intended.

Two weeks earlier, he had been woken before dawn and taken for a medical examination. He had bantered with the prison staff about the efforts they were making to ensure he was fit to be executed. But three hours before his appointed time, he was granted a reprieve: a fourteen-day stay of execution while an appeal court examined newly submitted evidence about his case.

Two weeks for his lawyers to fight for his life. Two more weeks for Richard Glossip to endure the permanent illumination of his concrete cell. Two more weeks to con-template what it would be like when the curtains were drawn back and the witnesses to his execution stared at him from behind the glass windows.

I was due to be one of those witnesses, one of six people he had chosen to be with him at the end. On 30 September, we were waiting in another room in the prison, as we had been two weeks earlier. This time it seemed certain the execution was going to proceed. Word had come from Washington DC that the US Supreme Court had refused to intervene. With all appeals exhausted, it could go ahead as planned.

I had accepted the invitation to be a witness months earlier, as a way of telling Richard Glossip's story – that of a man being put to death for a murder committed by someone else. My selection had led to arguments; another witness challenged my right to be there, and at one point I thought Glossip would withdraw the invitation. But he kept me on his list. Why did he want a British journalist to watch him die? I had asked him several times if he was sure; there were precious few choices he could make freely. Choosing who should be present at his death was one. I promised to be there, but only if he thought it would help, only if he wanted me there.

As I watched the clock tick ever closer to the time of his death, I was regretting my decision. But it was too late to walk away. This was a story unlike anything I had experienced in more than three decades as a reporter.

And it wasn't over yet.

CHAPTER 1

The Murder

January 1997

The murder victim was found face down, wearing a T-shirt with the slogan *Jesus Carried the Cross For Us*. Barry Van Treese died in room 102 of the motel he owned, the Best Budget Inn, in Oklahoma City. He had been beaten to death. The murder weapon was never recovered, but his car was found abandoned a short distance away, with tens of thousands of dollars inside.

Television cameramen arrived in time to capture the flashbulbs going off inside the room as the police photographer took pictures of the crime scene. Detectives began to question motel staff and some of the guests. The body had been lying there for around eighteen hours, covered by bedlinen, and the evidence suggested the victim had put up a fight. There was blood all over the floor, walls and door handle, and a bloody handprint on the mattress. The window had been smashed, but there were clear signs of an effort to tidy up. The broken glass had been stacked neatly in a chair, and a shower curtain had been taped over the window so the body could not be seen from outside.

Barry Van Treese was fifty-four years old and owned two motels in Oklahoma City and Tulsa. He lived in Lawton, ninety miles south-west of the state capital, with his wife Donna and their five children aged between five and sixteen. He also had two grown-up children from an earlier marriage. His wife described him as a real-life Santa Claus, whose children loved his bushy white beard and were upset on the one occasion he had shaved it off. He could be gruff, and had a temper, but friends considered him generous.

Van Treese had been a banker for twenty years. He'd completed a master's degree in banking and finance at Southern Methodist University in Dallas, and his last job was as a vice president of Boulder Bank in Tulsa, where he had more than forty staff. In 1979 he decided to set up his own business, and began to purchase motels in the state. At one point he owned and ran nine of them.

He hired managers to look after the businesses, but would visit regularly to collect the money and receipts. If he decided to stay the night in Oklahoma City, he would usually choose room 102 because it was one of the best furnished in an otherwise run-down motel, where rooms cost a little over $20 a night. Room 102 had a water bed. The motel, on the western outskirts of the city, attracted hookers and drug dealers, but it also had some long-term guests. It was busy, except in the winter months, and it made a decent profit. The manager usually picked up a monthly bonus of several hundred dollars on top of his salary.

Richard Glossip had been manager of the Best Budget Inn for almost two years. He was thirty-three years old and lived in an apartment next to the motel reception with his girlfriend, D-Anna Wood, who was in her early twenties. Glossip had never been in trouble with the police. He had no previous convictions. But within a few days of the murder of his boss, he would be in jail accused of plotting to kill him, and the following year he would be found guilty and sentenced to death. He was convicted even though everyone involved in the case agreed he did not physically kill Barry Van Treese.

There are conflicting stories about much of what happened in the twenty-four-hour period around the murder on 7 January 1997. But one key detail is not in dispute. Barry Van Treese was murdered by a nineteen-year-old drifter called Justin Sneed, who lived for free at the motel in exchange for helping with maintenance work. Sneed had gone into room 102 in the middle of the night, and repeatedly bashed the owner on the head with a baseball bat.

The police had Richard Glossip in their sights long before they extracted a confession from Sneed. His behaviour after Van Treese went missing had seemed suspicious. Officers were convinced he had played a part in the murder. At his trial, detectives and state attorneys would describe how and why they believed Richard Glossip had plotted to murder his boss.

The previous year had been a difficult one for the Van Treese family. Two bereavements within a short period of time had hit them hard, and for a while they didn't give the businesses their full attention. The motel managers in Tulsa and Oklahoma City were trusted to deal with any problems. But later in the year, when Donna Van Treese was going through the books of the Best Budget Inn, she became concerned that around six thousand dollars seemed to be missing. The prosecution would allege that Barry Van Treese intended to raise the discrepancy with Richard Glossip, who was already anxious that his boss would discover that many of the motel rooms had fallen into a state of disrepair.

Van Treese had arrived at the Best Budget Inn at around 5.30 p.m. on 6 January. He'd been seen by and spoken to the desk clerk, Billye Hooper, who was waiting for his arrival so she could get paid. She would recall that Barry had an abrupt manner but was not necessarily rude; he just got on with what he needed to do. He picked up the motel receipts and said he was going to his other motel in Tulsa, which was around a two-hour drive away.

When he got there, Van Treese told the manager of the Tulsa motel that he was unhappy about the way Glossip had been running things, and said he planned to fire him. He then drove back to the Best Budget Inn, arriving at around 2 a.m., and went to sleep in room 102.

The state's evidence for what happened next comes from the killer. Justin Sneed was said to be totally reliant on Richard Glossip for providing him with a room to stay in and food to eat. According to Sneed, Glossip came to his room at 3 a.m. and said he was worried that they were both about to lose their jobs and be forced to leave the motel. He asked Sneed to murder Van Treese, and promised to pay him several thousand dollars.

Sneed picked up a baseball bat he kept in his room and went to room 102. He opened the door using a master key he'd been given by Glossip. Van Treese woke up, but Sneed hit him with the bat. Even so, the owner tried to fight back, and in the struggle, the bat smashed a window and Sneed received a black eye. But the teenager continued to hit Van Treese more than a dozen times until he stopped moving. He claimed that he then went to the motel office and told Glossip what he'd done. They both went to room 102 to check their boss was dead. Sneed said he was told to take car keys from Van Treese's pocket, to collect money that was in the vehicle and then drive the car away from the motel to a nearby parking lot.

Sneed said he found four thousand dollars in the car, and returned to Glossip, who divided the money between them. Sneed tidied up the broken glass and taped a shower curtain over the window. He claimed Glossip told him that if anyone asked, he should say that two drunks got into a fight and smashed the window. He was told that when it was daylight he should buy Plexiglas to repair the window, and a hacksaw and trash bags to dispose of the body.

When Billye Hooper arrived for work, she was surprised to see Glossip awake so early. She noticed that Van Treese's car wasn't there and she said Glossip told her that the owner had gone to get some supplies for redecorating the rooms. A few hours later, Glossip and his girlfriend, D-Anna, went shopping.

After lunch, Hooper took a phone call from a neighbouring business to say that Barry Van Treese's car had been abandoned in their parking lot. The police were notified, as was Donna Van Treese, who was concerned that she hadn't heard from her husband. Hooper also called Cliff Everhart, an ex-cop who looked after security at the motel and who claimed to own a small stake in the business. When Glossip and his girlfriend returned from shopping, they drove around the neighbourhood with Everhart looking for any sign of Van Treese.

Justin Sneed had been seen around the motel for much of the day, and had been asked by Hooper and Everhart to search the motel rooms. By mid afternoon he had disappeared, and Sergeant Tim Brown, a local patrol officer who knew both Glossip and Everhart, was getting suspicious about what appeared to be conflicting details in Glossip's story.

Eventually, at around 10 p.m., Brown and Everhart decided to check room 102 themselves. They'd been told earlier that the window had been broken by drunks so hadn't connected it to Van Treese's disappearance. They forced open the door and found the body on the floor.

Glossip and D-Anna Wood were taken to the police station, but after being interrogated, they were allowed to leave. The following day, Glossip began selling some of his possessions and appeared to be getting ready to quit his job. After going to see a local lawyer, he was arrested, interrogated and then charged with being an accessory to murder.

A week later, after Justin Sneed was arrested and questioned, both men were charged with murder in the first degree. It was a charge that carried the death penalty, but only one of them would face execution. Justin Sneed agreed to testify against his co-accused and in return would be given a sentence of life in jail without the possibility of parole. Richard Glossip was offered a similar deal if he pleaded guilty to murder. He refused, even though he was putting his life in the hands of a jury. If convicted, he would join more than two thousand men and women whom American courts had decided were the worst of the worst and deserved to die.

CHAPTER 2

The Worst of the Worst

December 2014

The execution business in America was facing a crisis. A decline in public support, a fall in the number of sentences being imposed and carried out, and a series of mishaps in death chambers had led to predictions that capital punishment was doomed. But killing convicts has always been controversial.

On 6 August 1890, a new invention made its debut in New York that was supposed to replace hanging and bring the execution business into the modern world. William Kemmler became the first person to die in the electric chair, but many of those who witnessed his death were horrified. The *New York Times* report, under the headline 'FAR WORSE THAN HANGING', described it as an 'awful spectacle' and a 'disgrace to civilisation'.

Kemmler, who had killed his common-law wife with an axe, seemed amenable to taking his place in the history books. 'Gentlemen, I wish you all good luck. I believe I am going to a good place, and I am ready to go.' He sat down on the chair and allowed the electrodes to be attached to his body. 'Now take your time and do it all right, warden.

There is no rush. I don't want to take any chances on this thing you know.'

But the first burst of electricity, which lasted seventeen seconds, did not kill Kemmler, and a second attempt was made. This time the current was left on for more than a minute. A reporter fainted and the District Attorney groaned and rushed out of the room. The *New York Times* reported that 'the stench was unbearable'. The reporter speculated that it was likely to be the first and last such execution.

However, the electric chair soon became established as America's primary method of capital punishment, and was used for more than a century. All executions in America were temporarily halted for a decade until the US Supreme Court upheld its use in 1976. A database maintained by the Washington-based Death Penalty Information Center records 158 executions by electrocution since then. The most recent was in Virginia in 2013. Convicted killer Robert Gleason had requested the electric chair. The *Herald Courier* reported how he died:

> One man turned a key in a wall to activate the system and another man in an adjacent room started the electrocution. Gleason's body spasmed with each series of jolts, smoke rising from the mask. The jolts were administered at 9:03, and after five long minutes of silence a doctor in a white coat entered from a side room, put a stethoscope to his tattooed chest and then nodded that he was dead.

During the 1920s, many states adopted the use of cyanide gas. On the first occasion, prison officials tried and failed to kill inmate Gee John by pumping the gas into his cell while he slept. Only when it seeped out did they decide that a proper gas chamber was needed. And even when they succeeded at the second attempt, the area near the chamber was evacuated because there were concerns that gas was leaking.

Eleven men have been put to death using gas since 1976. The last time it was used was in Arizona in 1999. Walter LaGrand was given the option of death by gas or lethal injection. His half-brother Karl, who had also been convicted of the murder of a bank manager during a robbery, had chosen to die by injection a week earlier. The *Tuscon Citizen* reported that

> Cyanide pellets were dropped into the acid below the chair. The witness room fell silent as a mist of gas rose, much like steam in a shower, and Walter LaGrand became enveloped in a cloud of cyanide vapor. He began coughing violently — three or four loud hacks – and then, in what appeared to be his last moments of consciousness, he made a gagging sound before falling forward at about 9:15 p.m. The method of death is comparable to having a heart attack, according to prison officials.

Death by hanging, the approved method of execution in Britain throughout the twentieth century until abolition in the 1960s, was much less common in the United States. And since 1976, only three men have died on the gallows. The last was in Delaware in 1996, and was described by a reporter from the Associated Press.

> Billy Bailey, the 49-year-old murderer of an elderly couple, climbed onto a wooden gallows and was hanged early Thursday, becoming only the third convict in the nation to be executed this way in 30 years.
>
> Bailey closed his eyes, sniffled and said nothing before the black hood was placed over his head. His body twisted quickly in the wind once the trapdoor was sprung, then turned slowly beneath the 15-foot-high platform in the cold night air. He was pronounced dead 11 minutes later.

For a nation that loves guns, the United States has been surprisingly unenthusiastic about using them in executions. It remains an option in two states, but in modern times only three men have died by firing squad, all of them in Utah. Gary Gilmore, the first person to be executed after the reinstatement of the death penalty in 1976, chose this method, as did Ronnie Lee Gardner, the last prisoner to die in a hail of bullets, in 2010. According to the *Deseret News*:

> A black hood was placed over Gardner's head, and less than a minute later, five guns made two

booming sounds in quick succession. Gardner was strapped to a chair at six different places on his body: forehead, shoulders, chest, waist, wrists and ankles. On each side of the chair were 13 sandbags, nine of them stacked on top of each other. Behind the chair was a wood panel painted black.

After the shots were fired, Gardner's left hand clinched into a fist. The fist eased a little and his thumb stroked his forefingers again. Gardner's arm and hand continued to move for about two minutes, leaving some media members to wonder for a brief moment if he would have to be shot again.

The death by firing squad of Gary Gilmore in 1977 prompted a debate about what was the most humane method of execution. In Oklahoma, the state's medical examiner was asked to devise an alternative, because there was a feeling that animals were being put to death more humanely than humans. Within a few days, Dr Jay Chapman came up with the idea of using three drugs, an anaesthetic, a paralytic and a drug to stop the heart. His suggestion was adopted, although he has never been keen on his title, 'the father of lethal injection'.

'Chapman's protocol' was later copied across the country, but it was Texas that first put it into practice. On 7 December 1982, Charles Brooks Jr was put to death in Huntsville. The *New York Times* reported that 'The witnesses, all of whom

appeared shaken by the experience, indicated that Mr
Brooks's death did not appear to be painless.' Dick Reavis,
a reporter for *Texas Monthly*, wrote:

> He turned his head upward and yawned, then
> wheezed, and that was all, but another witness
> said Mr Brooks gasped and moved his stomach.
> The use of lethal injection has been widely
> urged as a 'humane' way of carrying out the
> death sentence. However, many physicians have
> protested that it is a violation of medical ethics
> to use drugs meant to save lives in order to
> end lives.

That issue has not gone away, but it didn't stop lethal injection
becoming established as by far the most common method
used to carry out the death sentence.

Brooks was the first prisoner executed in Texas since
1964, but the state quickly became the nation's leader in
capital punishment. In the thirty years since Brooks died,
more than five hundred inmates have been put to death,
all by lethal injection. The national total is now more than
fourteen hundred.

For a time, executions became almost routine. Every
year between the mid 1990s and 2007 there were at least 42
deaths across the United States, and in one year there were
as many as 98. But by 2015, the number of people put to
death had fallen to 28. The biggest factor in that decline has
been controversy surrounding the lethal injection process,

mostly because prisons have been finding it more and more difficult to obtain the required drugs.

Because death-penalty abolitionists had failed to get American courts to ban the practice, they began to look at an alternative line of attack, alerting international pharmaceutical companies that their drugs were being used in executions. Later they persuaded the European Union to impose strict export bans to stop drugs being sold to American prisons.

It's easy to understand why EU politicians would want nothing to do with the execution business; most democratic European nations abandoned the practice decades ago. The United Kingdom carried out its last hanging in 1964, and countries such as Italy, Belgium, the Netherlands and Norway stopped executions more than a decade earlier. East Germany, together with other Warsaw Pact nations, including Poland and Romania, were still putting people to death in the 1980s.

The last execution in western Europe was carried out in France as recently as 1977, and the method hadn't changed since the French Revolution. Hamida Djandoubi, a Tunisian immigrant, became the last victim of the guillotine, in a Marseilles prison. Many countries have not only abolished capital punishment, they have changed their constitutions so it cannot be easily restored.

The British-based human rights group Reprieve has led the way in lobbying pharmaceutical companies that either knowingly or unwittingly provide the drugs used in lethal injections. According to their director, Maya Foa, 'What we have seen is the debunking of the "humane" lethal injection.

Whilst these other methods look more barbaric, the lethal injection remains an incredibly cruel way to execute someone and it's really important that the American public and the public at large has been able to see that this was just a disguise. It was masking what was happening when you put someone to death.'

In 2011, the American firm Hospira took decisive action when it realised that one of its drugs, sodium thiopental, was being used as the first-stage anaesthetic. It simply stopped making it. Executives discussed other options, but decided that they couldn't guarantee that the drug, which was made at the company's plant in Italy, wouldn't find its way into prisons. They issued a statement withdrawing it from sale: 'We cannot take the risk that we will be held liable by the Italian authorities if the product is diverted for use in capital punishment. Exposing our employees or facilities to liability is not a risk we are prepared to take.'

With sodium thiopental no longer available, the prison authorities turned to pentobarbital, a drug used to treat epilepsy, made by the Danish company Lundbeck. When Lundbeck found out how the drug was being used, it imposed restrictions on its distribution.

The company's spokesman, Anders Scholl, explained to me how it had become embroiled in the death penalty debate. A Danish journalist had read a story in the *New York Times* that said Lundbeck's drug was now being used in executions. 'We had never provided pentobarbital on purpose for prisons so of course it was quite a shock. We are a company conducting research to save people's lives with severe brain diseases, so this was, from our view, the complete opposite.'

They responded initially by writing letters to the prisons asking them to stop misusing their product. When the letters went unanswered, they discussed withdrawing the drug from the market, just as Hospira had done with sodium thiopental. But that would have had an impact on patients who needed the drug. As Scholl said, 'Pentobarbital is used for people with severe epilepsy. It's a kind of sedative compound. You even have children suffering from severe epilepsy and they could potentially die if they couldn't get hold of the medication.'

So five months after they were first told of the misuse, Lundbeck executives restricted distribution. Purchasers had to sign written guarantees that they would not redistribute the drug. But the company found it deeply frustrating that prisons had simply ignored their requests. 'You have other situations where you have misuse of medication, when people use it for doping, and if that's the case you can work with authorities to try to stop it. But in this case it was actually the authorities who were doing the misuse. Other companies have contacted us because they have ended up in the same situation and we could tell them our story. And I know those companies have implemented the same system as us.'

Faced with another supply network being closed off, several states turned to compounding pharmacies to try to replicate the restricted drugs. Others looked for an alternative anaesthetic, and chose midazolam. But critics say it isn't strong enough to prevent prisoners feeling pain when the next two drugs are administered.

Robert Dunham, the executive director of the Death Penalty Information Center, says that even in executions that have apparently passed off without incident, it doesn't mean that inmates weren't feeling pain, because the paralytic drug prevents signs of pain being seen. But in some cases, the problems have been obvious.

'You've got inmates who are conscious, you've got inmates who are gasping. One description is that an inmate was flopping around like a fish against the restraints. That's someone who is clearly experiencing high levels of pain, and we know that the lethal drug is akin to being burned from the inside out. So that's someone who is experiencing a torturous and painful death. That's clearly improper. That's something all people of good faith and good conscience want to stop, and midazolam runs the risk that that's going to happen.'

The most infamous example of an execution involving midazolam was that of Clayton Lockett, in Oklahoma in April 2014. It marked a watershed moment in the history of Oklahoma executions. It wasn't just the length of time he took to die – forty minutes from the first injection to being declared dead – but the manner of his death was anything but humane and dignified. It led to international headlines and prompted President Obama to express concern, despite his qualified support for the death penalty.

Clayton Lockett was not a man who should have expected public sympathy. He had shot, but not killed, a nineteen-year-old woman who had witnessed her friends being attacked and raped. When his shotgun jammed, he and an accomplice buried her alive in a shallow grave.

There had been legal wrangling and several delays before his execution date. One of the reasons for it being postponed was that the Department of Corrections had been having great difficulty in procuring drugs. With its supply of sodium thiopental having been cut off, it followed Florida in deciding to use midazolam, which was readily available. A legal challenge delayed the execution by another week, so Oklahoma decided to schedule two executions on the same night, 29 April 2014.

Lockett was not willing to cooperate in his own death, and had resisted prison guards throughout his last day. Early in the morning he had refused to leave his cell for a mandatory medical examination prior to his execution. Staff tasered him when he resisted. A razor blade was found in his cell, and he had self-inflicted cuts to his arms.

Just under twelve hours later, he was strapped to the gurney in the death chamber, forty minutes before his scheduled execution at 6 p.m. A paramedic and a doctor were there to oversee it. The paramedic was having problems finding a suitable vein in Lockett's arms or legs to insert a needle. She tried and failed several times, and had to ask the doctor for help. After considering the jugular, they finally opted for the femoral vein in his groin. The needle they used was too short, but they didn't have a longer one so made do. A sheet was draped over Lockett, hiding where the intravenous drip had been inserted.

They were now running twenty minutes late, but the blinds in the viewing room were finally opened so that official witnesses and reporters could see the execution. Lockett had no final words, so Warden Anita Trammell simply announced, 'Let the execution begin.' In a neighbouring room, the plunger was pushed on the syringe of midazolam, and the drug began to flow through a tube into Lockett's body.

One of those watching was Katie Fretland, an American reporter who was writing for the British newspaper the *Guardian*.

> The restrained prisoner blinked and pursed his lips. At first he looked straight ahead, but after four minutes, he turned towards the witness area. By 6.30 p.m., his eyes were closed and his mouth slightly open, but when an official stood over him to check, it was clear something was wrong. 'Mr Lockett is not unconscious,' Trammell said.
>
> At 6.33 p.m., Lockett was checked again and declared to be sedated. But then, during the following minutes, Lockett lurched forward against his restraints, writhing and attempting to speak. He strained and struggled violently, his body twisting, and his head reaching up from the gurney. Sixteen minutes after the execution began, Lockett said, 'Man.'

Something was terribly wrong. The blinds were closed, preventing the reporters and witnesses seeing what happened next. But the full details were later revealed in the official report into the botched execution. Even though the two remaining drugs had been administered, Lockett's heart was still beating. When the warden pulled back the sheet, there was blood visible around Lockett's groin, and the area where the IV had been inserted was swollen. As the doctor tried to push the needle in further, blood squirted over him.

There was a brief discussion about whether to try to resuscitate the prisoner. Officials tried to ascertain whether he had been given enough of the lethal drug to kill him. Finally a decision was made to halt the execution. But ten minutes later he died anyway. At first it was thought, and reported, that he had died of a heart attack, but an autopsy revealed that enough of the lethal injection had finally made its way into his system and killed him.

The second execution that was due to be held that evening was postponed while officials tried to work out what had gone wrong.

The official report blamed the problems with inserting the IV line rather than the use of midazolam, which allowed the Oklahoma authorities to insist that it was a suitable anaesthetic. But there had been other adverse incidents when the drug was used, leading to criticism that it was ineffective at putting prisoners into a deep coma-like sleep.

Three months before the Lockett fiasco, Ohio took twenty-six minutes to execute Dennis McGuire using midazolam and hydromorphone, a combination that had never been used before. McGuire's spiritual adviser, Fr Lawrence Hummer, wrote an account of what he witnessed for the *Guardian*:

> At 10.30 a.m., three minutes into the execution, he lifted his head off the gurney, and said to the family who he could see through the window: 'I love you, I love you.' Then he lay back down. At about 10.31 a.m., his stomach swelled up in an unusual way, as though he had a hernia or something like that. Between 10.33 a.m. and 10.44 a.m. – I could see a clock on the wall of the death house – he struggled and gasped audibly for air.
>
> I was aghast. Over those 11 minutes or more he was fighting for breath, and I could see both of his fists were clenched the entire time. His gasps could be heard through the glass wall that separated us. Towards the end, the gasping faded into small puffs of his mouth. It was much like a fish lying along the shore puffing for that one gasp of air that would allow it to breathe. Time dragged on and I was helpless to do anything, sitting helplessly by as he struggled for breath. I desperately wanted out of that room.

McGuire, who had raped and killed his former girlfriend and her unborn child, was pronounced dead at 10.53. Another inmate who would attract little sympathy from the public because of the nature of his crimes was now being characterised as the victim of a cruel death because of the manner in which he was executed.

In July of 2014, there was an even more prolonged execution involving midazolam and hydromorphone. Joseph Wood took two hours to die, in what was described as the longest execution in American history. He was injected fifteen times. His attorney Dale Baich told me that Wood had read newspaper reports of what had happened in previous executions involving midazolam, and was worried. 'About three minutes after the process started, the physician/executioner came into the room and performed a consciousness check, and an announcement was made that the inmate was sedated. After that I noticed colour leaving Joe's face, turning to ash and then white.'

Thirteen minutes after the execution began, Baich says that Wood took a very deep breath and yawned. 'He was gasping and moving up against the straps that were restraining him. Two minutes later he did the same thing. That continued for the next hour and forty minutes. Usually the prisoner dies within ten to twenty minutes, and to see a person gasping and gulping for an hour and forty minutes was very disturbing.'

Another of Wood's attorneys, Robin Konrad, became so concerned that she phoned a federal judge asking him to intervene, but he feared that could do more harm than waiting for Wood to die. The execution became so notorious that CBS's *60 Minutes* broadcast a lengthy investigation, in which Arizona's Attorney General, Mark Brnovich, defended the length of time taken: 'I think two hours, three hours, four hours, when someone's on the death gurney and they're unconscious, I don't think they're worried about the time. In this instance it happened to take longer but that does not mean that it was botched.'

Dale Baich says he doesn't know whether Wood was experiencing pain or suffering, but he believes midazolam does not render a person unconscious.

Four years before turning to midazolam, Arizona had tried to purchase sodium thiopental from an unusual source. When the pressure group Reprieve found the name and address of the supplier in state documents, they investigated. The company, Dream Pharma, turned out to be operating out of an office within a driving school in west London. The drugs it supplied were used in two Arizona executions despite being illegally imported.

Bob Dunham from the Death Penalty Information Center told me, 'The market has opted out of the death penalty. It is now something that businesses do not want to be associated with for a variety of reasons. American pharmaceutical companies want to be servants of medicine, and that means keeping people alive. So they've either taken the drugs off the market in some instances, or they have issued edicts saying that they will not sell these supplies to prisons without assurances that they won't be used for executions. That meant that the main suppliers for the States were unavailable, so they looked abroad. But there's a problem there too, because if there's one thing that's clear in Europe, it's that the death penalty is a violation of human rights.'

With lethal injection proving to be so troublesome, some states have looked at returning to the firing squad, or in the case of Oklahoma, a new method. In 2015, the state voted in favour of using nitrogen gas, though legislators didn't specify whether it would be administered via a mask over the face or pumped into a sealed chamber. Having never been used in the United States, it would undoubtedly face lengthy legal challenges, but Oklahoma lawmakers wanted it to be available if lethal injection became impossible.

Bob Dunham says it is a flawed argument. 'I believe that the Oklahoma legislators think nitrogen gas will be swift and relatively painless. I do not think they were intending to create an alternative method of execution that was torturous. The problem is, they are engaging in human experimentation. The American Veterinary Medical Association says that nitrogen gas is not suitable for euthanising large mammals, which is what human beings are. It's not suitable for dogs and cats, who become aware that they are being asphyxiated before they lose consciousness. The association says you're going to need an extended administration of nitrogen gas to kill those animals because of panic and adverse reaction and they recommend it can be used only if the animal is sedated first. And that brings you back to the supply issue for the lethal injection process.'

So what is the alternative? When *60 Minutes* investigated the Joe Wood execution, they interviewed an Arizona appeal court judge who was opposed to lethal injection, but for very different reasons to the abolitionists. Alex Kozinski told the programme, 'Make it look like an execution.

Mutilate the body. And this would express the sense of that's what you're doing, that we're actually committing violence on another human being.'

He wanted a return to the firing squad. Or importing the guillotine, because, he said, that never fails. Wasn't that a barbaric idea?

'The death penalty is barbaric. And I think we as a society need to come face to face with that. If we're not willing to face up to the cruelty, we ought not to be doing it.'

Many campaigners argue that if executions were televised, a majority of the public would be so revolted that the practice would be banned. Bob Dunham believes attitudes are already changing.

'The folks in the United States who are most opposed are the youngest, people who are under thirty years of age. Support for the death penalty is also the lowest among African Americans and Latinos. As the United States continues to mature as a society, it's becoming more and more racially integrated, more culturally integrated, and those are the type of people who are opposed to the death penalty. Support is from a smaller and smaller set of groups who are getting older and older. It's looking as though the death penalty is your grandfather's punishment, not the punishment that the country is looking forward to in the future.'

But for the present, capital punishment remains legal in thirty-one out of the fifty American states, although only eight of those have carried out executions in the past three years. Until 2014, Oklahoma had been second only to Texas in the number of prisoners executed.

Abolitionists felt they were making progress in their campaign. What they needed was a case that would attract public sympathy, where the inmate's guilt was still in dispute and the death sentence seemed excessive. Eighteen years after he was accused of murder, Richard Glossip was about to become famous.

CHAPTER 3

The Interrogations

January 1997

With no physical evidence to tie Richard Glossip to the murder of Barry Van Treese, his interviews with police officers and the subsequent interrogation of Justin Sneed explain why he was charged with murder. The interviews with both men were recorded on camera, but only those with Glossip were ever shown in court.

Glossip's first interview began at 3.15 a.m., five hours after Van Treese's body had been found. He was questioned by Oklahoma City Police detectives Bob Bemo and Bill Cook; their subsequent report recorded that he appeared very nervous and on edge. The detectives read him his rights and asked him if he was happy to talk to them even though he didn't have a lawyer present. He said he was.

He told them how Van Treese had been at the hotel the previous evening, but said that after he left to go to Tulsa, he didn't see him again. He said he and D-Anna went to bed around 3 a.m. Around 5 there was a knock on their door and Justin Sneed was standing there. According to Glossip: 'He told me there was a couple of drunks that got wild and out of hand and they broke the glass in 102. So I told him, I said … well clean it up and the first thing in the morning put a piece of Plexiglas in there.'

Glossip said he had noticed that Sneed had a bruise on his face. The teenager said he'd hit his face on a soap holder in the shower. Glossip was talking freely, with little prompting from the police officers. He described how he had been suspicious when he saw the bruise. He volunteered the information that a few months earlier, Sneed had suggested a scam in which he would steal money from the motel and Glossip would allow him to get away with it by blaming someone else.

'I swear to you I had nothing to do with this shit,' he told detectives. 'I was at home in bed with my girlfriend, you can ask her, and when he knocked on the door I was as surprised as anybody. What was he doing out at five o'clock?'

Glossip said Sneed had been 'hanging around a lot of bad people', and he said Sneed would have been aware that Van Treese visited the motel regularly to collect the cash handed over by paying guests.

After a quick break in the interview, the detectives returned and began to put pressure on Glossip, picking up discrepancies in his story.

> Detective: We're going to get Justin … and if he brings your name up in this thing, we come back and you're going down for first degree murder, buddy, do you understand what I'm saying?

Glossip: Yes, sir, I wish you would find him 'cause I
swear to God I did not do none of this.

Detective: Well I'm going to tell you right now. The
first one that comes forward is the one that's going
to be helping himself. If you didn't do the actual
deed, buddy, then you don't have anything to worry
about.

Glossip: I told you, and this is the God's honest truth,
I had a hunch that Justin did it and that's as far as it
went. I do not know.

However, this wasn't the truth. Glossip had known Barry
Van Treese was dead because Sneed had told him he had
killed him. And Glossip had failed to alert the police, Donna
Van Treese or the other motel staff. It was a lie that was to
cost him his liberty and might ultimately cost him his life.

The interrogation continued, with Glossip insisting he
did not need to rob his boss because he'd always earned
his own money since he was a kid.

Detective: Well we don't want to put the wrong person
in jail.

Glossip: Thank you and I don't want you to put me in
jail because I am the wrong person.

Detective: I don't know exactly what happened, but I
think Justin's involved. You may be involved or you
may not be involved. If he puts you back in this,
you've got some serious problems.

Glossip: Then we'll go to court.

Detective: You betcha you will go to court.

Glossip: I know I will and I'll be fighting hard because I'm not in this, man. I'm really not in this.

Despite the officers' suspicions, Glossip was told he was free to go. He and D-Anna Wood, who'd been interviewed separately, went back to the motel. The following day, the two of them went to see a local attorney called David McKenzie, to seek advice about the situation. The lawyer reassured him, because he didn't believe Glossip was potentially facing a murder charge.

McKenzie recalls, '[Glossip] told me that the Oklahoma City Police homicide division was really putting the heat on him, threatening to arrest him if he didn't cooperate with their investigation. I explained to him that he was under no obligation to cooperate with them. He had agreed to take a polygraph exam and they were expecting him at 11 a.m. or noon, not long after our discussion. I advised him you don't have to take that.'

Glossip didn't pay the lawyer any money to retain his services, but McKenzie phoned the homicide department on his behalf and told them that he had Glossip in his office and he wasn't going to take the polygraph. He gave Glossip his business card and wrote on the back the words he needed to say to police if they contacted him again: 'I will not cooperate with you under any circumstances. I demand to be provided with counsel for any further questioning.' McKenzie says it was 'an unequivocal invocation of his right not to incriminate himself'.

But the lawyer didn't hear from him again until weeks later. As Glossip left the office, he was surrounded by several police officers, at least one of whom pointed a gun at him. McKenzie's office was on an upper floor of the building, and he didn't see what was happening. He only found out about the arrest from a newspaper report some days later.

Glossip says the police took McKenzie's card from him when he got to the police station. He told them about having an attorney, but he says Detective Bemo said, 'Well, we're going to book you in and arrest you now, because you can't talk to us now you have an attorney.'

Glossip says Bemo then told him he wouldn't be arrested if he just talked to them and told them what had happened, and agreed to take a polygraph. 'I believed him and trusted him,' he recalled. After taking the lie detector test, he was informed that he had failed it, though it was never submitted as evidence at trial. For the second time in twelve hours he was read his rights and questioned without an attorney present. The interview was again recorded on video. This time, right from the outset, his story changed and he told the officers, 'I know I should never have lied. You see my record, I've never been in trouble, man.'

The detectives again took him through the events leading up to Barry Van Treese's disappearance. Glossip repeated that Van Treese had left the motel to go to Tulsa and he wasn't aware that his boss had returned sometime during the night. Then he got to the part where Sneed knocked on his bedroom door.

Glossip: I knew something was wrong because I seen
his face and he was just rattled … he couldn't look
me in the face or nothing. And then he told me
what he did.

Detective: What did he tell you?

Glossip: He told me that he killed Barry.

The detectives asked him to describe what Sneed was
wearing and whether he was covered in blood. Glossip said
he wasn't. They asked about a motive.

Glossip: He thought Barry was going to throw him out
in the street. He said he got nowhere to go. But I
don't believe that was the only thing it was … I was
scared at that point, big time, 'cause I did not know
that Justin was going to do it and I couldn't believe
that he actually did it.

Detective: So what did you do then?

Glossip: That's when I told him to clean, to clean up
the glass. 'Cause I didn't want to touch nothing,
'cause I didn't want my prints on a damn thing.

But Glossip admitted that he had gone with Sneed to the
exterior of the room, and briefly held the Plexiglas over
the broken window.

Glossip: I asked him why he did it, I do remember
that. I said why did you do it? And I'm trying to
remember exactly what he said. Part of it was

> he thought Barry was going to throw him out.
> He didn't want Barry to see the rooms. He said
> something else but I can't remember what it was.
> He was mumbling so much ...

Detective: You didn't go inside the room?

Glossip: No.

Detective: Did you ever see Barry's body in the room
at all?

Glossip: No I did not, I swear.

Detective: But you knew it was in there.

Glossip: I had ... yeah, pretty much.

Detective: You knew it was in there, that's why you told
him to put the glass in.

Glossip: Well I was just covering the window, but yeah
I did. I didn't go in to make sure, but yeah I did.

This confession made Richard Glossip, at the very least, an accessory after the fact in the murder of Barry Van Treese. But he continued to deny any involvement in the murder itself. Officers Bemo and Cook asked him why he hadn't told them this the day before. Glossip said he was scared. He denied he was trying to cover up for Sneed, and said it was to protect his girlfriend, D-Anna. He didn't want her to get in trouble.

The detectives asked him what would happen when they arrested Sneed and he gave them a different version of events.

> Glossip: I don't know. I'm going to testify against
> Justin because that's wrong. I didn't have nothing

to do with Barry's death. Justin did it. I mean, I
guess I did. I covered it up.
Detective: Well I believe that ... you didn't have
anything to do with the actual murder.
Glossip: No I didn't and I didn't know it was taking
place either.

After a few more minutes the interrogation was brought to
a close, and they told Glossip he was going to have to spend
the night in jail. He protested and said he wasn't going to
run. But on 9 January 1997, Richard Glossip was locked up
in a cell. He has been a prisoner ever since.

The following day, a short piece appeared in the pages
of *The Oklahoman* newspaper.

> A southwest Oklahoma City motel manager was
> arrested Thursday as a co-conspirator in the
> beating death of the motel's owner. Oklahoma
> City Police said Barry Alan Van Treese, 53,
> of Lawton was found beaten to death Tuesday
> in room 102 of the motel he owned, the Best
> Budget Inn, 301 S. Council Road.
>
> Richard Eugene Glossip, 32, was arrested after
> a lengthy interview with detectives Thursday,
> police spokesman Sgt Roger Wagnon said. Glossip
> was in the Oklahoma City Jail on Thursday
> night. Wagnon said Glossip is considered a
> co-conspirator in the beating death but he may
> not be the killer.

It would be another five days before the killer was arrested, pushing Richard Glossip even deeper into trouble.

Justin Sneed hadn't run far. Despite having a couple of thousand dollars in his pocket, he didn't head for his childhood home in Texas. Instead he travelled just a few miles to hook up with some former workmates who were repairing roofs. But it still took the police a week to track him down and arrest him.

On 14 January, Detectives Bemo and Cook got their first chance to question him about the murder. Just as when they interviewed Richard Glossip, there was no lawyer present. But before they started asking him questions, Bemo told Sneed what they thought they knew about the murder.

Detective: The thing about it is, Justin, we think ... we know that this involves more than just you, okay? We've got witnesses and we've got other people and we most likely have physical evidence ... And right now the best thing you can do is to just be straightforward with us about this thing and talk to us about it and tell us what happened and who all was involved, because I personally don't think you were the only one.

Everybody that we talked to, they're putting it on you, okay? They're putting the whole thing on you and they're going to leave you holding the bag. In other words, if you just said you don't want to talk to us and you want to talk to an attorney we would march you down to the jail and we would book you in for this charge, and you would be facing this thing on your own. And I don't think it's just you.

I think there are more people involved and you can straighten out a lot of things. And I just don't think you should take the whole thing.

The detectives didn't just want a confession from Sneed; with Glossip already arrested and charged with being an accessory to murder, they needed Sneed to provide corroboration of his involvement too. They steered the conversation to how Sneed began working at the motel, and asked him the name of the motel manager.

Sneed: Rich. I don't really know his last name.
Detective: Okay, would you know it if you heard it?
Sneed: I think it starts with a G.
Detective: Glossip?
Sneed: Yeah, I think that kind of sounds right. I knew
it was some weird name.

The interrogation continued with more questions about working for the roofing team, and then how Sneed came to stay at the motel for free in return for helping with maintenance work. He told them he got along pretty well with the manager.

Bemo then asked him about the murder. Sneed said he didn't know what to say.

Detective: Well let me tell you, there's a lot of people,
   you know, when something like this happens,
   everybody tries to save themselves. Everybody wants
   to make themselves look as good as they can …
   Well they've made you the scapegoat in this. You
   know everybody is saying you're the one that did
   this and you did it by yourself and I don't believe
   that. You know Rich is under arrest, don't you?
Sneed: No I didn't know that.
Detective: Yeah, he's under arrest too.
Sneed: Okay.
Detective: So he's the one – he's putting it on you the
   worst. Now I think there's more to this than you
   being by yourself, and I would like for you to tell
   me how this got started and what happened.

Sneed said little, but denied killing Van Treese. The
detectives persisted.

Detective: Okay, now we're not – we're not bad
   people. We're not trying to bully you or pressure
   you, but we're telling you this, this is not going to
   get it. You're going to have to get straight with us,
   you're going to have to get straight with yourself
   and mainly you have to get it straight with the
   Almighty. But you need to do that now.

Sneed didn't respond, so the officers began to express
sympathy that he had to work for free at the motel and

comment how he was 'probably starving to death'. They said that whatever he told them, they would take it to the District Attorney and tell them he had cooperated. Finally they got a breakthrough in the interrogation.

Detective Cook: Is it all your idea, the whole thing?
Sneed: No, sir.
Detective Cook: Well okay, tell me.
Detective Bemo: You need to tell us about it.
Sneed: Okay. Rich told me that he would split the money we could get out of Barry. I think that's – his name was Barry.
Detective Cook: Right.
Sneed: That's what I was told his name was anyway. And he come and woke me up like at three o'clock in the morning and told me that Barry had just got there. And that – he told me that he knew where the money was and that he was sitting on like $7,000. And so we went into the room.

The detectives tried to ascertain whether both men had gone into the room, but Sneed said, 'I just went in', opening the door with a set of master keys that he used while working at the motel. He found Van Treese asleep.

Sneed: And then I just really meant just to knock him out, you know.
Detective: Did you hit him with something?
Sneed: Yes.

Detective: What?
Sneed: A baseball bat.

What Sneed was describing was a plot not to kill the owner, but to rob him. He told the officers he'd found the bat in a room at the motel, and when asked where it was now, said he'd thrown it in a dumpster.

Sneed: I just only like hit him two or three times. I
    figured I would just knock him out.
Detective: Did Barry put up a fight, Justin?
Sneed: Yeah. He danced around a little bit and then I
    kind of knocked him to where he was down on the
    floor and then I tapped him a couple more times
    and when he quit moving I kind of left him alone
    because I figured he was knocked out.

Sneed said he took Van Treese's car keys from the pocket of his trousers, which were lying nearby. He said he found cash in a brown envelope under the car seat and went to his own room, where he and Glossip shared it out: $1,900 each. He then claimed they returned to room 102 to check on Barry. At this point his story changed from being a robbery that got out of hand to a murder plot.

Sneed claimed that Glossip had asked him to kill Van Treese 'so that he could run the motel without him being the boss'. He said Glossip had promised him $7,000, and told him that once he was in charge of the motel he would rent some rooms without declaring the income, and give

Sneed the money. He was asked if they had both gone into room 102 to check Van Treese was dead. He said they had.

He then described how he moved Van Treese's car from outside the motel to another parking lot nearby. Later in the morning, he said, both he and Glossip fixed a piece of Plexiglas on the outside of the broken window, and Sneed taped the shower curtain over the inside. He said he fled the motel in the afternoon when police officers showed up looking for the missing owner.

The interrogation continued for several more minutes, focusing on what had happened to the clothes Sneed was wearing at the time of the murder. He said he'd hidden them in the motel's laundry room. The officers then took photographs of his hands and the bruise on his face. They offered him a coffee.

Sneed: So is this going to help me out any at all by telling you all this?
Detective: Well we'll just have to wait and see. This is definitely going to be better for you this way than it would be if you didn't say anything.

Sneed asked about the punishment for murder. He was told that the sentence for murder in the first degree was death. But the detectives also told him about the possibility of parole after forty-five years.

Sneed: Well I should look forward to the next forty years of sitting in a cell?

Detective: Oh well I don't know. But I'm going to tell
   you this, your old bud Rich was planning on letting
   you hang by yourself for this.
Sneed: Well I ain't going to hang by myself. I'm telling
   you all the truth.

The interrogation drew to a close. During the course
of it, Sneed had first denied being involved, then said he
planned to rob Van Treese and that he only intended to
knock him out with a few taps of the baseball bat. Then he
claimed he had been paid to kill him so that Richard Glossip
could take complete control of the motel. The story would
continue to evolve in the years ahead.

On 14 January, Richard Glossip had been charged with
being an accessory to murder. Two weeks later, like Justin
Sneed, he was charged with first-degree murder

CHAPTER 4

Selling a Story

January 2015

Sally shrugged. 'So what?'

I was hoping for a better response than that. I had what I thought was a great story. I wanted people to be as intrigued as I was. That's the nature of journalism. But Sally's eyes didn't light up. She didn't look curious. Not even a little bit.

'The jury found him guilty,' she said.

'Yes, but he's always maintained he's innocent.'

'But there must be loads of death-row cases like that. Why would we do this one?'

I couldn't even use the magic words 'he's British', which can often transform apathy into mild curiosity when trying to sell a story idea to an editor. Sally Arthy was in charge of planning foreign news coverage at Sky News. As such, she was used to London-based reporters pitching story ideas that involved getting out of the country for somewhere more exotic. Though in this case, Oklahoma in January could hardly be described as exotic. I persisted.

'But he didn't kill anyone. The guy who did the killing

got off the death penalty by agreeing to testify against him.'

'When's the execution?'

'Later this month.'

I told her I'd email her all the details. Even though I had been based in America for four years, and loved going back there when I could, I wasn't pitching to do this story myself. I thought one of our US correspondents might be interested. All I was doing was handing over what I thought was a decent angle on an ongoing story, one that I had stumbled across a few days earlier.

Saturday 27 December 2014 had been a quiet day in the Sky newsroom. The week between Christmas and the New Year is a period when output editors dip into the emergency supply of timeless features filmed a few weeks earlier to fill the bulletins when real news is in short supply. The lead story was the weather. Snow was causing some travel problems, and the railway network was 'in chaos' because of engineering works. The other stories were about NHS delays and the hacking of Xbox and PlayStation.

I'm one of several senior correspondents. We are senior because we're all over forty, have been in TV news for many years and can turn our hand to most subjects. We don't specialise in any particular area; we are jacks-of-all-trades and masters of none, other than our ability to make a two-and-a-half-minute TV report even when there is a dearth of pictures, interviews or details. At the weekend, only one of us is on duty. I'd been assigned a straightforward story as soon as I walked into the office at 8 a.m. Once it was completed, I had the rest of the day to kill unless something big happened to surpass the VT that was now running every hour.

I read the papers, and monitored Twitter, and then a story on the constantly updating news wires caught my eye. It was an Associated Press report on the resumption of executions in Oklahoma after a seven-month hiatus. The last execution, the previous April, had made international headlines because inmate Clayton Lockett had taken three quarters of an hour to die. Following a review of procedures the death chamber would be back in business on 15 January.

I've always been fascinated by death-penalty stories. Coming from a country that abolished hanging half a century ago, it seemed to me to be a barbaric practice, and it always struck me as bizarre that the United States was still willing to join the ranks of China, North Korea and Saudi Arabia as the leading exponents. During my time as United States correspondent I had reported on a couple of death-penalty cases, including that of John Muhammad, the Washington Sniper, who was executed for the murder of ten people in a three-week shooting spree.

When I read that the first Oklahoma execution since the Lockett fiasco was due to take place in just over two weeks, I wanted to find out more. I thought it had potential as a story we might want to cover, given how much publicity the last execution there had attracted. I went onto the website of the Death Penalty Information Center, the Washington DC organisation that lobbies against capital punishment. It maintains a database of everyone who is facing execution, as well as those who have already been put to death.

The 15 January execution was top of the list. Not only would it be the first in Oklahoma since the controversial death of Clayton Lockett, it would be the first in America during 2015. There was a lengthy list of names in the following months.

The man who was due to die on the 15th was Charles Frederick Warner. He had been convicted of raping and killing his girlfriend's eleven-month-old daughter. I winced. Even death-penalty opponents would struggle to drum up much sympathy for someone who had carried out such an appalling crime. His guilt was not in doubt. I wondered if there were other cases that might illustrate the continued debate over the death penalty. I didn't have to look much further. The next on the list was Richard Eugene Glossip, who was due to die on 29 January.

I searched for information and found a few stories on Oklahoma news sites, as well as a listing for a website that bore Glossip's name. Over the course of the next few minutes I discovered enough to intrigue me, and make me want to read more about his case. The fact that instantly stood out was that Richard Glossip was being executed for a murder committed by another man. It seemed extraordinary to me that he had been convicted almost entirely on the word of the killer, who then escaped the death penalty by pinning the blame on his boss.

On the website was a link to a story by Fox 25 in Oklahoma City. It featured an interview with Richard Glossip conducted by their reporter Phil Cross. For some reason the video would not play, but I was still encouraged to see that there had been some media access to the inmate.

I sent Phil a long email full of questions about the case, and then emailed Kim Van Atta, who was listed as the point of contact on Glossip's website. I didn't want to pester them with phone calls on a Saturday morning, but I planned to call them on Monday. I went home thinking that it had been a productive day. I hadn't actually spoken to anyone, or arranged interviews about the case, but I had a good feeling about this story. Even if there were complex legal issues that a British audience wouldn't fully understand, it seemed to me that the essence of the story was pretty stark. A man was about to be executed for a murder he had not committed.

Both Phil and Kim sent back positive responses by email, and we then spoke on the phone. They had both spent time in England; Phil had studied at Cambridge University, and Kim had lived in London during his youth. Both seemed keen to help a British reporter. Phil arranged to send me a link where I could watch the video of his interview.

The explanation of how Kim Van Atta came to be campaigning for a man facing execution was an interesting story in itself. He didn't know Richard Glossip before his conviction, and he had no connection with Oklahoma; he lived in New York and worked as a child healthcare consultant. The tenuous link that brought the two men together was a shared interest in music. Kim was a fan of the indie rock group Guided by Voices, and subscribed to an online forum about the band. One of the other forum members was an Oklahoma attorney called G. Lynn Burch, who was working on Richard Glossip's appeal against his conviction. Burch was keen to find Glossip a pen pal to give him some outside contact with the world and raise his spirits.

According to Kim, Glossip was reluctant at first, and Burch had to work hard to persuade him. '[Lynn] said he'd worked with a lot of defendants, but this was the first one who was so clearly innocent. He also said he had no friends, no family who'd really stayed in contact with him and would I consider writing to him? He thought we would get along particularly because we had a shared taste in similar music. I had no interest in being a pen pal to anybody, much less to someone who had murdered someone, so I had lots of conversations and thought about it for a good few months. I needed to be convinced that this was something that was going to be mutually beneficial.'

To his surprise, the two men formed a deep friendship, which was why, fifteen years later, Kim was doing everything he could to save Richard Glossip's life.

'When it started out, he didn't know me and I didn't know him. I look back at our early letters and they're sort of semi-formal. It's like feeling each other out. But within the course of six months or a year it started to deepen and I think primarily because the man is unbelievably decent, I mean he just really is. He thinks as much or more about others than he does about himself.'

Kim filled me in on the latest developments. The rules of the Oklahoma Department of Corrections (DOC) are that thirty-five days before his execution, a prisoner is moved from his regular cell, which he shares with another inmate, to an isolation cell close to the death chamber. In Richard

Glossip's case, that meant that he was moved on Christmas Day. He responded by going on hunger strike.

Kim now included my name in a joint email to all the journalists who'd expressed an interest in Glossip's case. There were only six, most of them based in Oklahoma. I was the only non-American.

In speaking with Richard last night, he wants me to tell you that since moving upstairs to the holding cell on Christmas Day he has not eaten. And he will continue to refuse food until there is either a positive outcome to the appeal, a stay, or until his execution. He has asked his attorneys to file a motion to prevent the prison from force feeding him.

At this stage, Richard wants, at the very least, for his death to have some meaning; for his death to help shine a light on the ease in which an innocent man can be executed. My fingers are crossed for a miracle, but at this point I think the train has left the station and nothing is going to stop it, and my friend will die. That's hard.

Kim was concerned that the already limited press interest in the case would evaporate if the Charles Warner execution on 15 January went without a hitch. Like me, he recognised that there was likely to be little public sympathy for such a heinous killer, and that his friend would be placed in the same bracket as Warner.

Even at this early stage, I realised that it was unlikely I would be able to secure my own on-camera interview with

Glossip, as he had already been moved to an isolation unit. And without an interview, I would not be able to persuade my boss to send me to Oklahoma to do the story. But I still thought it was worth pursuing. I knew that the campaign to end the death penalty seemed to be gathering momentum. The number of death sentences being imposed was falling. So too was the number of executions. It was one of those issues that rumbled on in the background, but the only time it forced its way up the news agenda was when an execution was botched, or there was an alleged miscarriage of justice. I believed the Richard Glossip case could tie both of those together: a state with recent history of malpractice in carrying out a death sentence, and a prisoner who on the face of it did not deserve to be put to death.

I emailed the press liaison officer for the Department of Corrections, who initially ignored my filming and interview request and then, after a few days, rejected it, saying that prison officials couldn't be interviewed because there was ongoing litigation following the Lockett execution. I received no reply to my email expressing surprise that the legal action meant they couldn't do an interview but they could still carry on executing people.

I wanted to speak directly to Richard Glossip, but although he had access to a phone, he couldn't make international calls. Even so, after a week of research, I decided I had enough to make a formal pitch to do the story. I sent an email to Sally on Sky's foreign desk just before 11 a.m. on 7 January.

As soon as I clicked send, I looked up at the TV to see that details were coming in about a terrorist attack in Paris, at the offices of the satirical magazine *Charlie Hebdo*. It looked serious. Five minutes later, I was told to head for Paris. Oklahoma's death row would have to wait.

When I returned to London a week later, I resumed my efforts to sell the Glossip story, but there was no interest. Everyone in the newsroom had been too wrapped up in the Paris attacks. I realised I would have to break the news to Kim. It's not uncommon for journalists to express interest in a story, talk to those involved, and then not broadcast anything. It can be pushed down or off the news agenda by a new, more dramatic, more topical event. Or we can simply decide that it's not quite as interesting as we first thought.

In this case I felt terrible, because it really was a matter of life and death. Someone was about to be executed, but my network didn't think the story was sufficiently interesting or different or relevant. Or to be more accurate, we didn't think it was worth investing time and money to report it. I couldn't really mount a strong argument why Sky News should take an interest in a case in Oklahoma that had no direct relevance to a British audience.

But when I phoned Kim to kill the story, he breathed new life into it by posing an unexpected question. He asked me how I would feel about being an official witness at Richard Glossip's death.

His words were all the more startling because his voice was on my car speakerphone. It had never occurred to me that if I was to report on Richard Glossip's execution, I might actually witness it. I was aware that a limited number of journalists were allowed to be present in the death chamber, but I had read that Oklahoma had reduced the number of seats available for reporters in the wake of the Clayton Lockett debacle. And priority would be given to local reporters rather than an outsider from Britain. Nevertheless, Kim was suggesting that I should be there at the invitation of the prisoner, rather than the prison. Condemned inmates are allowed to nominate a certain number of witnesses, just as family of the murder victim are also permitted to attend the execution.

I was stunned. I didn't know what to say. My first thought was revulsion at the prospect, but then came a rush of excitement. I'm well aware how disturbing it sounds to confess to being excited at the prospect of attending an execution. But in an instant I realised that this was how I could convince my bosses to allow me to cover the story.

There have been many times during the thirty-plus years I have been a journalist when I have felt adrenalin and excitement when the natural instinct as a human being should be to feel disgust or horror. 'If it bleeds, it leads' is how the news agenda is often summarised. I have never become so callous or uncaring that I would celebrate human suffering, but I admit that there have been days at work that have become more interesting and challenging as a result of someone else's tragedy. Witnessing a death, rather than reporting on its aftermath, is rare. I had seen people killed in accidents, natural disasters and war, but I had never, ever been asked in advance to witness a death. The idea of being invited to an execution was disturbing. But it was different. And that made it potentially newsworthy.

Kim's logic was that if Richard Glossip was going to die, then shining a spotlight on his death could have a lasting impact on the capital punishment debate. He had already done his best to ensure that the execution of his friend did not pass unnoticed, through his website and by contacting the media. And now one of America's best-known campaigners against capital punishment had also become directly involved in the case.

Sister Helen Prejean's book *Dead Man Walking* had become a best-seller and had been adapted as a movie. In 1995, Susan Sarandon had won the Best Actress Oscar for her portrayal of the nun who worked with death-row prisoners. Sister Helen was now in her seventies and hadn't attended an execution for fifteen years, but she had been touched by a letter she had received from Richard Glossip in which he asked for her help. Not only had she agreed to be his spiritual adviser and attend the execution if it went ahead; she would also be speaking to the media to try to prevent it happening. The only other people on Glossip's witness list were his attorneys and Kim, plus Crystal Martinez, another friend and campaigner from California who had been the first to suggest trying to enlist Sister Helen's support.

I relayed the new information to my colleagues. When I told them I'd been invited to witness the execution, I could see their eyes widen. They realised immediately that this was potentially a powerful way of telling the story, but there were ethical as well as practical questions that needed to be addressed. I was asked how I felt about watching a man die. I said that it wasn't something I wanted to do, but I felt strongly enough about the story to do it. I wasn't aware of another British reporter who'd ever been in such a position, and I believed I could offer a unique perspective on the death penalty.

I warned them that it wasn't certain I would be allowed into the prison. Kim still had to make sure that it wasn't too late to add my name to the list. It was possible the Oklahoma authorities could block my application. But even with those caveats, Sky News editors agreed I should go to Oklahoma to report on Richard Glossip's execution.

I began to make travel plans. It made sense to fly to Oklahoma via New York. That way I could see Kim Van Atta at home and film him talking to Glossip on the phone. I called Sister Helen Prejean, who seemed like a fizzing bundle of energy and was very enthusiastic that a British reporter was interested in the case. She agreed that my being a witness would help tell the story, and hinted that she'd been told that officials at the Vatican were keeping an eye on events in Oklahoma. It all seemed to be building momentum as a significant story.

But there was a strong chance that the execution would be postponed, keeping Glossip alive a little longer. This was an outcome I would welcome, but on the other hand, it would potentially kill the story I had planned to write. The United States Supreme Court had agreed to hear evidence about one of the drugs used in the lethal injection process. The case had been brought by attorneys for three Oklahoma inmates who were due to be executed in the coming weeks. Richard Glossip was one of them. There had originally been four prisoners in the lawsuit, but one was already dead; Charles Warner had been successfully put to death a week earlier. The case was not about the guilt or innocence of the prisoners, but about whether the anaesthetic used to sedate them at the start of the execution was effective.

Even with the possibility that the execution could be postponed, Sky still decided it was worth going to Oklahoma. The visit would give me the chance to make contacts that might help secure a place as a witness if and when it was rearranged. I was excited to be working on a story that I had found and pursued, persuading others of its merits, rather than a topic I'd been assigned. I am always more passionate about stories that evolve through my own research. And before I went to Oklahoma, I needed to know more about how Richard Glossip had ended up on death row.

CHAPTER 5

Trial and Errors

June 1998

Several dozen prospective jurors in the trial of Richard Glossip filed into the courtroom in Oklahoma City on the morning of 1 June 1998. It had taken seventeen months of evidence-gathering and preliminary hearings before the case was ready to go to court, but such a lengthy delay between the crime and the courtroom is not unusual. Glossip had been held in the county jail while he awaited his trial for the murder of Barry Van Treese.

District Judge Richard Freeman put the jurors at their ease, but warned them that jury selection was a 'long tedious process, and it gets pretty boring'. They'd face a lot of questions. He began by quizzing them on their jobs and family life, seeking reasons why they might not be suitable for this trial. Did they know anyone connected to the crime, or did their background make them biased because they'd been a victim of crime, or had found themselves on the wrong side of the law? He told them, 'This is a charge of first-degree murder and the state will be asking for the death penalty in this case. Now, don't get excited. We're going to talk about this in great detail. It always kind of excites people when you talk about a murder case and about the death penalty.'

Selecting a jury for a murder trial in the United States isn't a random affair. It's a meticulous process in which the prosecution and defence attorneys try to pick people they believe will be receptive to their arguments. And in some states like Oklahoma, there's another requirement. Jurors in murder cases have to be 'death qualified'. They have to assure the judge that they are willing to recommend that a convicted murderer should be executed, though they also have the option of sending them to prison for life, with or without the chance of parole. So each juror was asked in turn if they could fairly consider each of those options.

The first was a young woman who worked in a body-piercing parlour. She fell at the first hurdle, saying, 'Even if I knew all the facts and everything, I don't think that I could sentence someone to death.' She was excused. Her place was taken by a teacher. He told the judge that he would struggle to find a person guilty of murder knowing that it might lead to a death sentence. He too was excused. But the next twelve people all said they were willing to consider all options.

After a lunch break, the attorneys were given their first chance to exercise their right to ask a potential juror to be taken off the case. The prosecution used their first challenge to remove a nineteen-year-old man from the panel. No reason has to be given. His replacement was asked the question about the death penalty, and she said she was opposed to it. 'I have very strong beliefs against the death penalty. I'm a Christian, I consider myself a Christian, and if someone has done something wrong, then they'll have to answer through the eyes of God and that's what I believe.'

She was asked to leave the courtroom. And so the process continued throughout the rest of the day, and into the following one. More prospective jurors were dismissed because the attorneys saw or heard something they didn't like, and some of their potential replacements were also sent away because they admitted they were opposed to capital punishment. Eventually nine men and three women were selected. There's no requirement for the numbers to be equal. The jurors were told that they would probably not be needed until the middle of the following week. Richard Glossip might have been on trial for murder, with his life at stake, but his case was only expected to take up a week of court time.

The man in charge of prosecuting offenders in this part of Oklahoma was Bob Macy. Nicknamed 'Cowboy' Bob for his love of Stetson hats and string ties, his enthusiasm for pursuing the death sentence in so many murder cases made him one of the most controversial district attorneys in the country. On his office wall was a poster of the Wild West movie *Tombstone*, with the slogan 'Justice is Coming'.

During his time as DA of Oklahoma County, Macy had sent fifty-four people to death row, one of whom was just sixteen years old. Three of those he prosecuted were later exonerated. He'd put one of his trusted lieutenants in charge of prosecuting Glossip. He once praised Assistant District Attorney Fern Smith as 'the equal of any man in any courtroom in Oklahoma', despite her soft-spoken manner. A fellow lawyer described her as sporting a 'large silver bouffant hairstyle and suitably severe wardrobe'. Smith had been a home economics teacher before becoming an attorney. She opened the trial by reading out the charge.

'On or about the 7th day of January, 1997, AD, the crime of Murder in the First Degree was feloniously committed in Oklahoma County, Oklahoma, by Justin Blayne Sneed and Richard Eugene Glossip, who acting jointly, wilfully, unlawfully and with malice aforethought killed Barry Alan Van Treese by beating him with a blunt object inflicting mortal wounds which caused his death on the 7th day of January, 1997, contrary to the provisions of Section 701.7 of Title 21 of the Oklahoma statutes and against the peace and dignity of the State of Oklahoma.'

She introduced the jurors to the characters in her story, and the background to the crime, portraying Justin Sneed as a hapless homeless teenager who'd been preyed upon by the unscrupulous motel manager, who made him kill their boss. Then she introduced a motive for the murder, saying that it was the only way Glossip thought he could keep his job.

Smith promised, 'Our evidence will show that Mr Van Treese had become displeased with the management job that Mr Glossip was doing there at the hotel and was planning to fire Mr Glossip. Mr Glossip had a friend, an associate, someone that Mr Glossip could get to do his dirty work around the motel for him. His name was Justin Sneed. He's the co-defendant in this case. Mr Sneed was a desperate sort of a nineteen-year-old young man. He was homeless. And he stayed in a twenty-three-dollar-a-night room there at the motel free and that was his pay from Mr Glossip for doing whatever Mr Glossip wanted him to do around the hotel.'

The Assistant District Attorney told jurors that Glossip had frequently suggested Sneed should rob and murder their boss, but matters came to a head in January 1997 because Barry Van Treese had discovered that Glossip was embezzling money from the motel. Smith told the jurors that Sneed was young and impressionable.

'As a result of his agreement with Mr Glossip to murder Mr Van Treese, Justin Sneed will spend the rest of his entire life in the penitentiary. He'll tell you that he's going to escape the death penalty because of his cooperativeness with the police and his willingness to come into court and testify truthfully in this case, and he'll tell you that but for Richard Glossip, Barry Van Treese would be alive today and Justin Sneed wouldn't be spending the rest of his life in prison.'

The prosecution's opening statement had a clear narrative. Whether it was true or not, the jury were presented with a crime, a defendant and a motive. The case had been outlined by an attorney who had won more death-penalty convictions in Oklahoma than anyone else. By contrast, her opponent was a bumbling novice.

Wayne Fournerat had never defended anyone accused of murder, let alone someone who was facing the death penalty. His appointment was driven by who he knew, rather than how much he knew. Fournerat was already representing Richard Glossip's brother Bobby, who was facing drugs charges. It was Bobby's girlfriend who had recommended him. She ran an escort agency and Fournerat had defended some of the women who worked for her.

She advised Glossip he'd be better off with his own attorney rather than relying on a public defender. But while publicly funded attorneys might be overworked, they at least have experience of murder trials. Fournerat's baffling opening statement set the tone of an incompetent and muddled attempt to prove his client not guilty.

'Good afternoon, ladies and gentlemen. Richard Glossip did not cause the death of Barry Van Treese. In fact, Richard Glossip tipped Mr Van Treese off, but Mr Glossip made one mistake. He tipped the wrong person. He tipped off Mr Everhart of a problem, and as the evidence will be, Mr Everhart was the security guard and the evidence will be that prior to becoming a security guard at the Best Budget Inn, he had claimed that he owned the Best Budget Inn and in fact that Mr Van Treese owed Mr Everhart ten thousand dollars.'

Fournerat had decided that if he was going to get his client off the hook, he needed to find another culprit. But as he launched into an attack on the character of Cliff Everhart, the part-time security guard at the motel, the prosecutor objected and the two attorneys were told to approach the bench. When the judge asked him what he was doing, Fournerat told him, 'I'm going to show who the real murderers are.'

Judge Freeman asked him not to talk about his allegation that Everhart had a criminal record until they'd discussed it further, without the jury being present. He was allowed to continue his opening statement. He next suggested that Justin Sneed had a friend, 'they were boyfriend and boyfriend', called Richard Page. Page had been a guest at the motel on the night of the crime and had a previous conviction for murder. Fournerat was hoping to convince jurors that he was a more likely conspirator, but the prosecution again objected to him pointing the finger at someone else who was not on trial.

Fournerat resumed his speech to the jury but didn't have a lot more to add. He finished by saying, 'It's going to get real hot in here. This is a story of the innocence of one man, but it points in the direction of who the real culprits are and there are three. Three, ladies and gentlemen. I ask you to consider that and remember the presumption of innocence. Thank you very much.'

His opening address had been rambling and, at times, incoherent. He'd been interrupted twice on points of law. Richard Glossip's own explanation for the crime was that Sneed had attempted to rob Van Treese but ended up killing him. Fournerat had turned it into a conspiracy involving two other people, one of whom was a prosecution witness and the other a convicted killer whom he hadn't been able to track down.

The state called Barry Van Treese's widow Donna as their first witness. Fern Smith could have begun by getting her to talk about the tragic death of her husband, to win the sympathy of the jury. But instead she got straight down to business. She asked Mrs Van Treese how much Glossip earned. The prosecution were attempting to show how he lived hand to mouth and shouldn't have had $1,700 in his possession when he was arrested. But Donna acknowledged that he had earned hundreds of dollars in bonuses every month because business was good. This didn't sound like a negligent employee who feared he was about to be fired.

However, she then went on to say that she and her husband had reviewed motel records and worked out that the takings were around $6,000 less than they should be. She said that Barry had been angry and was planning to talk to Glossip about it. On 7 January, she became worried when she hadn't heard from her husband for nearly twenty-four hours. She phoned the motel and spoke to Glossip.

'I had asked him when was the last time that he saw Barry, and he had told me around 7.30 that morning, that Barry had left to go get supplies, paint and plumbing things to fix up one of the rooms.' She said that she then asked Glossip to take a look in all the motel rooms just in case her husband was working in one of them. She said he agreed to do so.

Mrs Van Treese was followed onto the witness stand by Billye Hooper, who'd been the desk clerk at the motel. She said Glossip appeared to be nervous when she arrived for her shift on 7 January, and was dressed for work earlier than normal, but she assumed it was because Van Treese had been visiting the motel. She said Glossip told her that their boss had left around an hour earlier, at 7 a.m.

Before she could go into further detail, Judge Freeman announced that it was getting late and they should adjourn for the day. She was told to return to court the following morning, and the jury filed out of the courtroom. However, that wasn't the end of the day's drama. Wayne Fournerat was ready to throw in the towel. The trial had lasted less than half a day, and already he felt incapable of securing a not-guilty verdict. He approached the bench without even consulting his client and made an extraordinary statement.

> Fournerat: Your Honor … I am informing my client
>   that I believe, based on the testimony, it would be
>   in his best interest to enter a plea.
> Judge: Say again.
> Fournerat: I said that I believe it is in his best interest
>   to enter a plea, a blind plea.
> Judge: Mr Glossip, have you discussed this …
> Glossip: No, I think we need to discuss this right now
>   because I'm not aware of this.

A blind plea means pleading guilty and throwing yourself on the mercy of the judge. If Glossip was to plead guilty now, the judge might give him some credit for owning up and saving the court some time, but he would still have free rein over the sentence, including death. Wayne Fournerat obviously thought the verdict of the jury was a foregone conclusion.

Judge Freeman gave Fournerat five minutes to talk to his client, but Glossip made his feelings clear to him. The attorney went back to the judge and told him, 'My client does not accept my advice, and I feel that is a shame that he doesn't.' Fournerat and the judge discussed how Glossip had previously been offered a plea deal in which he could have been given a sentence of life without parole. The defendant explained why he had rejected this deal: 'I don't care what the circumstances say, I'm innocent.'

Glossip confirmed he had willingly turned down the plea deal, and did not want to plead guilty now. The judge told him he didn't have to. The attorneys and the defendant were told to be back in court at 9 a.m. the following morning. Day one of the trial of Richard Glossip was over, but he seemed to be the only person who believed he had a chance of being acquitted. Even if Fournerat thought he was innocent, he didn't believe he would be able to convince the jury.

The following morning, Billye Hooper concluded her testimony. Under cross-examination she said that Barry Van Treese did not appear to be angry at Glossip on the day of his death, and that Glossip had always handed over all the motel's takings to the owner. She had no knowledge of any having gone missing.

Although the majority of guests at the Best Budget Inn stayed for just a night or two, the motel also had some long-term residents. The next witness, John Beavers, had lived there for nearly ten years. He described how he was awake on the night of the murder and was on his way to a nearby gas station to buy a drink when he heard breaking glass and muffled voices. He passed room 102 and saw the broken window, so thought he should report it. But when he rang the motel's doorbell, nobody responded.

The next witness was patrol officer Tim Brown, who'd been working in the area around the Best Budget Inn for fifteen years. During that time he had got to know Barry

Van Treese and Richard Glossip, and had become friends with Cliff Everhart, who had taken on the role of security man at the motel. On the afternoon of 7 January, Brown had spotted Glossip and Everhart looking in dumpsters in a parking lot, and stopped to ask them what was going on. They told him Van Treese was missing. Brown said he asked them when Van Treese was last seen, and Glossip said it was around 7 a.m. that morning.

Later, back at the motel, he was told about the broken window in room 102, but when Glossip said it had been caused by two drunks fighting, he didn't connect it to the disappearance, or search the room. Everhart said he had already asked Glossip and Sneed to look in all the rooms. Brown asked Glossip again when was the last time he had seen the motel owner, and this time Glossip told him he wasn't sure, but it might have been the previous evening.

Brown eventually decided he should take a look at room 102, and as soon as he and Everhart approached the broken window he could see blood on the glass. When they forced the door, they found the body underneath a pile of bedlinen. Brown didn't examine the scene; that would be the job of forensics specialists. He sealed off the room, and while he waited for detectives to arrive, he put Richard Glossip in his patrol car. Brown said he didn't ask him any questions, but that Glossip took a deep breath and said he should have told him about Sneed coming to his room in the early hours of the morning.

After a break for lunch, Cliff Everhart was the next witness to take the stand. He told the court that he was now a private detective, having previously worked as an investigator with attorneys defending capital murder cases. He said that when Barry Van Treese was first reported missing, he spoke to Richard Glossip and asked whether the motel owner had returned during the night from Tulsa. He was told he had.

Smith: Did he tell you that he had seen Mr Van
    Treese?
Everhart: Yes, ma'am. He said he had seen him.
    He'd come in and he'd questioned him about the
    window being broken on room 102.
Smith: Mr Glossip said that he had actually spoken
    with Mr Van Treese?
Everhart: Yes, ma'am.

Everhart said he had asked Glossip and Justin Sneed to search the rooms. He noticed that Sneed had bruising around his eye. Sneed told him he'd fallen in the bathroom. But as the day wore on and Van Treese had not been found, Everhart became more suspicious.

'At approximately 9.30 I met with Sergeant Brown again at the gas station, the Sinclair next door, and we were discussing the different stories that Mr Glossip had told both him and myself, and we decided that we needed to personally check room 102 because there was something that just didn't seem right about it.'

It was the inconsistencies in Glossip's timeline that had aroused the suspicions of Everhart and Brown. He had told them he had seen Van Treese around 7.30 that morning, but then said he had meant 7.30 the previous evening.

Fournerat now began to cross-examine Everhart, probing his background. He suggested he'd been fired from a previous job as a police investigator, but the judge prevented him from delving deeper into the details. Everhart said he was a part owner of the Best Budget Inn, but was unable to produce any paperwork to back up this claim. The cross-examination drew to a close, with the witness escaping relatively lightly despite Fournerat trying to suggest he was a conspirator in the murder.

Chai Choi, a forensic pathologist, testified in great detail about the injuries to Barry Van Treese's body and concluded that he'd been hit on the head nine times. She said the cause of death was 'lacerations of the head with blunt force', which caused a brain injury and he bled to death. She said Van Treese would not have died immediately but could only estimate that he might have lived for between one and five hours. She was asked whether he could have survived such an attack. 'Yes,' she said. 'He would have been able to survive if prompt medical attention such as to prevent loss of blood and to replace the loss of blood.'

This would have a major impact on how the jury viewed Richard Glossip. Even if they were unsure whether he had encouraged Sneed to commit murder, this evidence suggested that he could at the very least have intervened to prevent Van Treese's death. If he had called the police when Sneed first woke him and told them he had killed the motel owner, medical help could have been summoned and

Van Treese might have survived. It made Glossip appear to be callous and uncaring, even though he argued that he hadn't believed Sneed.

A technical investigator from the Oklahoma City Police Department was the next witness. Joseph McMahon had examined Barry Van Treese's car, a 1987 silver Buick Lesabre, and opened the trunk, which had been locked. Inside, he found one of the enduring mysteries of this murder case: $23,100 in cash, some of the notes covered in blue dye, the kind of stain left by a detonation in a cash box to foil a bank robbery. McMahon wasn't asked for an explanation about why the money was stained, but later witnesses would be questioned about it.

The next witness was Melissa Keith, a forensic chemist, who went through her findings after analysing samples collected from the body of the murder victim. Wayne Fournerat asked if she had found anything showing that Richard Glossip had had anything to do with the crime. She said no. He went through every one of the fifty-six items she had examined asking her the same question: 'Is there anything that indicates my client had anything to do with the murder of Barry Van Treese?' Fifty-six times she said no.

It was to be Fournerat's most effective moment in the trial. He was able to hammer home one of the key points in the Glossip case: that there was no forensic or physical evidence linking him to the murder scene. The prosecution would argue that that was because he made sure that only Sneed was involved in the actual murder.

The next prosecution witnesses were police officers. First,

David Mauk described how he had arrested Richard Glossip as he left the office of his attorney David McKenzie. He said that Glossip was found to have $1,757 in his possession. The prosecution claimed it was the money stolen from Van Treese. Glossip said he had raised the cash by selling off some of his possessions so he could afford to hire the attorney, but could provide no corroboration such as statements from those who paid him.

The second police officer was Bill Cook, one of the homicide detectives who had interrogated Glossip. He told the court that in his twenty-six-year career he had investigated a couple of hundred murders. He described visiting the murder scene, and how he had decided to interview Richard Glossip because of inconsistencies in his story. The videotape of the interrogation was played in court. After it was over, the blue dye on Barry Van Treese's money was discussed. The detective said they had checked to see if it was linked to a robbery but could find no evidence, so the cash was handed over to the Van Treese family. The mystery of the stained banknotes was never solved.

Detective Cook was asked about other possible suspects in the murder investigation. He said that a guest staying on the second floor had left 'rather mysteriously', and that they had looked into the background of Ricky Page, a convicted murderer who was rumoured to have stayed at the motel, but could find no evidence linking him to the crime and ruled him out of the inquiry. When the detective had finished, the court adjourned for the day, and the week. It was Friday afternoon, and Judge Freeman sent the jurors home with the usual reminder not to discuss the evidence with friends and relatives.

Before the trial resumed on Monday morning, there was a legal argument about the admissibility of the video showing Richard Glossip's second interrogation. Despite being told by attorney David McKenzie that he was under no obligation to talk to detectives, Glossip had agreed to be interviewed. Judge Freeman was troubled that the interview had proceeded notwithstanding McKenzie's advice. In an attempt to clarify this, he tried to phone McKenzie to ask him what had actually happened seventeen months earlier, but because he couldn't track him down, the jury were allowed to see the second video, in which Glossip retracted his previous version of events and told detectives about Sneed's late-night visit to his apartment.

However, despite the jury now having watched both of Glossip's interrogations, they were not permitted to view the interrogation of Justin Sneed. Fournerat wanted jurors to hear how Sneed didn't mention Glossip having a role in the murder until the detectives told him that Glossip was already in custody and blaming him, but the judge wouldn't allow it. He didn't rule it out completely, but knowing that Justin Sneed was due to testify in court later that afternoon, he decided the jury should hear what Sneed had to say first. Fournerat agreed to postpone his request to play the video, but when the time came, he failed to ask again. This omission would have serious repercussions.

Instead the defence attorney focused on what he claimed was false prosecution evidence. Detective Bemo told the court he had spoken by phone to a William Bender, who he said was the manager of Barry Van Treese's motel in Tulsa. Bender told the detective how, during his visit to Tulsa on the night he was killed, Van Treese had spoken openly about being unhappy with the way Richard Glossip was running the Oklahoma motel, and said he was going to fire him. Detective Bemo used that information as a motive for Glossip to want Van Treese murdered.

But Fournerat claimed there was no William Bender employed at the Tulsa motel, and said the manager was called Marty Baker. Fournerat pursued his own theory about the true identity of the man on the end of the phone.

> Fournerat: Have you ever spoken to Cliff Everhart on
>   the telephone?
> Bemo: I may have one time.
> Fournerat: Was the voice of Bender and the voice of
>   Everhart similar?
> Bemo: No, I don't think so. I don't recall, though. I'm
>   not sure if I've talked with him or not.

Fournerat was insinuating that Everhart had impersonated the manager in order to provide a motive for murder. However, not only was he wrong in describing Bender as a 'fictitious person', but the prosecution were quickly able to prove it to the jury, making him look even more foolish. After a brief recess, Donna Van Treese returned to the stand and explained that Billy Bender was the husband of Marty Baker, the manager of the motel. They ran the business as a couple but only Baker's name appeared on documents.

Wayne Fournerat's credibility had been torn to shreds. He tried to salvage the situation by asking to see motel records showing the name Bender, but the judge put a stop to it. Whatever his feelings about the performance of the attorney, Judge Freeman believed that Glossip was still getting a fair trial. It was time to move on and hear from the prosecution's star witness, the man who knew more about the murder of Barry Van Treese than anyone else.

Although Justin Sneed had admitted his role in the murder, his conviction and formal sentencing was on hold until after the trial of Richard Glossip, and like Glossip he had been held in the Oklahoma County Jail. When he was brought into court wearing his prison uniform, he was asked to identify Glossip. Glossip stood as Sneed pointed his finger at him.

Sneed told the court that around 3.30 a.m. Glossip had come to room 117, where he lived, and offered him 'seven grand' to kill Van Treese. He said it wasn't the first time he'd asked him to do it, claiming that it happened almost every time the owner visited the motel. 'Five or six times,' he added moments later. 'He was trying to tell me that I was going to get kicked out of the motel and that he was going to get kicked out of the motel. And then he basically just told me that if he was me, he would take a baseball bat, which I had in my room, and just go rush him while he was asleep.'

Sneed said he thought about it for an hour, and then went to room 102 and let himself in using the master keys that Glossip had given him when he started working at the motel.

Sneed: I went in with my baseball bat, and basically
    when I opened the door, Mr Van Treese woke up,
    and then I just hit him with the bat. And then he
    pushed me and I fell back into the chair, and that's
    how the window ended up getting broke because
    the bat hit the window. And then I just – Mr Van
    Treese was trying to get out of the room, and I just
    grabbed the back of his shirt and slung him on the
    floor and then hit him a couple more times.
Smith: Do you know how many times you hit him?
Sneed: No I don't. Maybe about ten or fifteen, I guess.
Smith: Did you hit him because you intended for him
    to die?
Sneed: Yes, I did.

Sneed said he stayed in the room for around thirty minutes
until he was sure Van Treese was dead, then went to Glossip's
apartment. He said that both of them went back into room
102 and spent about twenty minutes there. He said Glossip
watched him tape a shower curtain over the broken window.
Sneed then removed Van Treese's car keys from his trouser
pocket, went to the vehicle, and found around $4,000 under
the front seat. He brought it back to Glossip, who said he
wanted to split the money between them.

Sneed claimed that Glossip told him to buy not just
Plexiglas to fix over the window, but also a hacksaw and
some acid to try to dispose of the body, though no evidence
was produced to back up the claim. He then went through
the events of the day that the jury had already been told

about: the discovery of Van Treese's car, and the search for the owner himself. The only new detail he added was that Glossip told him to leave the motel later that evening as the search intensified.

Fournerat's cross-examination was the only opportunity to discredit Sneed as a credible witness. The fact that Sneed was a self-confessed killer meant that the jury should already dislike him. He got Sneed to acknowledge that he had been a methamphetamine user, though Sneed denied having taken drugs on the night of the murder. But he failed to question Sneed about the way the detectives had interrogated him, and how his story had changed from being a robbery to a paid killing. Nor did he make another request to play the video of the interrogation, which showed the role the detectives played in persuading Sneed to implicate Richard Glossip. Fournerat would later claim that it wouldn't have helped Glossip's case, and said the version of the video he had been given was a redacted copy, and not the full interrogation.

He suggested to Sneed that if he had been following Glossip's order to kill, now he was following the state's orders to testify against him. Sneed insisted he was telling the truth. Fournerat failed to uncover anything of interest and his cross-examination drifted to a close. The state concluded its case. The next day the jury would hear from the defendant for the first time, and though the burden of proof was on the prosecution, Richard Glossip would have to come up with a plausible explanation for his actions if he was to convince them he was an innocent man.

CHAPTER 6

A Weak Defence

May 1998

Richard Glossip's defence got off to a terrible start. The trial resumed the following morning with another attempt by Wayne Fournerat to bring it to a premature end. Just as he had done on the first day of the trial, he wanted his client to admit he was guilty, rather than put the decision in the hands of the jury. Before the jury took their places in the courtroom, he addressed Judge Freeman.

'Your Honor, I'd like to make a record that it is my professional opinion that Mr Glossip would be well served by entering a blind plea. I have informed Mr Glossip of that and I believe at this time it would be the appropriate thing to ask Mr Glossip and get his response on the record as to whether he is interested in entering a blind plea.'

He turned to his client. 'I believe that that would save your life because it is in my professional opinion that the jury would definitely come back with guilty.'

Glossip's opinion was that Fournerat was a lousy attorney, telling the judge, 'I would also like to put something on the record. Mr Fournerat, in my opinion, has not represented me the way that I wanted. I have repeatedly asked him to ask witnesses certain questions. He has denied me that, so in my opinion, I haven't even been represented the way I would want to be represented. In my opinion I haven't gotten a fair trial.'

Judge Freeman asked Glossip whether he wanted to enter a plea. He said no. Then there was an extraordinary exchange between the defendant, his lawyer and the judge.

Fournerat: Mr Glossip, you have told me that you want the death penalty, is that correct?

Glossip: If you're going to convict me of something I didn't do, yes, I do.

Judge: Now wait a minute. Let me ask you, are you planning to testify?

Glossip: I was going to, yes.

Fournerat: And it's my legal advice, Your Honor, that he not testify.

Judge: Are you going to tell the jury you want the death penalty?

Glossip: No.

Judge: Oh, okay. I wouldn't do that if I were you.

Glossip: No, sir. I'm just saying if you convict me of a crime that I didn't even commit, then, yes, you may as well go all the way.

Judge: Now, that's fine to be talking that way between friends, but I don't believe I'd tell that to the jury.

Glossip: I also want to make a record that I want to terminate Mr Fournerat.

Judge: Well, I don't think that would be very smart
    this morning, do you, when your case is about to
    begin?

Glossip: I'm not being defended properly. It would be
    a mistake on my behalf.

Judge: I'm not going to permit that. You're not going to
    terminate him on the date your defense is going
    to begin.

Richard Glossip was fighting for his life, but he had no
confidence that his attorney was going to help in that fight.
Finally, after more legal discussions, the first defence witness
was called. It was Glossip's former girlfriend, D-Anna Wood.
Their relationship had ended shortly after he was charged
with murder, and within weeks she had found a new lover.

She told the court that she had dated Glossip for around
five years, and though they both lived and worked at the
motel, only Glossip was on the payroll. She helped with
checking in guests and other duties, and knew the owner,
Barry Van Treese. She told the court that Van Treese was
always pleased with Glossip's efforts and she had no reason
to believe he was going to fire him.

The lawyer moved on to the night of the murder. D-Anna
said she and Glossip had gone to their apartment close to
the motel reception at around 2 a.m. They'd watched TV,
had sex and gone to sleep. They were woken up sometime
around 5 a.m. She described how she heard a loud scraping
up and down the wall outside. Glossip got out of bed and
went to the door, returning a few minutes later. 'I said, "Who

was that?" and he said, "It was Justin," and I said, "What did
he want?" And he said, "Two drunks broke a window and I
told him to clean it up."'

She said they went back to sleep and she didn't wake up
until around noon. She told the court they went shopping,
and that Glossip bought her an engagement ring that cost
just over $100. While they were in Walmart, he was paged
to say there was a phone call from the desk clerk at the
Best Budget Inn. D-Anna Wood said that they were told
there was an emergency at the motel and they needed to
get back there.

Assistant District Attorney Fern Smith began her cross-
examination. During it she asked D-Anna whether she
had told the police she was sure Richard Glossip had not
committed the crime.

'I don't believe he did,' D-Anna replied. 'He's not that
kind of person.'

She was asked about items that Glossip had sold to raise
money in the aftermath of the murder. She said he'd sold an
entertainment system, a futon and some vending machines
that earned him extra revenue at the motel. She was asked if
she was surprised that he had $1,700 in his possession when
he was arrested. She told the court she didn't remember.
Glossip's attorney interjected and tried to clarify what the
money was for.

Fournerat: Now, what was the intent of selling off
    the vending machines, the candy machines, the
    furniture and stuff like that, what was the intent?

Wood: My birthday was coming up and I wanted
    breast implants.

Wood told the court that she had now moved on, and
no longer visited Glossip in jail. Neither attorney pursued
details of her new life, but within a few weeks of the murder
she had become romantically involved with an older man
called Jim Gainey, who was a friend of the Van Treese family.
Her new lover paid for her to have the breast implants.

The second and, as it turned out, final witness for the
defence was Richard Glossip himself. After a few preliminary
questions about how long he'd worked at the motel, his
attorney asked him about the night of the murder. Glossip
said that Barry Van Treese had come to collect the week's
takings, and to pay him and his desk clerk Billye Hooper.
He testified that Van Treese did not mention anything about
discrepancies in the takings.

He then gave his version of what happened when Sneed
woke him up in the middle of the night. 'At first he told me
two drunks broke a window so I told him to fix the window.
He's the maintenance man. And as he turned to walk away,
I noticed he had some marking on his right eye and I asked
him if he got hit. And he said, "No."

'I said, "The drunks didn't hit you?" And he said, "No."
I said, "Where are the drunks now?" And he said he ran
them off. And as he was still turning to walk away, I said,
"Come on, Justin." I said, "Really, what happened to your
eye?" He then looked at me and he said he killed Barry. So
I then turned around and I looked. There's a big picture

window where Barry always parked his car, and I looked to see if Barry's car was there and it wasn't. So at that time I didn't believe what he was saying, and then I went back into the bedroom.'

After Glossip described how Sneed had asked him to help fix the window the following morning, Fournerat asked him why he hadn't told anyone about Sneed's early-morning 'confession'.

Fournerat: Didn't you think it was unusual that someone would say I just killed Barry Van Treese?

Glossip: Not from Sneed. When I looked out the front window, like I said, and I didn't see Barry's car, I didn't believe him.

But when it was clear that Barry Van Treese was missing, he still said nothing. He said he thought about it, but decided to keep quiet. 'I told D-Anna, I said I think I should tell the police officers and Cliff what Justin had told me, and she said that until it was proven I shouldn't say a thing. So I didn't.'

Glossip told the jury that he didn't think anyone was in room 102 when he was helping fix Plexiglas to the broken window. But that was different from what he had said during his second police interrogation, when he had told detectives that even though he didn't go into the room, he was pretty sure the body was in there. The jury would have heard him say that when they watched the interrogation video, and the prosecution would challenge him over that discrepancy.

When Assistant District Attorney Fern Smith began her cross-examination, she focused on how Glossip could have manipulated Sneed to do his bidding, because the younger man was totally reliant on Glossip's generosity. She accused him of not only knowing about the murder, but instructing Sneed on how to do it.

> Smith: Isn't it true that it was you who told Justin Sneed that he should use a baseball bat to kill Mr Van Treese?
>
> Glossip: No, ma'am. I had no ill feeling toward Barry Van Treese and I never would have ever told anybody to do anything to him.

The attorney pointed out that his story didn't match what he had told Officers Bemo and Cook in his second interrogation.

> Smith: Isn't it true you helped Justin Sneed install the Plexiglas window in room 102 knowing that Mr Van Treese was lying dead, brutally murdered, inside room 102?
>
> Glossip: No, I helped Mr Sneed put the Plexiglas on the outside of the window, but I did not know Barry Van Treese was inside that room, no, I didn't.
>
> Smith: Isn't it true you did not contact the police because you were the mastermind behind the murder?
>
> Glossip: No, ma'am.

Smith: Isn't it true that instead of calling the police or at least checking it out, isn't it true that you then began to help Mr Sneed cover up Mr Van Treese's murder?

Glossip: No, ma'am, I did not.

The prosecution needed to establish a motive to explain why Glossip would have hired Sneed to murder his boss. The Assistant DA suggested that he feared he was about to be fired.

Smith: And isn't it true you knew Mr Van Treese was upset with your management of the motel?

Glossip: No, ma'am, that's wrong.

Smith: Isn't it true that you were concerned that Mr Van Treese was going to find out even more about your poor management of the motel if he stayed for a few days and observed the rooms at the motel?

Glossip: He stayed there before, ma'am. No, that's not true.

Smith: Isn't it true that you knew that if Mr Van Treese was out of the way that you could gain management of the motel from Ms Donna Van Treese?

Glossip: I already managed the motel.

Smith: Isn't it true you knew that if Mr Van Treese wasn't murdered on January the 7th of 1997, that you were going to lose your meal ticket?

Glossip: No, ma'am, I can get a job. I wouldn't hurt
   nobody for a job, ma'am. It isn't worth it.
Smith: Isn't it true that you lied to the police about
   Justin Sneed telling you some drunks broke out the
   window in 102?
Glossip: No, ma'am, he did tell me that. I just told
   them the first part of the story and didn't tell them
   the last.

The biggest challenge facing Glossip and his attorney
was to convince the jury he was being honest in court, even
though he admitted that his actions in the aftermath of
the murder, and in his first police interrogation, had been
dishonest. The questions and answers were coming swiftly
as Smith tried to find discrepancies in his story and trip him
up in his testimony. The intensity of her questioning was in
stark contrast to how Wayne Fournerat had cross-examined
Justin Sneed.

Smith: Isn't it true you took advantage of Mr Justin
   Sneed's youth and vulnerability when you duped
   him into murdering Mr Van Treese?
Glossip: No, ma'am, I do not.
Smith: Do you admit that you lied to the police?
Glossip: I admitted I didn't tell them the whole truth
   in the beginning, yes, I do.
Smith: Isn't it true that you're just as likely lying to the
   jury now?

Glossip: No, ma'am, I'm under oath and I'm telling
this jury the truth.

The questions became repetitive, and so did the answers.
But finally the cross-examination came to an end with a
suggestion that robbery could not have been the motive
for attacking the motel owner.

Smith: Well, Mr Glossip, isn't it true if all you and
Justin Sneed wanted was money, all you had to do
was break the window to the car and get the money,
but that wasn't good enough, you wanted him
killed, didn't you?
Glossip: No, ma'am, I didn't want money, nor did I
want anything to happen to Barry. I already had my
own money.

There were a few more questions from Wayne Fournerat,
but the defence of Richard Glossip was over in less than a
day. Fournerat didn't make another attempt to have the
video of Justin Sneed's interrogation played to the jury, who
never saw for themselves how Sneed had been cajoled into
changing his story to fit the detectives' theory.

The following morning, in her closing statement, Fern
Smith went over the evidence she had presented in the trial,
and sought to contrast Justin Sneed and Richard Glossip.
'Glossip is clever. You saw him on the witness stand. You
saw him on these videotapes. He's very clever. Mr Sneed is
not so clever.'

When Wayne Fournerat had his last chance to talk to the jury, he again raised theories about who else might have been involved, and continued to claim that Cliff Everhart was 'the fictitious Mr Bender'.

Finally the talking was over, and the jurors were sent to consider their verdict. While they deliberated, they had several questions and requests that were relayed to the judge. They asked if they could see the video of Justin Sneed's police interrogation, but the request was denied because it hadn't been introduced as evidence and played to them previously in court.

Some jurors might have been unsure about finding Glossip guilty of murder. At one point they asked for a definition of 'reasonable doubt'. Judge Freeman declined because he felt it was self-explanatory. The jurors also asked for a transcript of Detective Cook's testimony, but were told they would have to rely on their collective memory of what he had said. Refusing to 'read back' the testimony is normal practice in Oklahoma courts, though defence attorneys argue that's a denial of the due process of the law – why would you want to leave jurors unsure of what has been said? They are also forbidden from taking their own notes.

Finally, they asked if Glossip's knowledge of the murder, and his failure to alert the authorities, constituted his becoming a principal to first-degree murder. The answer that was sent to them was 'You have all the law before you necessary to answer the question.'

Six hours after they had begun their discussions, the jurors filed back into court. The foreman announced that they had found 'Richard Eugene Glossip guilty to the crime of Murder in the First Degree'. Each of the other members of the jury was asked to confirm the verdict, and all of them did. Glossip says he felt like throwing up. While the jury were deliberating, Fournerat had told him he thought they would return a verdict of not guilty. Glossip believed him.

The jurors were sent home. The following day they would decide on what sentence they should impose. To pass a death sentence, the state had to prove that the murder was 'especially heinous, atrocious or cruel' and that the defendant constituted a continuing threat to society. Donna Van Treese was called back to the witness stand, and made a heart-rending victim impact statement: 'Due to this senseless and horrible act, I am a widow at thirty-eight with five children to raise on my own and trying to explain to them why their daddy will never be coming home again.'

She explained how she had taken the children to the funeral home to say goodbye to their father, and how her daughter was hardest hit by the experience. 'She did not want to leave her daddy. She told him – she told me that she did not want him to be alone. Bridget stood at the casket and patted her daddy's chest. I had to explain to her that her daddy was in heaven with Jesus and was not alone. That what she was seeing was only his earthly body and that the daddy that she loved, the one that loved to play and laugh, that was his spirit and his spirit was in heaven with God. Then with my help, she kissed his cheek and said I will love you forever.'

Richard Glossip's mother Sally was called to give mitigating evidence. She talked briefly about her son's childhood and education, and his working life. She said he had never committed an act of violence. Wayne Fournerat thanked her and said he had no further questions. Judge Freeman interrupted him and called him to the bench to tell him, 'May I suggest to you that you ask her something about his life having value to you, and that she would request the jury to spare it?'

The judge was telling him how to do one of the most basic aspects of his job. Fournerat returned to Mrs Glossip and said there were a few questions he'd forgotten. Once again his inexperience and incompetence had undermined his client's chances of escaping the death sentence. After finally eliciting a few more answers from her, he called her son to speak.

Richard Glossip talked about his background, and was then given the chance to plead for mercy. 'Please don't take my life,' he said. 'I made a mistake, but I'm not guilty of this.' He said he accepted responsibility for a part of Donna Van Treese's pain. 'All I can say is I should have done something about this and I didn't. But I didn't want Barry to get hurt at any time for nothing, and I'm asking you to forgive me and I'm sorry for all the pain that you went through.'

After closing arguments, where the prosecution pressed for the ultimate punishment and the defence asked for the chance of rehabilitation, the jury was sent out again. This time, they were faced with three choices. Life in prison with or without the possibility of parole, or death. They chose death.

Glossip says he was in shock, and it took a few days for the news to sink in. He was bitterly angry at Fournerat, saying the way he had handled the sentencing phase was even worse than the trial itself. He was told that just before he presented his mitigating evidence, Fournerat was still outside the courtroom asking other attorneys for advice on how to proceed.

Richard Glossip believed he hadn't received a fair trial, and over the next three years, a new lawyer would attempt to have the verdict overturned.

CHAPTER 7

Two Sides of America

January 2015

Richard Glossip was due to be executed in four days. I was on my way to meet the attorneys and campaigners who were trying to prevent that happening. My first stop was New York City, but the weather was threatening to scupper my travel plans. A massive snowstorm was forecast to hit within twenty-four hours. I wasn't the only one concerned about my onward flight to Oklahoma City. When I arrived at the apartment of Glossip's close friend Kim Van Atta, snow was already falling heavily, and he and his wife were on the phone trying to bring forward their flights by a few hours to avoid the worst of the blizzards.

Despite many phone calls in the previous days, this was my first chance to meet Kim and interview him. He's in his mid sixties, with white hair and a bushy white moustache. He has what I'd call a kind face, or maybe that's just because I know about his generous nature. I mean, why else would he have spent more than a decade helping a death-row prisoner who was neither a relative nor even a friend when they were first introduced?

Sky's New York-based cameraman Jake Britton quickly set up his equipment to record an interview. We only had about twenty minutes before Glossip was due to phone Kim, and we needed to be ready to film the call. I asked Kim why he was so convinced that his friend was not guilty of murder.

'From the very beginning it was the trial transcript. It was just clear that there was no way that he did what they said he did. There's nothing that suggests he is guilty to me. I tend to think that simplest is usually the most accurate and the simplest motive here is a robbery gone bad as the killer said at the beginning. Richard was in the wrong place at the wrong time.'

According to Kim, the motive was preposterous – killing his boss would not have given Glossip control of the motel, and even if he was about to lose his job, he had a strong employment history and could have found another one. He'd never been fired or been in trouble with the police.

On the website Kim set up to raise public awareness of the case, there is a short autobiography of Richard. He wrote his story in prison, then mailed it to Kim, who laboriously typed it up. During the course of that narrative, Glossip pays tribute to his friend in New York, explaining how Kim and his wife have helped him:

> As time went on he and his family would make me feel like I was a part of the family, which was truly amazing. It was truly a blessing to have the chance to meet such great people. I

owe them my life. They made this horrible
thing more tolerable. I really didn't think that
people like him and his family were still out
there. It is so hard to come up with the words
to express to you how incredible this family is.

I read those lines to Kim and asked him for a response.

'I'm honoured he would say that. His friendship has meant
as much to me as I think mine has meant to him. It's been a
true two-way relationship. He is incredibly supportive. Any
time I have had difficulties or problems with jobs et cetera,
he's been somebody I could vent with.'

He said he would miss their chats 'if the worst happened',
and that although he had agreed when Glossip asked him
to be a witness to the execution, he would be a reluctant
one. Even as an atheist, he was glad to have the spiritual
support of Sister Helen Prejean, as well as her experience
as a campaigner.

'She's been amazing. She has got good connections all
over. It's only in the last six months that I've got involved
in that aspect of his case. Prior to that we were told by our
attorneys not to talk to press, not to lobby or advocate.
Richard and I both followed their advice. Now we think
we're kind of stupid. But then it came to the point where
the attorneys said yeah, do whatever you want because we
are pretty much reaching the end of things that we can do.'

After the interview was over, Jake filmed some of the
hundreds of pages of letters from Glossip, stacked in a neat
pile. Then, a little earlier than arranged, Kim's mobile rang,

and for the first time I heard the pre-recorded message that always preceded Glossip's voice.

'This is a Global Tel Link pre-paid call from RICHARD GLOSSIP, an inmate at Oklahoma State Penitentiary. This call will be monitored and recorded except for privileged calls with attorneys.' The message continued with various options to accept or reject the call, and an update about how much money was still available on the account. Finally Richard's voice filled the room, thanks to the speaker we'd connected to the phone so that we could record the conversation.

'Good morning,' said the voice from Oklahoma.

'Good morning, Richard,' replied Kim. 'I'm glad you called a little early. It's madness here. My flight this afternoon was cancelled until tomorrow because of the blizzard coming in, and the earliest one would be on Wednesday, so we're going to make a mad dash to the airport right after we're done talking. Hopefully I'll get on a plane at eleven thirty.'

I briefly wondered whether a man due to be executed in three days would consider travel problems caused by snow in New York a big deal, but a delay would have major implications for both men. It might mean that Kim didn't get to see his friend on the eve of his death. Kim handed the phone to me so I could interview Richard.

'Hi, Richard, I hope you can hear me all right?'

'Hi, how you doin'?'

I've interviewed prisoners before, in jails in places as diverse as England and Afghanistan. Some of them were murderers. But this was the first time I'd spoken to an inmate who was facing execution. I was conscious of being sensitive in my tone while still probing for answers. I began by asking about Richard's latest legal challenge to the execution date, and whether he was optimistic it would succeed.

'I am because it would be kind of strange for them to say in one breath, "Okay, we're going to hear your case because of the merits of the case, whether or not it's humane to use this drug on inmates," and in another breath to say, "We're going to carry on killing people." That would be a ridiculous ruling. Everybody asks me will I be happy with a stay, and I say no, I want my freedom back. The stay allows me an opportunity to continue my fight. I got to tell you, man, the last week has been really incredible. We've gotten so much press and the story is getting out to a lot of people in a lot of different countries, not just the United States. And it does give you a lot of hope that this week is going to be a good one and not a bad one.'

He spoke about Sister Helen Prejean getting involved. He sounded energised by the mention of her name. 'Oh man, it was definitely a breath of fresh air. This lady is so amazing. She makes you feel like everything is possible. To be honest it didn't look as if people would listen, and all of a sudden here we are with almost thirty thousand signatures and all these people are out there fighting to free me. It's just really incredible. And it just shows that all the work that I put into the last eighteen years, people are finally beginning to look and see that this case is not what the state said all along.'

I was keen to explore his relationship with Kim, though of course he knew that his patron was sitting beside me, listening in to our conversation.

'If Kim hadn't been in my life I wouldn't have made it this far. He kept me strong and kept me sane. We lost a lot of battles and it got to the point where you're thinking, man, something's got to go right soon, you can't lose everything. We never thought in a million years that it would get to this point. Kim and Mary and the whole family have kept me really strong over the years.'

He told me that he wanted Kim to be a witness in the death chamber because of their close friendship, and because Kim was the first person, other than his attorney, to really believe he was innocent. 'He kept me motivated and kept me strong, so I want him there in the end because of the strength and courage he's given me over the years.'

These were poignant answers to some very personal questions. As a television interviewer, you can quickly identify the best sound bites for inclusion in a report. If you haven't prompted strong, articulate answers, you keep asking variations of the same question. But the sound bites were coming thick and fast from Richard Glossip.

Time was running out. We needed to leave for the airport as soon as possible. I wanted to end our conversation on a lighter note by getting him to talk about something you wouldn't expect to hear from a man who had a date in the death chamber in just three days. I'd heard he was a fan of British TV comedy, and in particular the venerable BBC series set in Yorkshire about a group of elderly friends.

'*Last of the Summer Wine* is, I think, one of the most incredible shows that was ever made. Because you've got these three old guys, and my favourite character is Compo because he tells you that you can lead a life so simple that you don't need fancy cars or homes or stuff like that. He can lie in the grass on a hill or have a cup of tea or something silly. And I just love watching that show because it makes me feel you can enjoy life no matter what happens to you. It's helped me a lot.'

'And you can laugh even at this dark time?'

'Oh yeah, I laugh every day. Someone asked me the other day – do you have good days and bad days? And I told her honestly, I try never to have a bad day. I wake up and I try to find the good in every day no matter what it is. And a lot of the guards watch me, and think I'm weird because I'm laughing and stuff. But I think it's the only way to do it. If something happens and I should be executed, I don't know what's on the other side of death, but I know one thing, I don't want to go out hating people or being angry at the world for what happened to me. I just want to go out peacefully and knowing that there's something, hopefully, on the other side that makes it all worthwhile.'

It was an eloquent way to finish. As I thanked him for talking to me, I realised how lucky I was to have found such an articulate prisoner to contribute to the death-penalty debate. Kim had now confirmed what I had feared: that it was too late to add me to the list of official witnesses at the execution. I would have to rely on being selected in a ballot to be a media witness. But I was confident that my contact with Glossip, plus interviews I would record in Oklahoma, would still help tell a powerful story.

Kim's wife Mary had phoned a cab and it was waiting outside. It would take ten minutes for Jake to pack away his camera equipment, lights and cables, but we didn't have time to wait. I was meeting another cameraman in Oklahoma. So Kim told Jake to carry on packing and slam the door on the way out – we needed to go.

At La Guardia Airport, the snowploughs were hard at work and the flight to Oklahoma City managed to take off in the nick of time before what the media had dubbed Snowmaggedon really took hold. By contrast, Oklahoma was unseasonably warm, with the temperature almost touching 80°F. I met up with my cameraman Dickon Mager, who had flown in from Washington DC and seemed happy to be working with me rather than filming Snowmaggedon in New York. Dickon and I had worked together many times before, in the UK, Israel and America. He's very good at his job: thoughtful, methodical and with a great eye for pictures.

Our first task on Tuesday morning was to go to a news conference being staged at the Oklahoma State Capitol, where Sister Helen Prejean was to speak out about the Richard Glossip case. The Capitol houses Oklahoma's legislature as well as the Governor's office. It's a grand building, but the news conference was in the tiny press room.

Diehard campaigners from the Oklahoma Coalition to Abolish the Death Penalty were assembling. I introduced myself, but even though they welcomed me warmly, I didn't get the impression that they were particularly excited or impressed that a reporter had come all the way from London to be there. And for good reason: it was more important for them to make an impression closer to home. They needed people in Oklahoma to put pressure on the state governor, who had the power to delay, though not cancel, an imminent execution. Their best hope was getting their views heard in the local media.

As cameras were hoisted onto tripods and reporters filed into the room, I sought out the one person I knew: Phil Cross, the Fox 25 reporter who had been so helpful and encouraging by phone and email. I arranged to talk to him on camera later. Then Sister Helen Prejean walked into the room. She was wearing a dark business suit with a large crucifix around her neck, and like many of the campaigners she had a lapel badge with a red line through the words *Death Penalty*.

Sister Helen and I had spoken on the phone and exchanged emails prior to my visit. She speaks with the slow drawl of her native Louisiana, but with the energy of a New Orleans jazz club. And she effortlessly combines the good character that you'd expect of a nun with the street sass of someone who knows how to handle herself in a rough crowd. She's in her mid seventies but has lost none of her drive and passion, despite three decades of fighting the death penalty and often being on the losing side.

In the public mind there are two Sister Helen Prejeans: the real one, who has visibly aged with the passage of time; and the fictional one, played by Susan Sarandon, who never gets older no matter how many years have passed since *Dead Man Walking* became a hugely successful movie.

She took her place in a line-up behind the lectern with fellow speakers. They were joined by several supporters carrying signs saying *Don't Kill For Me*, including a mother holding a baby. A photo of Richard Glossip's face behind bars was on the front of the lectern. Kim Van Atta arrived and squatted on the floor directly in front of the microphone. He held up his phone so the person on the other end could hear what was being said. It was Richard Glossip on the line.

Local politicians, church leaders and Glossip's attorney were among those who would speak before Sister Helen. I was struck by something that one of them said. The Reverend Adam Leathers attacked the death penalty, saying that Jesus Christ had himself been a victim of capital punishment. It was a challenge to those in Oklahoma who take their lead on morality from the churches they attend every Sunday. Many Christians in the state support Old Testament justice.

When Sister Helen took her turn addressing the media, she quickly outlined her credentials for being one of America's most outspoken critics of capital punishment, saying, 'I've accompanied six human beings to execution. Richard Glossip would be the seventh man I would be with to be killed by the state.'

She said the 'eyes of the world' were on Oklahoma and 'people don't understand how the people of Oklahoma could allow this to be done in their name'. She told reporters that Pope Francis was watching and praying for all those involved. 'There is no humane way to kill a conscious human being. People I've accompanied to execution all died inside their minds a thousand times before they were strapped into the electric chair or to be lethally injected.'

She highlighted the fact that one of the other speakers in the room was Bud Welch. On 19 April 1995, Bud's only daughter Julie went to work in her office in a federal building in downtown Oklahoma City. Just after 9 a.m., a huge car bomb was detonated, destroying the building and killing Julie and 167 other men, women and children. The bomber, Timothy McVeigh, had a grudge against the federal government. He was convicted in a federal court, and four years after the Oklahoma City Bombing he was executed, one of only three people in modern times to be put to death by the US government rather than an individual state.

Bud Welch opposed the execution, and has campaigned against the death penalty ever since. He's even become friends with McVeigh's father. He said, 'It took me almost a year to realise that revenge was not part of the healing process. That's how I came to be opposed to the death penalty before Timothy McVeigh was sentenced to death and I reached that in my own mind about a year after Julie's death.'

He told me that when he attended meetings of family members of victims, people would ask him how he could oppose the sentence. 'I would say to them, the day we take Tim McVeigh from his cage and kill him is not going to be part of your healing process. I had so many people a year, two years, three years after his death come to me and say, "You were correct."'

Most death-row cases drag on for many years, but McVeigh's execution came relatively quickly. 'He asked for an execution date. He was a volunteer. I don't think the federal government really wanted to execute him. I just felt really bad for his dad, Bill McVeigh, and his younger sister Jennifer. I had met with them, and found them to be delightful human beings. I could see the grief in their eyes about the upcoming execution. After it, Bill McVeigh and I had one thing in common: we had both buried our children.'

The campaigners moved from the news conference to the Governor's office, bringing with them an online petition that by then had more than thirty thousand signatures in support of a stay of execution. A large portrait photo of the Governor, Mary Fallin, dominated the lobby of her offices, and this was the closest anyone would get to her. She was unwilling or unable to meet Sister Helen and the others, so a member of her staff was dispatched to take delivery of the petition for the benefit of the cameras that had crowded inside.

Afterwards I caught up with Mark Henricksen, one of the attorneys trying to keep Richard Glossip out of the death chamber. 'Whatever one's dispute about the guilt or innocence issue, it is undisputed that he did not have a sufficiently broken moral compass to go and take someone else's life. He's not even alleged to have been at the crime scene when Barry Van Treese was killed by Justin Sneed.'

Henricksen argued that his client did not even come close to the definition 'the worst of the worst' that separated most convicted killers from those who would pay the ultimate price for their crime. 'Prior to his arrest Richard Glossip was never involved in any accusation of crime and in his seventeen years in Oklahoma's death row, he has never been accused of violating any of the prison regulations. That kind of personal background of no criminal history and no in-prison violations makes him sort of remarkable. Clearly he is not among the worst of the worst. It is a peculiar distortion of justice that we have a killer planning to live out his days in a medium-security prison, and we have a non-killer who is scheduled to die in two days. It is a further example of how unjust the death penalty is as applied in Oklahoma. It is basically a bad-luck lottery.'

But it was too late for Henricksen to plead in court for clemency or innocence. Those appeals had been rejected. The only avenue he had left was to fight against the method of execution. He highlighted the botched execution of Clayton Lockett and accused the state of human experimentation. 'It appeared the condemned was suffering, gasping and conscious. We should not use these human beings as lab rats for Oklahoma's attempt to find a constitutionally acceptable death-penalty protocol.'

Comparing prisoners to lab rats ensured that particular answer would find its way into my TV report. The local TV crews were, like me, still conducting interviews an hour after the news conference was over. Because Glossip had called Kim Van Atta so that he could listen to the news conference, a couple of reporters took the opportunity to record his voice, with their microphones pressed close to the phone's tiny speaker. He told them he was still optimistic of a reprieve.

I arranged to meet Sister Helen outside the building to record our interview. We talked about her first execution in 1984, when she was spiritual adviser to a man called Elmo Patrick Sonnier. He was put to death in the electric chair having been convicted of killing a teenage couple, though there was some doubt as to whether he or his brother was the actual killer. The crime was in Louisiana, where the law says that only the person who commits a murder can receive a death sentence. If Richard Glossip lived there, he could not have been sentenced to death for the murder of Barry Van Treese.

Sister Helen told me that nobody protested about the Sonnier execution. 'What I saw that night set my soul on fire. Outside the prison I vomited.'

She decided to write about her experiences in that case, together with that of another electric-chair death she witnessed, a man called Robert Lee Willie. When her book, *Dead Man Walking*, became a movie, the two cases were merged to create a fictionalised inmate called Matthew Poncelet, played by Sean Penn. By the time the film was made, lethal injection rather than the electric chair was the norm, so the climactic scene shows the inmate being killed with drugs.

Sister Helen believes that this method is for the benefit of those carrying out the killing rather than the prisoner. 'Why use a paralytic if anaesthesia puts the person under? It's to stop them flailing around. It's to save the witnesses from seeing the suffering.' She argues that if the anaesthetic truly renders the prisoner unconscious, then a second drug to stop them moving around is superfluous.

I asked her why she had agreed to be with Richard Glossip when she hadn't attended an execution in a decade.

'It was the simplicity of his letter. He wasn't overstating. He wasn't exaggerating. It was a short letter: "I'm innocent. I just want everyone to know I'm innocent." So I was drawn to that. I believe he really is innocent. There is an integrity and simplicity in him. I bolted awake in the middle of the night and thought, what am I going to do for him? It's not just to accept the death penalty, comfort him as he dies … you've got to resist things that are wrong. You have to actively unmask the evil and then you've got to resist it. I swung into action. I knew then I had to get the word out about Richard Glossip.'

Up to then, his lawyers had been reluctant to chase publicity. But now they had no choice. And there was nobody better to attract media attention than the author of *Dead Man Walking*. 'I'm hopeful. I know that as long as Richard is alive, we can pursue the case of his innocence. The world focusing on a place, including what's happening with you, with Sky, helps spread the word and create the atmosphere for it to become more possible.'

She smiled when we finished recording. 'Did you like that I gave Sky a little namecheck there?'

Oh yes, she knew how to work the media.

Later that evening, once it was dark, Dickon and I arrived at a location central to the story: 301 South Council Road, Oklahoma City. The Best Budget Inn has now become the Super 40 Inn, but it's the same motel where the lives of Richard Glossip, Justin Sneed and Barry Van Treese became fatally intertwined. I had toyed with the idea of booking a room so that we could have a valid reason for being there. I had even considered asking specifically for room 102, but I knew that might have aroused suspicion. The manager could have told me to clear off.

I decided to see how much we could video without attracting attention. That way, if we were asked to leave, we would at least take away some material to work with. But nobody from the motel approached us to ask what we were doing. Perhaps they hadn't seen us. I had time to stare at the building, and wonder what really happened that night in January 1997.

CHAPTER 8

From Birth to Death Row

1963–2004

Richard Glossip jokes that he's from a hillbilly family. His mother was only fifteen when she married his dad. He was the seventh of sixteen children, born and raised in Galesburg, Illinois, a city of around thirty thousand people, two hundred miles from Chicago. His father served in the military during World War II, and then worked as a coal miner before moving from Kentucky to Illinois in search of a better job.

Richard's only bad childhood memory is having his bike stolen. That, and occasional beatings with a stick from his mother when she needed to enforce discipline in their chaotic household. 'The kids came so fast that it seemed like they just appeared out of nowhere, the house just seemed to get smaller and smaller. One day I'm sharing a room with one brother, and the next it was four.'

By the time he was a teenager, it was a madhouse. Eight boys, eight girls, and though he loved them all and wouldn't have traded the time he had there, by the age of fourteen he had had enough. He attaches no blame to his parents for making him want to run away. 'They were great, anyone who can have sixteen kids and keep them fed and clothed and love each and every one of them deserves to be patted on the back and given a medal.'

He left because he had no privacy or time for himself, but he exchanged it for a life sleeping on park benches. Eventually he began to stay at a friend's house, returned to school and got a part-time job in a restaurant. At the age of fifteen, he met and fell in love with a black girl who was a few years older, and they moved in together. 'At first it was a little rocky because I never took into account the race issue, especially for that time. I took a lot of crap from white and black people who thought that what I was doing was sick. But we fought through and made it work.'

They got married using a false birth certificate because Richard was only sixteen, and soon he was a teenager with two daughters, Christina and Ericka. He says he loved his girls, but some of his friends and family still gave him a hard time for being in a mixed-race relationship. 'I was getting tired of the stares and the wisecracks I would get from people. I still tried to stick it out but it was getting harder.'

He took a job as a delivery driver for Domino's Pizza, but his boss spotted his potential and encouraged him to get into their trainee manager programme. He says he became Domino's youngest manager, with a store in Rock Island, Illinois, which was soon taking more than ten thousand dollars a week. He was moved to a bigger store, but there was another change in his life too. He had met another woman, called Missy King, and he left his young family to be with her. They decided to make a fresh start in Oklahoma, where

Richard's parents had moved after they'd retired. Two more children followed, Tori Lynn and a son, Richard junior.

Richard specialised in taking over pizza delivery outlets that weren't performing, and turning the business round. 'I'm a workaholic. I worked 24/7 even on holidays. If there was a chance I would do even just a little money on those days, I would open. Every penny counts when you get bonuses.'

Just when life seemed perfect, the pizza store he was working at was sold, and he found himself out of work. For a couple of years the family moved around, with Richard taking jobs with other pizza businesses in Iowa and Nebraska, but Missy became homesick and they returned home. At his latest restaurant, one of the workers he hired was D-Anna Wood. They had an affair, and his wife found out. 'Missy was a wonderful person, wife and mother. She truly didn't deserve that. Losing her was truly a huge mistake on my part. The day I met Missy at the attorney's to sign the divorce papers has to be one of the hardest things I had to do.'

He returned to Oklahoma, taking D-Anna with him. He became manager of a motel, but quit when it ran into financial problems. However, it wouldn't be long before he was back in business. Cliff Everhart, who had looked after security at the motel, told him a friend was looking for someone to run the Best Budget Inn, and introduced him to Barry Van Treese.

Richard went to take a look, and wasn't impressed. 'This place was pretty nasty. The rooms were run-down and dirty. The outside of the motel wasn't kept up. And the bulk of the business was from hookers, crack and meth users.'

He told Van Treese what he expected to be paid, and that he needed supplies to be able to mend and clean the property. Van Treese agreed. Richard spent a few dirty, tiring weeks steam-cleaning carpets and replacing broken sinks and toilets. Half a dozen rooms were uninhabitable, but within a month, he'd fixed them, and some nights the motel was sold out. He says everyone told him the motel had never looked better, and Van Treese was impressed. 'Barry would make comments like he wished he could clone me, and even bragged to other family members.'

Just over a year later, in the summer of 1996, he met two brothers from Texas who were staying at the motel while working on roof repairs in the area. He knew them as Wes and Justin Taylor, but Justin's real surname was Sneed. They asked if they could help out with maintenance in return for a free room, and Richard agreed. Shortly afterwards, Justin's older brother decided to return to Texas.

Business was good, and Van Treese let Richard get on with the day-to-day running of the motel without interfering. Richard says that Van Treese was aware that Justin Sneed was working there, although a curious incident occurred one night when the owner was staying at the motel. According to Richard, Van Treese woke at 5 a.m. to find Sneed standing over him, claiming he was there to clean the room. Richard told Van Treese that he hadn't instructed him to do so, and offered to fire him. He says Van Treese told him not to. Later came Sneed's suggestion that he could rob the motel and that Richard would report that someone else had done it. 'I said, "You're joking, right?" He said he was. I know now I should have taken it more seriously.'

The following month, Van Treese was dead and Sneed and Glossip were in jail. Richard called his brother Bobby and told him he needed an attorney. A couple of weeks later, Wayne Fournerat showed up. Richard says he was relieved. He'd been warned that a public defender would be more likely to push for a plea deal and he was adamant that he was innocent of murder.

D-Anna came to visit him a few times in jail but eventually admitted that she was now in a relationship with a friend of the Van Treese family. On a subsequent visit she showed off the breast implants that her new lover had paid for. 'Salt in the wound, man. Salt in the wound,' said Richard.

As a man who had never been in prison, it took him some time to get used to life in the county jail. He would spend his days walking around the common areas, chatting and getting to know the other inmates. One man in particular became his friend. Earl Frederick had been convicted of murdering a man, but had the verdict overturned on appeal. He was awaiting a new trial, and he passed on his experience of life inside.

Richard says that Frederick taught him to respect the prison guards, because they would then respect him. He credits Frederick for helping him get through those tough first few months of imprisonment. Earl Frederick was later convicted a second time. He had stabbed a man to death with a screwdriver during a drunken fight. Richard believed he should have been convicted of manslaughter, but Frederick didn't argue with the verdict, or with the punishment. He told Richard he didn't want to spend his days in prison, or continue with what he called 'this horrible life'. He dropped his appeal and was executed in 2002.

After his own conviction and sentence in June 1998, Richard quickly discovered what it was like to be a death-row prisoner. He says he was freaked out because the guards in his jail yelled, 'Dead man walking!' as he came through the door. 'I had never been this scared in my life.' Being convicted meant a transfer to a much tougher prison regime. A week after he was formally sentenced, he was transferred to Oklahoma State Penitentiary. He was woken at 3.30 a.m., strip-searched and then put into a van. He claims that one of the guards who was driving him to the prison in McAlester told him he wished he would run so he could shoot him.

However, the camaraderie of death row meant that other inmates gave him shampoo, toothpaste and cigarettes when he moved into his new cell. They told him they did it for all the new guys. Needless to say, however, the state penitentiary was not a welcoming place. 'I truly hated it there. It was a very eerie place. The cell to me felt like I was in a tomb. Your cell from floor to ceiling was concrete. Your bunks were cement slabs. The door was metal with a thick Plexiglas window two inches wide and three inches high with large tubed bars on the outside. You have no direct sunlight in your cell. You could only tell the sun was out because you could see it on the so-called yard, which was cement floor and twenty-foot-high cement walls with a steel grating over the top. You could see the sun through the holes in the grating. You could not, however, see anything going on in the outside world. No trees or grass, no people except for staff. No cars, et cetera. You had to do whatever you could to occupy your mind or it could really get to you.

'When the guards would do their counts, which was every hour, you would hear the metal clanking from opening and shutting doors. Inmates screaming and hollering, beating on their doors. It was very eerie and wasn't easy to get used to, especially if you had not gone through anything like this before. It makes it twice as bad knowing that you shouldn't even be there in the first place.'

Nor was he getting on with his cellmate, Jack Walker, who seemed to enjoy telling him the grisly details of how he had almost decapitated his girlfriend. Richard eventually asked to move to another cell. Walker was executed three years later. Richard's new cellmate, Robert Lambert, had burned two people alive in their car. His accomplice was executed but Lambert had his death sentence commuted because he was deemed mentally ill.

Legal moves seemed to be heading in the right direction for Richard. He needed a new attorney to replace the incompetent Wayne Fourncrat, but he had no money, so he had to rely on the appointment of a public defender from the Oklahoma Indigent Defense System. OIDS sent two attorneys to visit him in prison, who told him about the difficulty of winning the right to appeal. Richard was unimpressed at their attitude. After they left, he asked for access to a telephone, and called the OIDS office. He demanded someone who would fight to prove his innocence. A few days later, a letter arrived from a new attorney called G. Lynn Burch, who said he planned to visit him in prison in a couple of weeks.

When they met, Richard was immediately impressed. Burch announced that he would start going through the trial transcripts to start working on an appeal, the previous attorneys having failed to file the necessary paperwork. Richard was relieved to have Burch taking over, especially when the attorney told him to phone him every week to check on progress. Burch says he hit it off with Glossip straight away, because he believed his story and realised 'I have an innocent client.'

Burch successfully argued that there were grounds for an appeal, and the Oklahoma Court of Criminal Appeals appointed a district judge called Twyla Gray to oversee it. She was later to remark that Wayne Fournerat was 'the most incompetent counsel that any of us have ever known or heard of', and she called the trial 'bizarre'.

When Burch presented his list of complaints, the appeal court accepted his arguments. The conviction of Richard Glossip was overturned and a retrial was ordered. The appeal court ruled that 'Trial counsel's conduct was so ineffective that we have no confidence that a reliable adversarial proceeding took place.'

There was no shortage of evidence of Fournerat's incompetence. Among the points highlighted were his lack of preparation, the incident where he called the Tulsa motel manager a 'fictitious person', his failure to prepare for the penalty phase of the trial, and having to take advice from the judge when Glossip's mother was on the witness stand.

The appeal court came to the conclusion that Fournerat had expected Glossip to plead guilty and wasn't expecting to have to defend him in court.

But the most serious error was his failure to show the inconsistencies in Justin Sneed's version of events, particularly by not playing the video of his interview with detectives. 'Trial counsel's failure to utilize important impeachment evidence against Justin Sneed stands out as the most glaring deficiency in counsel's performance. Evidence of counsel's failure to utilize the videotape of Justin Sneed is also apparent from the trial record.'

Judge Gray noted the numerous inconsistencies between Sneed's trial testimony and his videotaped confession. She identified at least seven material inconsistencies and noted at least five things in Sneed's trial testimony that he had completely omitted from his videotaped statement.

David McKenzie, the attorney whom Richard had first approached for advice, also said that Fournerat was 'the most incompetent attorney I've ever comes across'. He called it a 'crazy system where you are licensed to try death-penalty cases with absolutely no practical experience. Innocent people die based on the incompetency of lawyers.'

Fournerat was later struck off the Oklahoma District Bar Association, and his career as a trial lawyer was ended. In 2010, he tried and failed to take legal action against the authors of an article that criticised his handling of the case. To this day he is active online in discussing the Glossip case, and I spoke to him as part of my research. He argues that drug deals played a part in the Van Treese murder, but his theories are rejected by the other attorneys who have worked with Richard Glossip.

There were other aspects of the trial that were criticised by the appeal court judges. A lesser offence of accessory after the fact should have been available to the jury if they felt Glossip was not guilty of murder; and at least one member of the jury had brought a copy of the Bible into the room while they were deciding on a verdict. The law insists that juries should only be influenced by the evidence, not religious scripture.

Richard got the news that he'd won his appeal in a phone call from Lynn Burch.

'I was so happy and I thanked him. He also told me that he would be doing my trial as well, which took one hell of a load off my mind. He told me that it would be a month or so before they took me back. Now the time I was doing didn't seem so hard any more, it was truly great to know that maybe this time they would do the right thing and I would be given my life back.'

With his conviction for murder overturned, Richard was removed from death row at the state penitentiary and sent back to the county jail in Oklahoma City, pending a new trial. He became a trusty, with responsibility for cleaning, and it gave him the chance to talk to other inmates. His policy of treating guards with respect, in the hope that they would treat him the same way, seemed to work. One of the guards he befriended was Scott Husband, who contacted me when he heard I was reporting on the Glossip case, asking to be a character witness.

Husband began working at the jail in October 2003, when Richard was the prisoner entrusted with helping to keep his section of the jail clean. He didn't realise he had been convicted of murder and was astonished when he found out. 'He said to me, "Don't worry, I ain't going to kill you, I wouldn't hurt anybody." He was a great guy. He cleaned tables, mopped floors, cleaned showers, and after he left and another inmate took over, we thought, we miss Richard. He was a hard worker. He was always in a cheerful mood.'

Richard was happy, because he was sure he was on the path to being exonerated. Even though he was still facing a new trial, he was confident he would be found not guilty. He was so certain that he would win his freedom that a few months before his case returned to court, he turned down another offer that would have saved his life, just as he had rejected a plea deal before his first trial.

Lynn Burch, his attorney, was keeping all his options open. He was trying to secure a not-guilty verdict, but his primary task was to keep his client alive. He asked the District Attorney's office whether they would consider a plea deal. It was a routine question, one he would always ask, even if his client's guilt was not in doubt. A deal would save the court time and money by avoiding a trial. Burch sensed that his appeal court victory had made the DA's office nervous about winning a retrial. They had already replaced Fern Smith as the prosecutor. He described her replacement, Connie Smothermon, as 'very aggressive and better on her feet' than Fern Smith.

The controversial DA, 'Cowboy' Bob Macy, had retired, and his successor, Wes Lane, agreed to a plea deal. If Richard Glossip pleaded guilty to murder, he would receive a life sentence, and crucially, it was *not* life without parole. Because he had already been in jail for nearly a decade, he would be eligible to apply for parole within ten years, and the court would recommend it be granted. He would almost certainly be a free man by around 2016.

Lynn Burch told him of the deal on the table, but Glossip said no. 'Richard rejected it on the basis that he cannot confess to something he didn't do.' For Glossip, the decision was straightforward. He was not involved in the murder, so he refused to say he had been. He and Burch debated the offer, but his mind was made up. Burch, though, had mixed feelings. 'Part of me was disappointed, because it would have been a great relief to know that they weren't going to take his life. But on the other hand, I completely understood that he felt that he had justice going his way after the successful appeal.'

By this time, Burch had been Glossip's lawyer for almost three years. They'd formed a friendship, as well as a professional relationship. 'We were close. We talked about how long we'd known each other, and he understood why it might be in his best interests to do that. But he was adamant.' Within three months, however, their partnership was brought to a dramatic and controversial end.

Burch was in the final stages of getting ready for the new trial. There had been pre-trial hearings to discuss the evidence and the start date. He and his co-counsel had gone to visit Justin Sneed in prison to talk about his version of events, bringing with them crime-scene photos. Burch says Sneed was 'cool as a cucumber' as he recalled the murder. 'I remember when he came in and sat down, there was no whiff or air that he was this easily malleable man-child or whatever the heck they've characterised him as, that he would do the bidding of other people.'

Sneed was enthusiastic about the medium-security prison in which he was an inmate. He praised the quality of the food, and how he was able to have meals alongside his visitors. But after the visit was over, he alleged that Burch had threatened him, and made a complaint. The District Attorney's office raised it with the judge who was due to hear the case. It meant that the trial of Richard Glossip would have also heard accusations of intimidation by his lawyer.

'I was infuriated. It was a lie,' said Burch. Although his co-counsel could have refuted the claim in court, Burch decided that the row would become 'a ridiculous sideshow and a procedural nightmare. The jury would be entreated to conclude that the defendant's lawyer is a lying manipulative criminal, just like his client.'

Burch decided he had no alternative but to withdraw from the case. He was bitterly disappointed. He had immersed himself in the case and visited Glossip at least once a week.

They talked about sport and music when they weren't discussing the trial. They had built what he calls a 'trusting relationship', and it was Burch who introduced Richard to Kim Van Atta, who would become his closest friend. After months of painstakingly working through the evidence, he was convinced that his client was innocent, and as confident as he could be of proving him not guilty of murder. 'I think there was no evidence to tie Richard to it, and their alleged motive is ridiculous, so then I'd cross-examine the crap out of the people who were lying about Richard being involved.'

Even now, a decade later, Burch is frustrated that he came close to representing Glossip at trial, only to be denied. He's also angry when lawyers and campaigners who later became involved in the case criticise the standard of legal advice the prisoner received. He felt he had laid the foundations of a solid defence, although he hadn't decided whether or not Glossip should testify in his retrial.

'Richard understandably had a lot of frustration and anxiety built up in him because of what he'd been through over the last few years, and so I had concerns about him being able to contain his emotions. I did have concerns that if you put him on the stand and let him get cross-examined about things like the money, he would get angry and I did not want the jury to see that. But Richard is articulate. I know he would have wanted to testify.'

The new trial was delayed to allow a new defence attorney to read into the case, but Glossip would have to do without the lawyer he trusted when he faced a second jury.

CHAPTER 9

Different Jury, Same Verdict

May 2004

All the key figures in the courtroom in Richard Glossip's second trial had changed except one. Glossip himself was the only survivor from the original trial. He had new attorneys; there was a new assistant district attorney to prosecute him; and a new judge to keep them in line. On 11 May 2004, the Honourable Twyla Mason Gray – who'd overseen Glossip's successful appeal – gathered ninety-one prospective jurors into her court and began the long, tedious process of finding twelve men and women who would sit in judgement.

Judge Gray introduced the assistant district attorneys as Connie Smothermon and Gary Ackley. Silas Lyman and Wayne Woodyard, public defenders from the Oklahoma Indigent Defense System, were now representing Glossip. More than seven years had passed since the murder of Barry Van Treese, and even though his conviction for murder had been overturned, Glossip had spent that entire seven years in jail. It had been three years since he won his appeal, but the controversial replacement of Lynn Burch as his attorney had brought further delay to the already painfully slow legal system.

As the judge spoke to the prospective jurors about their experience of crime and the law, she uncovered many who had a more extensive criminal record than Glossip himself prior to his arrest in 1998. Some had been convicted of drugs, alcohol or shoplifting offences. Others had close relatives in jail; one had a father serving thirty-five years for drug offences under the three-strikes rule that added extra jail time for repeat offenders. Another was related by marriage to a murderer who had been executed in 1990.

As usual, they were quizzed about their attitude to the death penalty. One woman wrestled with her conscience throughout the day before finally saying, 'I don't understand how the world would be a better place putting somebody to death.' By contrast, a man was also excused because he was so pro-death-penalty that he couldn't contemplate sending a murderer to jail. Eventually, after two and a half days of questions and answers, a jury was assembled of seven men and five women.

Prosecutor Connie Smothermon had joined the Oklahoma District Attorney's office five years earlier to head up their domestic violence unit. But she had also prosecuted murder cases, and other violent crimes. She began her opening statement by painting a picture of Richard Glossip as a man with a comfortable life that was being threatened because he was about to be fired. She claimed that his 'gravy train was coming to a halt. And the only way to stop that was to eliminate Barry Van Treese.' But her outline of the events from January 1997 would have been familiar to those who had attended the first trial.

Silas Lyman's opening statement for the defence was very different from Wayne Fournerat's rambling address six years before. He was experienced at defending those facing a murder charge, and he spoke calmly about the presumption of innocence and the need for the jury to base a verdict on the evidence they would hear. This time there were no other suspects, and no conspiracy. Just Justin Sneed, 'acting alone'. Those words were used repeatedly. Lyman claimed that Sneed was the sole killer and that Glossip only found out about the murder after the event. He concluded that 'the evidence will show that Richard Glossip was guilty of a mistake in judgment in not telling what he knew, when he knew it'.

Donna Van Treese was again the first witness. She told the court she had remarried the previous summer, but she wore her first wedding ring on a necklace. She explained that the deaths of both her mother and Barry's mother within a few weeks in 1996 had diverted their attention away from the motel businesses. They had left Richard Glossip to take care of things, checking in with him by phone and visiting the motels only every second week. But after Christmas and New Year, they decided to resume a more active role, particularly as they were concerned about apparent discrepancies in the accounts.

She went on to say that some of her financial records had been destroyed when a water leak flooded her home. Other copies had been given to Glossip's original attorney, Wayne

Fournerat, back in 1998 and were never returned, but she said they showed that just over $6,000 was missing from the motel. After the murder, she visited the place and said it was in a 'horrid' condition. Every room needed something doing to it, and she was amazed that people were staying there. It looked as if nothing had been done for six or seven months. She said that if she had known before, she would have fired Richard Glossip.

However, under cross-examination, Donna Van Treese acknowledged that she and her husband would give staff the chance to rectify mistakes, and only if they didn't improve would they lose their jobs. She said that she had spoken to Richard Glossip on several occasions about financial discrepancies, but she had not felt the need to fire him.

Having suffered the blow of having Glossip's conviction overturned, the DA's office had worked harder at tracing witnesses ahead of the second trial, so several people were testifying for the first time. John Prittie had been staying right next door to the murder scene, in room 103, on the night in question, and described being woken by voices in the next room, and the sound of breaking glass. He thought they were male and female voices. When it went quiet, he went back to sleep without alerting anyone.

In the 1998 trial, D-Anna Wood had been one of only two witnesses for the defence. In 2004, she testified again, though this time she was called by the prosecution as a potentially hostile witness. In the intervening years she had married and her name was now D-Anna Garmendez. On the stand, she was less forthcoming with answers than she had been in the first trial. Sometimes she said she couldn't remember, or she didn't know. Most of her answers were just a few words. She seldom managed more than one sentence.

Her story tallied with the version of events she had given in 1998, but it had to be dragged out of her bit by bit. At one point the judge had to check one of the jurors hadn't fallen asleep, because his eyes were closed. During her testimony she agreed that she had advised Richard to say nothing to the police about Justin Sneed until they were sure Barry Van Treese was dead. She didn't believe he had anything to do with the murder.

After D-Anna had completed her testimony and the jury had been sent home for the day, defence attorney Wayne Woodyard complained to the judge about a prosecution tactic. As statements were made by witnesses, some of the quotes were written on large sheets of paper and displayed in the courtroom, remaining there after the witness had left the stand, in full view of the jury. Woodyard argued that they were selective parts of the testimony.

But Connie Smothermon defended her use of the posters, saying it was a record of the 'various spins that the defendant had put on his version of the facts'. Judge Gray didn't see anything wrong with the posters and denied the motion to have them removed.

The following day, motel guest John Beavers reprised evidence he first gave in 1998. He had lived in room 245 at the Best Budget Inn for ten years, up to and beyond the murder of Barry Van Treese, and had got to know both the owner and Richard Glossip well. 'Richard seemed like a real go-getter,' he told the jury. 'He was always working hard. It seemed like he always had plans to do this, that and the other. I can't give you any specifics, but he always seemed to have some project going on at the property.'

Billye Hooper, the motel receptionist, also returned to court to testify. She said Van Treese had a good relationship with Glossip, commenting, 'It seemed like when Rich first started, him and Barry got along very well. He did a really good job. He was doing a lot of maintenance and trying to fix the place up and I couldn't observe any problems going on between him and Barry.'

At one point she mentioned that sometimes Glossip would express his relief when his boss left the motel after a lengthy visit. Connie Smothermon wrote on her display board, 'Expressed pleasure when Barry was finally off the property.'

Hooper described Justin Sneed as quiet and polite and said he wasn't aggressive. She thought he and Richard were 'very close'. She didn't believe Justin Sneed would have murdered Van Treese of his own volition, because he hardly knew him. She told the court she had had a heart attack in August 1996 and was off work until October. During that time, Glossip and his girlfriend had to do her job. Hooper said she didn't feel that Glossip wanted her back at the motel, and when she did return to work, she became suspicious that rooms were being rented and not accounted for.

When Hooper finished her testimony, the defence made another protest about the display of poster-sized quotes. Wayne Woodyard asked for them to be removed, saying they gave undue influence to testimony and it was improper. At the very least he felt they should be removed after the witness had completed his or her evidence. Once again Judge Gray refused, saying he was only objecting because it was damaging to the defendant's case. She suggested the defence could adopt the same tactic. Later, Woodyard would ask to take photographs of the posters so they could be used as evidence in any future appeal. The judge said no.

The next prosecution witness had not been called to appear at the first trial, an omission that had led Richard Glossip's woefully inadequate attorney Wayne Fournerat to suggest he was a 'fictitious character'. But William Bender was real, and his testimony supported the prosecution's claim that Glossip was about to be fired from his job.

Bender and his wife had run Barry Van Treese's motel in Tulsa, which the owner had visited just hours before he was killed. He said Van Treese was usually in a jovial mood, but not that night. He described him as 'all puffed up. He was upset. He was mad. He was all red in the face.' He related how Van Treese had made a point of checking the booking records of the Tulsa motel, and the state of the rooms, because he was unhappy with what he had found at his Oklahoma City motel.

Bender claimed that Van Treese had given Glossip an ultimatum. 'He said he had given [Rich] the time it took for him to get to Tulsa and back to come up with the weekend's receipts that were missing and if he came up with that, he was going to give him another week to come up with the registration cards and get all the year-end receipts together.'

According to Bender, if Glossip failed to do so, Van Treese was threatening to call the police. He also claimed that the owner had asked him to take over the running of the Best Budget Inn, though he said he would have turned down the job because his family were settled in Tulsa.

The following day, Bender heard from Donna Van Treese that her husband was missing. A day later, he phoned the Best Budget Inn to find out whether he had turned up. He said he spoke to Richard Glossip, who told him the owner was dead, and he himself had been questioned by detectives. 'He said he was beat to a bloody pulp. They found him cold as ice, dead as a doornail.' Connie Smothermon made sure she wrote down all those phrases on her poster collection.

Bender said he asked Glossip if he had killed Van Treese. He said Glossip denied it, but said he knew who had. He told Bender that the murder of their boss had scared him so much that he 'feared for his life'. That was why, he said, he hadn't gone to the police.

Jackie Williams had been the housekeeper at the Best Budget Inn. She told the jury how Glossip had hired her, and she was given a free room in return for working there. Williams said Glossip told her to stay in her room out of sight when Barry Van Treese was visiting. She also told the court that on the morning after the murder, Glossip told her to clean only the upstairs rooms, not the ground floor, where room 102 was located. But under cross-examination, she agreed that in her original police statement she had said that it was Justin Sneed who told her to clean the upstairs rooms.

Kayla Pursley had lived at the motel, and worked at

the gas station close to it. Her testimony was important in backing up the state's description of Justin Sneed as being impressionable and under Glossip's control. She told the court that Sneed used to play with her young sons, and said he was very childlike. 'He didn't make a lot of decisions. You had to tell him sometimes what to do. He didn't eat unless you kind of told him to eat,' she said.

On the night of the murder, Sneed came to the gas station for a drink and cigarettes. Pursley said his demeanour was normal. A couple of hours later, fellow resident John Beavers came by and said that he'd walked past room 102 and the window was broken. Pursley phoned the motel's front office, but there was no answer.

At breakfast time the following day, she saw both Sneed and Glossip in the motel reception. She testified that Glossip told her that he and Justin had thrown out two drunks for breaking the window of room 102. She overheard him say he was going to help Sneed fix the window and clean the room, which she thought was unusual because he didn't normally do that. As she walked past 102, she noticed blood on the broken glass and asked Glossip about it. She said he told her that someone had got cut while cleaning up.

Kayla's ex-husband Michael Pursley followed her onto the witness stand, and told the court that he too had asked Glossip about the broken window. He said Glossip had told him they had the address of the people responsible for the broken window and would bill them for it.

Officer Tim Brown repeated his testimony from the first trial, though this time he admitted that he had known

Richard Glossip so well from his regular patrols of the area that he was sometimes invited in to eat with the motel manager. Brown conceded that Glossip had always been straight with him, and he'd got to know him as a friend. He said his behaviour on the day of the murder seemed no different from any other time they had spoken.

The court heard from several police employees who had collected and processed evidence from the scene, including fingerprints. There was no forensic evidence linking Richard Glossip to the scene of the murder, but Justin Sneed's fingerprint was found on two pieces of broken glass, the Plexiglas covering the broken window, a door handle and the waterbed. His palm print was also found on a light switch.

Forensic pathologist Chai Choi again described in detail Barry Van Treese's injuries, saying that he died from head injuries and blood loss, and that it would have taken more than an hour for him to die. She mentioned that as well as the injuries caused by the baseball bat, there were minor cuts to his hand and elbow consistent with a knife.

Making his first appearance in the witness box was Kenneth Van Treese, Barry's brother. He described how Barry would 'go ballistic' if he was annoyed, but said that the amount of money that was supposed to be missing from the motel's accounts would not have concerned him. He described the $6,000 as being the equivalent of four hours' revenue over an entire year.

However, he did say that Van Treese would have been angry about the condition of the motel. Kenneth had taken over the running of the business for two months after the murder, and told the court, 'The motel looked more like a whorehouse than a motel.' He said there were used syringes and used condoms in the parking lot, and only half the rooms were rentable because of broken plumbing and no heat. He said the place was 'absolutely filthy', but that was cured by 'soap and elbow grease'.

Kenneth Van Treese had visited the motel the year before the murder and met the staff, including Richard Glossip, who, he said, 'struck me as being a very bright, aggressive young man and I was very proud of Barry for having hired him'. But when asked about the condition of the motel in January 1997, he said that Barry 'should have fired his ass'.

Part-time security guard Cliff Everhart returned to court to testify. His story was the same as in 1998, though this time he claimed to have been privy to Barry Van Treese's plan to fire Glossip, telling the jury, 'He was going to be given a choice, walk out the door or go to jail.'

On 26 May, Justin Sneed was taken from prison to the courtroom to testify again on behalf of the prosecution. Although his basic story remained the same – he wouldn't have committed murder if it hadn't been for Richard Glossip – there were some significant changes to his testimony. This time he said that it was Glossip who'd suggested staging a fake robbery at the motel; Glossip had told detectives when he was first arrested that Sneed and his brother Wes had floated the idea.

The amount of money he said Glossip had promised him for carrying out the murder also changed. Sneed said it was because Glossip kept offering more. 'At one point, like I said, when it all started it started out like $3,500 and then it jumped to like $5,000 and then it jumped to $6,000 then it jumped to $7,500. I mean, it just kept climbing every time we started talking about it.' On the morning of the murder, he testified, he was offered $9,000 or $10,000.

Sneed claimed that he had been on the verge of killing Van Treese a couple of months earlier, while he was fixing TVs in the motel, but backed out. He didn't say anything about this incident in either his police interrogation or the first trial. And when he described the actual murder, he mentioned another new detail: that he had tried to stab the owner with his pocket knife, as well as beating him with the baseball bat.

That new detail about the knife, which had not emerged in any previous statement from Sneed, led to a complaint from the defence that crucial prosecution evidence had been withheld from them. They asked for a mistrial but were quickly overruled by the judge.

And then came another new piece of the story. Sneed testified that Glossip came into room 102 with him after the murder and took a hundred-dollar bill from Van Treese's wallet. And yet his fingerprints were not found. Sneed offered an explanation: 'Because now that I look back on it, he seemed to be real careful about not touching anything and having me try to do everything.'

Another discrepancy was the time Sneed said he fled the motel. He was insistent that it was midday, and that he did so because Glossip told him to run. 'He seen me walking the top tier and came running up the stairs to – and was telling me that I needed to leave and that I needed to leave right now, that no matter what, I just needed to get my stuff and leave.' Yet other witnesses had described how Glossip wasn't at the motel at midday; he was shopping with D-Anna. Even the prosecution's timeline had Sneed at the motel until at least 3 p.m.

There were further changes to Sneed's story. He said that he and Glossip had gone into room 101 to get a shower curtain to tape over the broken window. Investigators had assumed the shower curtain had come from 102, because the one that should have been in the bathroom there had been removed. If it was the best-equipped room in the motel, it would surely have had a shower curtain. Sneed was asked to explain the discrepancy, but said he couldn't.

At various points Sneed was read a transcript of his police interview from January 1997, to highlight changes to the narrative. But for some reason the defence did not attempt to show the jury the video of the interrogation, even though the failure to show it in the 1998 trial was highlighted as a major error. This baffles many observers of the Richard Glossip case, but neither of the defence attorneys involved in the second trial has been willing to offer any explanation.

Glossip was letting his frustration show. His tendency to react verbally to evidence he disagreed with led Connie Smothermon to complain to the judge, saying, 'I know Mr Glossip has opinions, but when he is objecting so loud on evidentiary rules that I can hear it, I would just ask that he keep his comments to his attorneys and not to me. I have put up with it for three weeks and I'm tired of his comments that I have to listen to while I am up here.'

Wayne Woodyard responded that it was prejudicial for the DA to make such a public rebuke in front of the jury, but the judge simply warned the attorney to tell his client to behave. A jury will make up their minds based on everything they see and hear in a courtroom, not just the evidence presented to them. They are less likely to sympathise with a defendant if he appears angry or disinterested, or if his behaviour is criticised by a court official. Glossip had been in jail for seven years, despite protesting his innocence. It was natural for him to feel strongly about evidence he disagreed with. But anger and frustration would not put the jury on his side.

Bob Bemo, the detective who had interviewed both Sneed and Glossip, returned to give evidence, and the videotapes of the two Glossip interviews were played to the jury. Afterwards Bemo was asked his opinion about the two personalities.

'I think that Richard Glossip is a very intelligent individual. He's a very manipulative individual. Justin had none of those qualities. As a matter of fact, he was kind of a pitiful person. I mean, he was kind of an individual that you felt sorry for.'

Bemo denied having coerced Sneed with his line of questioning in his interrogation, but of course the jury had not viewed the videotape so would not have even been aware of it. When he had completed his testimony, the court adjourned for the weekend. On Monday morning, the prosecution would complete their case and the defence would have their chance to present theirs.

Before the jury took their seats on Monday, the judge and the attorneys discussed whether or not Richard Glossip would speak in his own defence. He was asked to stand; he said he did not wish to testify, and that it was his own decision. His verbal irritation at the evidence and the rebuke from Connie Smothermon about his behaviour may have helped convince his attorneys that he should stay silent. Even though he had handled cross-examination well during his first trial, he was advised not to open himself up to persistent questioning from another combative prosecutor. But by failing to testify, he ensured that the jury would never hear his version of events in his own words.

Glossip's lawyers told the judge that they felt the state had presented insufficient evidence to corroborate a charge of first-degree murder. They asked that the jury should only consider a charge of accessory to murder. The judge overruled the motion.

The defence offered no witnesses on behalf of Richard Glossip. They had failed to find anyone they felt could make a positive contribution to his case. His previous attorney, Lynn Burch, had found people who knew Richard, but when they spoke about him, they mixed positive comments with negative ones. Those types of witnesses made Burch nervous, so he would not have chosen to put them on the stand. The jury would decide Glossip's guilt or innocence based entirely on whether they believed witnesses brought by the state.

In his summing-up, Silas Lyman told the jury that 'there is no evidence to prove a contract' between Glossip and Sneed, just the word of Justin Sneed. He wanted them to focus not on what happened after the murder, when Glossip made a 'bad decision', but on whether there was evidence to show that he knew in advance of the murder. Lyman, who'd been told by the judge to speed up his final comments, poured scorn on the inconsistencies in Sneed's story, and ended by reminding the jury that they could find Glossip not guilty of murder, but they could also consider the lesser charge of accessory after the fact.

Connie Smothermon concluded by saying it was nonsense to suggest that Justin Sneed had acted alone. She claimed that the new details that had emerged from Sneed during five hours of testimony were a result of her asking more questions than had been done in the past. She told the jury, 'It's not enough we got the bat boy. It's time to convict the coach.'

The jury were sent out just before 5 p.m. According to one of the jurors I've spoken to, everyone around the table took it in turns to give their view and the consensus was that Richard Glossip was guilty. However, when they took their first vote, three of the female jurors voted not guilty because they wanted to have a longer discussion about the evidence, to reassure themselves that they were making the right decision. Two of the women changed their vote relatively quickly, while the other held out a little longer.

The juror who provided this insight into the deliberations did not want to be identified, but explained to me why they reached their verdict. 'We just really felt that Barry Van Treese wouldn't be dead but for Richard Glossip, even though he didn't swing the baseball bat. We felt Justin Sneed was coerced.'

The juror felt Sneed was a convincing witness. 'I found him very believable. If he was lying, he was in the wrong business. He should have been an actor because he would have been an Academy Award winner.'

After a little more than five hours, the jury returned to the courtroom to deliver the guilty verdict. Their next task was to decide on the severity of the punishment. Members of the Van Treese family gave impact statements that the juror said were very powerful. 'The impact testimony was gut-wrenching, especially when his daughter got up there and said, "He'll never be able to walk me down the aisle." The judge was crying. The only three people who weren't crying were Richard Glossip and his lawyers. I wanted to ask the judge if I could be excused for a while because it was horrible.'

Despite that, the juror's initial instinct was that Glossip should be given life without parole, and several others agreed. They felt that he didn't deserve to die because he hadn't been the one who wielded the baseball bat. But after some intense deliberations, they all agreed on a death sentence to punish the man they regarded as the mastermind. 'We wanted to send out a message about what would happen if you sent people out to do your dirty work. It got hairy during that phase. One female juror had a panic attack and couldn't breathe. We put a cold towel on her face. The sense of responsibility was weighing on her.'

The jurors decided that before they returned to the courtroom, they should take it in turns to articulate their decision. They went round the table, each of them uttering the word 'death'. 'There were a couple of women who found it hard to speak it. It wasn't that easy. I knew he was guilty and the punishment was just, but it's still hard to take someone's life.'

After the verdict, Glossip phoned Kim Van Atta with the news. Although they'd been writing to each other for three years, they'd still not met face to face. They'd both agreed that it would be more useful for Kim to donate money to Glossip's prison account so he could buy food and other essentials, rather than spend it on a trip to Oklahoma. And based on the successful appeal, and Glossip's pre-trial optimism, Kim had assumed that acquittal was a foregone conclusion. He was so shocked at the outcome, he needed time to digest the news, and told Glossip to phone him back later. That response led Glossip to think that Kim would no longer believe in his innocence and would end their friendship, but when they spoke again, Kim assured him he would stick by him. He was still convinced that there had been a miscarriage of justice. If anything, it would bring them closer together.

For the next decade, prison life would settle into a slow, tedious routine, interspersed with various legal challenges as Glossip's case worked its way through the appeals process. After his conviction, he was sent back to Oklahoma State Penitentiary's death-row wing. His execution wasn't imminent, because challenges to his conviction and sentence would take years to resolve in state and federal courts, but he and his fellow inmates lived next to one of the country's busiest death chambers.

In the seventeen years between the murder of Barry Van Treese and Richard Glossip's first scheduled execution date, one hundred men and three women were put to death in Oklahoma. There was no reason to suppose that Glossip would escape the ultimate punishment, unless a court ruled in his favour.

In April 2007, the Oklahoma Court of Criminal Appeals rejected several grounds for complaint from Glossip's legal team. One of them was the prosecution's tactic of writing quotes from witness statements on posters and keeping them on display in the courtroom. Even though the appeal court strongly criticised Judge Gray's refusal to allow photographs to be taken as proof of what had been written, the posters themselves were ruled to be 'harmless'. The juror I spoke to said they had no bearing on the jury's decision.

Another tactic deployed by those trying to overturn a conviction is to blame their attorneys for doing a bad job at their trial. Glossip's new publicly funded attorneys criticised the actions of their predecessors, including Lyman and Woodyard's failure to play the video of Justin Sneed's interrogation. But even though it had been highlighted as grounds for appeal after the first trial, this time it was rejected.

The Oklahoma Court of Criminal Appeals has five judges. Three of them agreed that Richard Glossip had received a fair trial and that his conviction should stand. But two of the judges disagreed, and explained why. Judge Charles Chapel and Judge Arlene Johnson were opposed to the use of the posters as an aide-memoire to the jury – particularly as the jurors had been told not to take their own notes and to rely on their collective memory of the evidence. They argued that that amounted to a continuous summing-up of the evidence throughout the trial, and could not be described as 'harmless'. However, Judge Chapel did acknowledge that there was enough circumstantial evidence to supplement Sneed's testimony, particularly Glossip's failure to fully account for all the cash in his possession when he was arrested.

The 3–2 majority indicated that there were concerns about a miscarriage of justice, but not enough to reverse the guilty verdict. The Oklahoma court system had concluded that the death sentence should proceed. Richard Glossip's next avenue was to appeal through the federal court, which rules whether state law has infringed the standards of United States justice. The federal court starts from the assumption that the state judgment was correct, unless it can be demonstrated otherwise.

An appeal was filed with the Court of Appeals for the Tenth Circuit, which handles cases from Oklahoma, Wyoming, Utah, Colorado, Kansas and New Mexico. Similar objections were raised about the use of posters and the failure to play the videotape. But once again, the court rejected the complaints. In the case of the video, the federal court concluded that 'the officers' questioning was not sufficiently manipulative' to have influenced Sneed's answers. It also ruled that even though the defence attorney hadn't played the tape, he had still highlighted discrepancies during his cross-examination of Sneed.

On 25 July 2013, the federal court rejected Glossip's appeal. An execution date was getting closer.

CHAPTER 10

No Mercy

October 2014

Richard Glossip had one final chance to plead for his life, but he didn't do himself any favours by failing to give a plausible explanation for his actions in the hours after the murder. He needed to persuade a majority of the five members of the Oklahoma Pardon and Parole Board to recommend that the Governor reduce his sentence from death to life in prison. But they were unanimous: Richard Glossip deserved to die. He blames his lawyer for bad advice, but even Kim Van Atta was annoyed that Glossip had failed to make the most of his appeal for mercy.

The three-hour hearing took place on 25 October 2014. It was held at the Kate Barnard Community Correctional Facility in Oklahoma City, but Richard Glossip was 130 miles away in the state penitentiary in McAlester. He would be allowed to have his say via video link, but he wouldn't hear the lawyers and witnesses talking about him. And he wouldn't hear the verdict.

Three board members are appointed by the Governor, and one each by the senior judges on the state Supreme

Court and Court of Criminal Appeals. They're supposed to be independent, but with some experience of the judicial system. The chairman of the board was Marc Dreyer, a former federal drug agent who'd become a Baptist minister. Richard Dugger was a former district attorney and Lynnell Harkins a retired attorney. Both were in their seventies. Vanessa Price was a retired police officer.

The most controversial appointment in the context of Richard Glossip's hearing was Patricia High. She was a former prosecutor in the District Attorney's office and had been involved in the early stages of Glossip's case, appearing on behalf of the DA in pre-trial hearings in 1998. Glossip was angry and worried to find that she would have a say in deciding whether he should live or die. Many months later, when I contacted the board's chairman Marc Dreyer to talk about the hearing, he said he hadn't known of her previous connection to the Glossip case. He told me that if he had, he would have asked her to recuse herself from taking part in their deliberations and vote.

There were around a dozen members of the Van Treese family present. Glossip's friend Kim Van Atta had flown in from New York for the hearing. Glossip was represented by attorneys Mark Henricksen and Kathleen Lord. Journalists are allowed to attend hearings, just like a court trial. Only one turned up: Graham Lee Brewer, a reporter with *The Oklahoman*. His report appeared on page 14 of his newspaper.

Brewer recalled, 'I've been to several clemency hearings and they're very formulaic. They generally start with a discussion of the inmate's childhood or how he got a bad go, trying to set the stage to say that this guy never got a chance to be a law-abiding citizen because his childhood was so poor. That didn't happen with Glossip at all.'

It was a deliberate tactic by attorney Mark Henricksen. He said that Richard Glossip had had a happy childhood. The family might have had financial needs, but it was a good home life. Instead he focused on what he argued was the injustice of Glossip's trial, while his colleague Kathleen Lord argued that the evidence was circumstantial.

Assistant DA Seth Branham hit back. 'We would have loved to have forensic evidence, DNA, that sort of thing, connecting Glossip. Sometimes you have pure circumstantial cases. Now, in this case, it's not a pure circumstantial case. You have Justin Sneed, and I would submit to you when you look at the total evidence, this is not a weak case. It all points back to Richard Glossip.'

Barry Van Treese's brother Kenneth spoke on behalf of the family and told the board how he had taken over the running of the Best Budget Inn after the murder and had to clean up room 102. Graham Lee Brewer, the journalist present, told me that 'Kenny's testimony was very powerful. That image of him wiping the blood off the walls when the police had gone was really powerful to me. He started to cry at one point. The whole victim's side of the room were in tears.'

Kenneth Van Treese concluded with a plea: 'Consider clemency, then reject the idea of clemency. It's a bad idea. If anybody ever deserved to be executed, Richard Glossip deserves it.'

The chairman of the panel, Marc Dreyer, told me that, looking back, the victim impact statement had made a big impression on him, and on his colleagues. He said that during his time on the board, they had only recommended three death sentences to be commuted. In all three, the family of the victim had opted not to press for execution, the inmate had spent a long time in prison and 'there was clear evidence that they had turned their lives around'. Not that the recommendation of mercy had any impact. In all three cases, the Governor had dismissed the vote for mercy and the executions had gone ahead anyway.

After Kenneth Van Treese's emotional testimony, there was a break while the equipment was set up to allow Richard Glossip to speak. Back in McAlester, he'd been led to a room in the prison that was used for video links. He sat at a desk with the flags of the United States and Oklahoma behind him. When the hearing resumed, he was allowed to make a statement and began by offering his condolences to the Van Treese family. 'But I do also want to say that I did not plan and I did not participate in the death of Mr Van Treese, and I would have never, ever paid for someone to do anything like that.'

The panel began to question him about the murder. Why hadn't he told the police where the body was? Graham Lee Brewer said his answers were 'very unconvincing'. He told me, 'Richard's answer was "I really don't have a good answer for you. I think I was just scared." The board were surprised. "You don't have an answer? That question is everything." Once he said that, it was all downhill from there. He's had a lot of time to think about it. Either he got nervous or had trouble conveying how he felt that day, but he seemed really reserved. He wasn't very eloquent or passionate.'

Looking back on that day, Glossip says he hadn't been properly briefed. 'Mark Henricksen misled me. He told me that I had three minutes to speak so he said keep it short and just say a couple of things. So I took him at his word and then I get there and I find out I had a lot more time than that. If I'd have known that, I'd have been so much more prepared to answer whatever questions they had and it kind of threw me off.'

Marc Dreyer agrees. He told me that he was surprised by the brevity of Glossip's answers. 'I don't believe it would have changed the outcome, but the advice he got was not as helpful as it should have been. He was allowed to have thirty minutes to talk, not including questions from the board.'

Instead his appearance was brief. According to the official record, the hearing resumed at 4.31 p.m. Glossip spoke, the panel questioned him; the members of the board discussed the case and then voted 5–0 to reject clemency. They signed their names on the record and the meeting adjourned at 4.44 p.m. The session had lasted just thirteen minutes from start to finish. Richard Glossip wasn't permitted to listen to the verdict. He was already being led back to his cell.

Given the 5–0 vote, Dreyer says Patricia High's involvement made no difference to the board's recommendation. He says they voted as they did because they heard no compelling evidence to make them want to commute the sentence.

'His attorneys tried to portray him as a victim. That is
not going to be effective in a court of last resort. It would
have to be so significant that the Governor would be persuaded to agree with our decision.'

The decision wasn't relayed to Richard Glossip. His lawyer
asked his secretary to ring the prison, but for some reason
he never got the call. Several hours after the hearing, he
rang Kim Van Atta, who had to break the bad news. But
Van Atta was also angry because the clemency hearing had
been told that Richard had failed several polygraphs. He
said Richard had never mentioned he'd taken lie detector
tests. They argued. 'When I went to visit him in prison the
next day, he's looking depressed. The first thing he says is
"I don't mind being turned down for clemency. What was
worse was you not believing that I'm innocent."' Kim had
to reassure him that he still believed he had nothing to do
with the murder.

They decided to drum up some attention from the media,
though there had been little interest up to now. Within a
few weeks, Oklahoma's Attorney General set 29 January as
Glossip's execution date. Once that happened, it became a
current news story rather than a throwback to an eighteen-
year-old murder. And some reporters began to sense that
this wasn't a straightforward murder conviction.

Four weeks after the clemency hearing, Phil Cross was
told to report to Oklahoma State Penitentiary. He'd been
a reporter for Fox 25 in Oklahoma City for nine years,
but he'd never been invited into the prison before. He'd
requested an interview with Richard Glossip, but hadn't

expected to be given permission. He couldn't remember any Oklahoma death-row prisoner being allowed to conduct a TV interview before.

Phil had never heard of Richard Glossip until he received a typed and signed letter from him in June. Time was running out for Glossip and he was becoming desperate, but getting the attention of busy journalists can be difficult. 'I get jail mail all the time from a variety of different inmates,' Phil told me. 'But I've never received anything from death row before. He wrote one letter and I kind of brushed it off a little because you usually don't get a lot of access to those inmates. The second letter I got I decided to look into it a little bit more.'

The second letter was handwritten, and Phil was impressed with the way it was worded. He requested permission from the Department of Corrections for an interview, but wasn't optimistic it would be granted. He heard nothing for several weeks, and admits he'd almost forgotten about it when out of the blue he got a call from the DOC to say that the interview would happen the following week. Two local print journalists and another TV network had also been granted interviews.

Richard Glossip knew nothing about his impending media appearances until that morning. A guard came to his cell with a waiver form for him to sign, agreeing that he was willing to talk to the reporters. He was then taken to the visitors' area for a series of interviews that would take several hours to complete. In the month since the clemency hearing, there'd been an intriguing development that Glossip was keen to talk about in his press interviews.

A message had been posted on the website created by Kim Van Atta. It purported to come from Justin Sneed's daughter Justine, who was only two years old when her father was convicted of murder. Kim asked his fellow campaigner Crystal Martinez to follow it up. She contacted Justine and persuaded her to write a letter to the parole board. The letter arrived too late for consideration, but essentially it said that she believed Richard Glossip's version of events, and that her father had implicated Glossip to save himself.

There would be arguments in the months ahead as to the authenticity of the letter, and efforts would be made to persuade Justine Sneed to swear an affidavit. But when the reporters came to interview Glossip that day, he was excited that this could be a breakthrough in his case. If Justine's story was true, it could be classed as new evidence, which was essential if a court was to consider granting a new appeal.

Phil Cross's interview was conducted with bars and reinforced glass between them, with the prisoner's voice barely carrying through a metal grille. The only concession was that they could give a radio microphone to a guard, who would then attach it to Glossip's clothing for a clear audio recording.

Glossip began by laying the blame on Justin Sneed for implicating him in the murder. 'I've never been in trouble in my life, with the law, with anybody. I've never hurt anybody in my life and I wouldn't ever. His own daughter is helping me to try and prove my innocence because of comments that Justin made to her. When Justin was first arrested, he told the police it was a robbery went bad. All these years later, his daughter asked him the same question and he said the same thing: it was a robbery that went bad. So I mean he keeps contradicting himself, telling different stories, different versions of stories. But I believe the first one and the last one.'

Sneed's daughter's intervention was certainly a potentially huge development, and for weeks reporters and defence attorneys would attempt to corroborate her story, but she didn't respond to requests for interviews. Phil Cross listened intently to what Glossip said, but he was also studying his body language, trying to form a judgement about the veracity of what he was being told.

'It was really difficult to hear him, so my photographer turned up the volume on the speaker of the camera. I got the gist of what he was saying, but some of the specific wording I didn't pick up on until I listened back to the interview in its entirety afterwards. So I found myself looking at his expression and his posture, and all these non verbal cues to pick up mood and what he was thinking.'

One of the reasons Phil Cross was intrigued by Glossip's story was that he was the only Oklahoma death-row inmate who hadn't actually killed anyone. Putting to death men or women who have persuaded others to carry out a murder is relatively rare. The Death Penalty Information Center records eleven such executions in recent American history. Only one of them was in Oklahoma: in 2001, Marilyn Plantz conspired with her lover to kill her husband so she could collect insurance money; both of them were executed. There have also been nearly a dozen cases where men have been executed even though it was their accomplice who fired the fatal shot, often during a robbery.

Glossip's case is not unique, but it is still unusual. 'They admit that I had nothing to do with the killing itself. But yet here we are. I'm on death row and it's just ridiculous, it doesn't make any sense. I'm truly innocent. I made some really bad decisions after the fact. I'm not saying I didn't. But I think I paid for them with seventeen years of my life.'

Cross asked him about the mistakes he was admitting to having made.

'When it finally came to light about what happened, I didn't do nothing about it. That's my fault. I should've. So here I am stuck in this thing now and it's just looking bad on me. Because I didn't do the things I should have done immediately. But I paid for that.'

He might not have paid the price if he could have afforded a good lawyer. It's a frequent complaint from those opposed to capital punishment that defendants who have to rely on overworked or less experienced attorneys will always be at a disadvantage. Each time Glossip lost a legal battle in the courts, his publicly funded attorneys would turn the case over to someone else within the system. Glossip had little control over his own destiny, but he would always be told to trust the advice of the attorneys and wait for the justice system to run its course. Now he had no choice but to disregard the lawyers who had told him not to talk to the press.

'What has our country become when you start letting innocent people be executed for crimes they didn't commit? I'm just hoping that somebody will stand up out there, besides the people that already are, and help me to get the

Governor's attention to ask her to look into this. She can see for herself that I shouldn't be here. I've never been in trouble in my life, ever. Never been to jail, never been to prison, none of that, and here I am on death row.'

They discussed the murder and his possible motive. Glossip gave an answer that I would use a lot in my reports over the coming year. It wasn't just what he said, it was how he said it. There was a conviction in his voice that impressed me. 'I'm truly sorry for what happened to Barry, I am. But I had nothing to do with it. I truly had nothing to do with it. I would not hurt Barry in any way, shape or form and I surely wouldn't have had someone else do it for me.'

He reminded Phil Cross that he could have avoided the death penalty almost ten years earlier. 'They even offered me a straight life sentence before my second trial and I told them no. At the clemency hearing one of the panel asked the DA and the Attorney General, why did you offer him that deal? Both of them said, "Well, the case wasn't that good." It wasn't that good because I didn't commit a crime.'

He finished the interview with a direct appeal to Justin Sneed, who he hoped would see him on TV. 'Are you willing to let an innocent man die just so you don't have to go to death row? I'm asking him to step up and do the right thing. Because if he don't that's exactly what's going to happen. I mean an innocent man is going to die for a crime he didn't commit.'

Phil ended the interview and thanked the prisoner. 'I walked out wondering what's next and if I would ever hear from him again. He could be dead in a few weeks.'

The interview prompted some minor audience reaction, but the story remained low-key, and it wasn't picked up by the US national media. When I interviewed Phil two months after he'd spoken to Richard Glossip, he was still struck by how the prisoner had behaved on camera. 'He came across as very genuine, very honest, soft-spoken. When you talk to him, his eyes are bright. He makes really good eye contact with you. He expresses remorse for what happened. Even to the point where he says, "I'm sorry for what happened to Barry." He still has that personalisation. He definitely believes in his innocence. Whether it's true or not, he's definitely come to the point where he believes it. He doesn't show any of those signs of deception where he's shifting his eyes or showing no emotion.'

Phil was hooked. In the coming months, he would dig deeper into the evidence. It wasn't just a good story for a journalist; it was also a powerful case study for those campaigning against the death penalty. Richard Glossip wasn't a career criminal. He seemed like an ordinary guy. In the months ahead, the details of his case would be debated across the country and around the world. It would become a potent weapon in the battle against capital punishment.

CHAPTER 11

Hello or Goodbye

January 2015

Supporters of the death penalty in Oklahoma were growing restless. The arguments over lethal injection were holding up executions, so they had come up with a new way to kill prisoners. They proposed and passed a law to use nitrogen gas, claiming it was a humane method because it was used to kill pigs in slaughterhouses. State Senator Ralph Shortey was one of those in favour, and agreed to meet me to discuss why.

'It's cheap,' he said. 'Nitrogen is abundant. Seventy-eight per cent of the world's atmosphere is nitrogen. You know our bodies are used to it, so whenever nitrogen is introduced to a human being there's no rejection, the body doesn't try to reject the nitrogen, but when you start reducing the oxygen levels then basically what happens is that your brain stops functioning. When your brain stops functioning, the rest of your body stops functioning as well. It's very painless.'

For someone so knowledgeable about this method of execution, Senator Shortey didn't seem to have done his homework on either global attitudes to capital punishment or Richard Glossip's case. I asked him if he could name any other countries around the world that continued to execute prisoners. He couldn't. I listed a few: Iran, China, Saudi Arabia, North Korea. I asked if he was happy that the United States was a member of this exclusive club. He said the fact that dictatorial regimes used the death penalty didn't make it wrong.

'The people of Oklahoma overwhelmingly support the death penalty. We had it on a ballot initiative years ago and it was supported by over eighty per cent. And we have an obligation as a state to ensure that the people's will is met. On a personal side, I support the death penalty because in certain cases there is no alternative. If we are talking about remediating someone who rapes and murders an eleven-month-old child, I don't want that person to be remediated. I don't want that person to be a part of society. That person is inherently messed up, and really the best alternative is that person is no longer a part of society.'

I pointed out that Richard Glossip hadn't killed anyone. Senator Shortey didn't know that. I filled him in on the details and asked him if it sounded just. He replied that justice had been half served; he thought Justin Sneed should have been given a death sentence too. And he wasn't fussy about the method, telling me, 'I support the lethal injection. I support hanging. I support whatever it takes that the state deems is necessary to effect that death. And if it got to the point where we did not have the technological advancements to have lethal injections, then I would support hanging or beheading or whatever it would take to make sure that person, in the end, meets his justice.'

He said Glossip had been given a trial, and numerous appeals, and it was time to carry out the sentence because it was a deterrent to others. And apart from anything else, it removed someone who 'has no place in society'. He quoted the example of Clayton Lockett, the Oklahoma prisoner whose botched execution had attracted international headlines the previous April. 'He murdered an unarmed person. He said in his statement that as he was burying this girl alive after he had shot her twice with a shotgun, he kept putting the dirt on her to stop her from screaming so much. That person is not fit for society.'

I thanked the senator for his time. I was taken aback by some of his comments, but he was affable, and at least he was prepared to make his argument in front of a TV camera.

Two years later, in March 2017, Senator Shortey would get an unexpected insight into Oklahoma's judicial system. He was arrested in a motel room with a teenage boy and charged with engaging in child prostitution. Shortey, a married man with three children, resigned from the Senate. When I heard who he had hired to defend him, I had to smile. By a remarkable coincidence, it was the same attorney I had interviewed immediately after leaving Shortey's office back in January 2015. I needed a legal expert to explain Oklahoma's death-penalty laws, and Ed Blau had been recommended because he was working in the District Attorney's office when Glossip's case was being tried.

Blau was everything I could have wanted from an expert interviewee. Not only was he very familiar with the Glossip case, he looked every inch the successful American attorney.

He was square-jawed, wearing a smart business suit and expensive leather cowboy boots. And if he felt he hadn't delivered a word-perfect answer, he wanted to do it again to get it absolutely right.

'Oklahoma as a state is very conservative. It is religiously conservative and it's politically conservative, and that same conservatism lends itself to issues like capital punishment. Supporters of the death penalty here in Oklahoma, which is the vast majority of the state, they look to the Bible, they look to the Old Testament, and they look to their churches. And when a church is in favour of the death penalty, clearly the adherents are very likely to follow it.'

Generally speaking, the east and west coasts of America are the most liberal parts of the country. The closer you get to the middle, the more conservatives you'll find, and the more right-wing their views. Oklahoma has more in common with Texas than just the seven-hundred-mile border the two states share.

'I believe there's a little bit of a Wild West mentality,' Blau told me. 'A lot of Oklahomans see themselves as frontiersmen. If you look at gun ownership, if you look at people who carry guns, it's extremely high. And that hang-'em-high, Old West justice mentality carries on to this day.'

We discussed the ongoing debate about execution methods. The Eighth Amendment to the United States Constitution bars cruel and unusual punishment, such as extreme pain that causes lingering death. While the firing squad and electric chair remained legal in some states, 'evolving standards of decency have led us to lethal injection'. The end result might be the same, but lethal injection was more palatable to the general public. And if that method had to be abandoned, state governments would keep finding alternatives until the death penalty itself was ruled to be unconstitutional by the US Supreme Court.

According to Blau, 'The reason this case is getting so much scrutiny is because it is a death-penalty case. People are convicted of murder and other crimes all the time based on accomplice testimony and based on circumstantial evidence – that's what the law is in the United States. However, when you're giving somebody the ultimate punishment, we've become accustomed to there being more – a confession; videotaped evidence; a mountain of evidence. And in this particular case if you're looking at it through the lens of the death penalty, the evidence does not appear to be substantial enough to warrant that.'

I wanted to know why he thought two different juries would have found Richard Glossip guilty. I've quoted his answer many times when people have asked me the same question.

Because jurors in murder cases in Oklahoma have to be 'death qualified', defence attorneys will always struggle. 'What that means in practice is that people who would more likely be liberal or open-minded or defence-oriented, they are automatically excluded from the jury panel because if somebody is a hundred per cent opposed to the death penalty, they're not allowed to sit on that jury. By its very nature the panel of jurors are going to be more conservative and more likely to convict than a jury in a robbery case or any other type of case.'

In Blau's opinion, the prosecution will always have a built-in advantage when trying to prove guilt in a murder case. 'That's the ultimate irony in a death-penalty case in that while the general public believes those should be the ones where you have the fairest jury, by its very nature the jurors who sit in a death-penalty case are going to be more conservative and more likely to convict than on any other type of jury.'

That hang-'em-high mentality that Ed Blau believes still exists in the state is more prevalent among jurors in a murder trial than when trying more minor offences. He didn't know it then, but if his future client Ralph Shortey went to trial on child prostitution charges, his jury would probably be more representative of society than Richard Glossip's.

As I completed my interview with Blau, officials at Oklahoma State Penitentiary were making final preparations for the execution of Richard Glossip, which was due to take place at 6 p.m. the following day. The prison is located in McAlester, a two-hour drive east of Oklahoma City. McAlester has a population of under twenty thousand, and around a quarter of them are employed either making bombs or looking after prisoners. The McAlester Army Ammunition Plant supplies virtually all the non-nuclear munitions used by the US military. The penitentiary holds up to seven hundred prisoners, including nearly fifty on death row. Eighty-three per cent of inmates are considered violent offenders.

The prison is often dubbed Big Mac, and for nearly seventy years it hosted an annual rodeo in which the inmates were allowed to participate. As you drive into town, you pass a statue of a uniformed prisoner astride a bucking steer. The arena within the prison walls where the rodeo was staged is now crumbling and unsafe. The show closed in 2010.

Sister Helen Prejean was about to meet Richard Glossip for the first time. I wasn't allowed inside the prison to film their meeting, but I had arranged to meet her outside the entrance to Unit H, the death-row section of the jail, which is on the far side of the complex from the main entrance. I hadn't called the prison authorities in advance to say that my cameraman and I were planning to film there. Frankly, I'd assumed they would refuse permission, but I hadn't expected to simply drive into the jail unchallenged. The relaxed security surprised me. After all, there was an execution due to take place here within twenty-four hours. Perhaps the prison authorities shared our expectation that a stay of execution was due to be announced by the US Supreme Court.

I carried on driving through the complex, past the rodeo arena, and pulled into the parking lot for Unit H. Almost as soon as I arrived, so did Sister Helen. As I approached, she was talking to a middle-aged woman. Sister Helen said hello and introduced me.

'Have you met the warden?'

Anita Trammell had been running the penitentiary for two years and had been in charge of the Clayton Lockett execution in April 2014 that had gone so badly wrong. 'A bloody mess,' she called it at the time. I expected her to be less than hospitable to a journalist, but she seemed prepared to relax the rules a little. She didn't tell me to stop filming, and she didn't order us to leave, but she declined to be interviewed.

Then family members began to arrive. Among them were Glossip's niece Billie Jo Boyiddle, and Christina Glossip-Hodge, his daughter from his first marriage. She now lived in Maryland and hadn't seen her father since she was thirteen. Both were wearing white T-shirts with Glossip's face and his website address on the front and PLEASE HELP FREE AN INNOCENT MAN in large letters on the back. They had both been at the event at the State Capitol the day before, but I hadn't had time to introduce myself.

Kim Van Atta had told me that one of the reasons he had become so closely involved with Richard Glossip was that he didn't have any close family or friends. So I asked both women why they had lost touch with him. Christina said they'd gone their separate ways after the break-up of her parents' marriage, but she wanted to fix it now and was looking forward to seeing him. Billie Jo didn't like my question. She told me that she had visited him in jail when he was first arrested and had attended his trial. She hadn't been to visit him lately, but she had stayed in touch through letters and phone calls. 'We've tried to get people involved all of this time,' she said, 'but nobody was interested. It was just "he's a death-row inmate, he's guilty". But he's not and now everybody is listening.'

As the relatives walked towards the entrance to Unit H, Kim and Mary Van Atta emerged. They had already spent a couple of hours with Richard Glossip that morning. They said the warden was being sympathetic and allowing them

ABOVE. Barry Van Treese, the owner of the motel, the Best Budget Inn, in Oklahoma City. He was murdered on 7 January 1997. (Oklahoma state evidence files)

ABOVE: The Best Budget Inn on the night of the murder. (Oklahoma state evidence files)

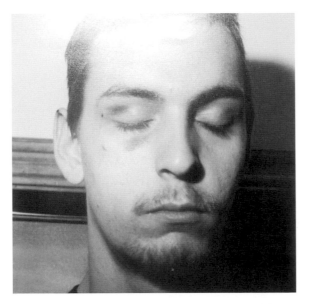

ABOVE: Justin Sneed after his arrest, with bruising around his eye following the scuffle with Barry Van Treese. (Oklahoma state evidence files)

ABOVE: Detectives Bob Bemo and Bill Cook prepare to interrogate Justin Sneed, who would change his account of events several times. The video was never shown to jurors. (Oklahoma state evidence files)

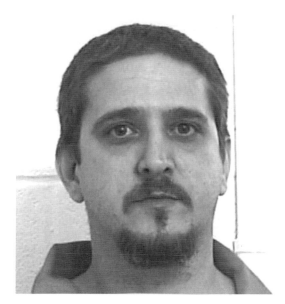

ABOVE: A Richard Glossip mugshot in 2004. (Oklahoma Department of Corrections)

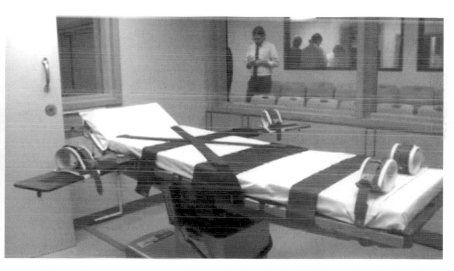

ABOVE: The media are given a tour of the death chamber in Oklahoma State Penitentiary, October 2014. It was refurbished following the Clayton Lockett execution controversy, in which the death-row prisoner was given an untested mixture of drugs. (Sky News)

ABOVE: Richard Glossip speaks to death-penalty campaigner Sister Helen Prejean, January 2015. (José Vazquez)

ABOVE: Kim Van Atta, the pen pal who became Glossip's best friend. (Sky News)

ABOVE: Media interest in the Glossip case after the US Supreme Court hearing in April 2015. (Sky News)

ABOVE: Oklahoma Attorney General Scott Pruitt defends the death penalty, April 2015. He later became a member of President Donald Trump's cabinet. (Sky News)

ABOVE: Attorney Don Knight's first news conference after being brought onto the case by Sister Helen Prejean, July 2015 (Sky News)

ABOVE: Ian Woods talks to Richard Glossip on 15 September 2015, the eve of his second scheduled execution date. (Sky News)

RIGHT: Advert placed in Oklahoma newspaper by Virgin boss Sir Richard Branson on 16 September 2015, the day of the second scheduled execution. (Sky News)

BELOW: Fox reporter, Phil Cross, Sister Helen Prejean and Ian Woods outside the prison following the stay of execution on 16 September. (Sky News)

ABOVE: Ian Woods and other witnesses arrive at Oklahoma State Penitentiary for Glossip's third scheduled execution on 30 September 2015. (Sky News)

ABOVE: Relatives of Richard Glossip celebrate his unexpected reprieve. (Sky News)

to enter in small groups to be able to see him face to face, rather than with reinforced glass between them. His final meal was also due to be delivered while they were inside. The prison gives condemned men a twenty-five-dollar allowance to order whatever they want on the eve of their death.

Everyone went inside, leaving Dickon and me alone to wait for developments. A stay of execution had been widely predicted, but the family and friends still didn't know whether they were saying a final goodbye or preparing for a celebration. It turned out to be the latter. After a couple of hours, Mark Henricksen phoned the prison with the news that the Supreme Court had granted a stay for at least three months, until after the justices had heard evidence about the lethal injection controversy.

A few minutes later, Sister Helen came rushing outside shouting, 'Richard's going to live!' She relayed how the news had been broken to him, and how excited and relieved everyone was to hear it. Gradually the others began to emerge from inside, all smiles and talking over each other about what they had seen and heard. One of them was Crystal Martinez, whom I hadn't met before. She had long been an active campaigner against the death penalty, who wrote supportive letters to prisoners. Richard Glossip was one of the first to write back, and they had become close. Martinez, a large, ebullient woman, had been instrumental in generating publicity about the case, it was she who had suggested getting Sister Helen Prejean involved. Now the two women were turning what could have been a solemn farewell into a party.

'It was wonderful! Talk about exciting. Oh my Lord.'

'Such a relief!'

'We can breathe again. It was a good day.'

The immediate consequence of the stay of execution was that Glossip was moved out of solitary confinement, from a cell where the light was never switched off and where he was monitored twenty-four hours a day. He had been there since Christmas Day, deprived of his MP3 player and the music he loved to listen to. Kim had been inside the prison with him for several hours and said, 'It was clear to me that the guards who were with Richard, none of them wanted to be with him if this happened tomorrow. They would have had an enormously difficult time.'

Glossip's family and friends got into their cars and left the prison. Dickon and I headed to our hotel to edit my report, which would be broadcast the following morning. In it I told the story of the crime, the conviction, the sentence and the stay of execution. I ended with the words: 'Richard Glossip may live to see the summer, but Oklahoma remains committed to executing him as soon as the law allows.'

It wasn't the dramatic account of being a witness at an execution that I had originally planned. But I believed I had laid the foundations for a story I could build on in the coming months. I planned to attend the US Supreme Court hearing in April, and if Glossip's attorneys were unsuccessful, that would mean a return visit to Oklahoma later in the year.

CHAPTER 12

Supreme Indifference

April–June 2015

For more than a decade, a stark black-and-white photograph of the US Supreme Court has hung on the wall of my living room in south-west London. The tall columns of its famous frontage uphold a carved inscription that is both timeless and uplifting: *Equal Justice Under Law.* I took the picture in 2004 while I was living in Washington DC. I wasn't much of a photographer, but I was embracing the new era of digital photography, which flattered complete amateurs like me into thinking we could be artistic.

I had walked or driven past the US Supreme Court building hundreds of times. And yet I was unfamiliar with what went on behind its impressive frontage. In my four years as US correspondent, there hadn't been a single case newsworthy enough to demand the attention of this British reporter.

So at 9 a.m. on 29 April 2015, I walked up the steps for the very first time. And yet I nearly didn't make it. The date had been marked in my diary for three months, ever since Richard Glossip had been granted a stay of execution to allow the court to take up the arguments against the lethal-injection drug midazolam. I had suggested to my bosses at Sky that I could be sent to the States for a few weeks around the date to allow me to cover the case, and whatever else was making news in America.

In fact, there was so much other news, I almost missed the court hearing. I began the week in Colorado reporting on another death-penalty case – the trial of the man responsible for a shooting massacre in a cinema. James Holmes had killed twelve people who had been watching the Batman film *The Dark Knight Rises*. He was eventually found guilty of murder, but despite the slaughter he'd inflicted, he was not sentenced to die. A single juror objected to the death penalty, and under Colorado law, a death sentence has to be unanimous. Instead he was jailed for life. It was a result that satisfied opponents of capital punishment, but it was another indication of the inconsistent sentencing in different parts of the country.

I spent only one day at Holmes's trial because of another major story. Baltimore had been engulfed in riots following the unexplained death of a young black man in police custody. The night before the US Supreme Court hearing, I was being tear-gassed as police tried to clear the streets of protesters. If the rioting had persisted, I would not have been able to leave the city. Thankfully, calm was restored, and I caught an early train to Washington DC, arriving just before the hearing was due to start.

I had heeded the court etiquette and worn a jacket and tie. I would have done anyway, but it's unusual to be issued with an official dress code. I collected my accreditation, and met up with Phil Cross from Fox 25, who had flown in from Oklahoma City to cover the hearing. He was excited to be there. It was rare for a local news reporter to be sent to the nation's capital.

We had been allocated numbered seats, and lined up in order to be escorted into the courtroom. The media seats are to the side of the raised platform where the nine justices sit. Naturally, reporters who cover the court on a regular basis, and those from networks and the big city newspapers, have the best seats. Phil had been given a good view too, a few rows in front of me. I had been placed directly behind a pillar. If I leaned left or right I could get a partial view of the lawyers, but I couldn't see any of the seats where the justices would sit.

I was next to a legal blogger and someone from a Christian website. Clearly Sky News didn't hold much sway in the accreditation department. I took note of a couple of empty seats that offered a better view, and as everyone stood for the entrance of the justices, I took my chance and moved. I could now see the judges, though the lawyer representing Oklahoma's Attorney General was hidden behind another pillar.

There are nine justices. At the time of this hearing, the longest-serving member was Antonin Scalia, who had been appointed by President Ronald Reagan in 1986. Less than a year later, Scalia died suddenly, causing months of arguments over who should replace him. For a generation, the court had leaned to the right, with four conservatives and four liberals, plus Anthony Kennedy, who was harder to pin a label on, but who tended to side with his conservative colleagues.

Republican presidents nominate justices with a conservative track record; Democrats choose liberals. The appointments are for life, so to preserve the status quo, justices who want to retire aim to do so when a like-minded president is in the White House. President Obama had already nominated two new liberals during his time in office, and there wasn't expected to be another vacancy until after a new president took the oath in January 2017. Scalia had a reputation as the most outspoken conservative on the bench, with a sharp tongue that cut through legal arguments he didn't like. His death gave Obama a rare opportunity to make another appointment that could reshape the court's decisions for a generation. However, Republicans in Congress refused to even consider the appointment in an election year, and the vacancy remained unfilled.

Chief Justice John Roberts opened the day's proceedings: 'We'll hear argument first this morning in Case 147955, Glossip v. Gross.'

And that was the first and last time Richard Glossip's name was mentioned. This was not a debate about the merits of his case, or his guilt or innocence; it was a debate about how he and two other Oklahoma inmates should be killed. Kevin Gross was the chairman of the Oklahoma Department of Corrections, and this was a hearing to argue that his officials should be banned from using midazolam as the first stage of the lethal-injection cocktail.

It's a tough job for an attorney to make their case in front of America's most senior judges. It's called an oral argument not just because they have to argue that the law is on their side, but because the justices argue back. Attorney Robin Konrad had first-hand experience of an execution using midazolam. She had been a witness at a prolonged execution in Arizona a year earlier, and had phoned a judge midway through to try to get it halted. She had barely begun her Supreme Court comments, however, when she was interrupted by Justice Scalia, in combative mood, who picked her up on a comment, and challenged her to justify it. It set the tone for what seasoned observers of the court described as unusually bitter and tetchy exchanges.

Scalia argued that the only reason midazolam was being used was because 'the abolitionists have rendered it impossible to get the hundred per cent sure drugs'. Justice Samuel Alito also laid into those who'd been campaigning against aspects of the death penalty. He said the court had ruled that capital punishment was constitutional, but protesters were still free to lobby legislatures and courts to get that decision changed. 'Until that occurs, is it appropriate for the judiciary to countenance what amounts to a guerrilla war against the death penalty which consists of efforts to make it impossible for the states to obtain drugs that could be used to carry out capital punishment with little, if any, pain?'

Chief Justice Roberts wanted to know about alternative methods of execution and to find out if Ms Konrad found firing squad or gas chamber more acceptable. She said it was hard to argue that in the abstract. The court was splitting along predictable ideological lines.

When Konrad had completed her half hour of being cross-examined, it was the turn of Oklahoma's solicitor general, Patrick Wyrick, who reassured the court that midazolam was a suitable drug. But Justice Elena Kagan was concerned that if midazolam wasn't strong enough to induce a coma, then the third drug in the lethal-injection cocktail could deliver intense pain. 'People say that this potassium chloride, it's like being burned alive. We've actually talked about being burned at the stake, and everybody agrees that that's cruel and unusual punishment. So suppose that we said, we're going to burn you at the stake, but before we do, we're going to use an anesthetic of completely unknown properties and unknown effects. Maybe you won't feel it, maybe you will. We just can't tell. And you think that that would be okay?'

Wyrick said they had provided evidence that midazolam was regularly used as an anaesthetic in painful and invasive procedures. But Justices Kagan and Sotomayor continued to challenge him, to such an extent that Wyrick was granted an extra five minutes to complete his argument. He was allowed to finish uninterrupted. Robin Konrad was also granted extra time, and spent much of it arguing hypothetically about whether being burned alive at the stake would be unconstitutional even if the victim was rendered completely unconscious.

Listening and making notes as America's most senior judges discussed burning at the stake, I couldn't help conjuring up images of the Salem witch trials of 1692. Even in that climate of public hysteria and a demand for scapegoats, there was no suggestion that those accused of witchcraft should be burned alive. That would have been too much of a grisly spectacle. The Salem witches were hanged. Now, more than three hundred years later, American courts were still discussing the best way of killing the condemned.

After just over an hour of heated debate, the Supreme Court adjourned. A decision wouldn't be made public for several months. The attorneys involved in the proceedings assembled on the court steps to make comments in front of the waiting cameras. Robin Konrad was first to speak, but was brief and hesitant and failed to deliver the kind of succinct sound bite that would get her into a TV news report.

By contrast, the spokesman for Oklahoma was a seasoned politician. Attorney General Scott Pruitt said he was confident they'd proven that midazolam was constitutional, though he accepted that it was the state's third choice behind drugs that were now difficult to acquire. 'The state of Oklahoma went through a very thoughtful process and sober process of selecting midazolam. Pentobarbital and sodium thiopental have been used in the past. If we had access to those, we would use those drugs. We do not. We continue to try to access those drugs. We cannot. I think the petitioners are fundamentally attacking the death penalty more so than the use of midazolam.' Pruitt accused abolitionists of using 'threats and intimidation to cause the manufacturers to not export that drug to the United States', and said that Oklahoma 'birthed and gave life to the lethal injection process as the most humane way to carry out capital punishment'.

I headed back to Sky's Washington bureau. I'd arranged for Richard Glossip to phone me to get his reaction. I now had an American number, which was on the prison's list of approved contacts, and I'd deposited money in an account to pay for his calls to me. Even though the hearing wasn't about the circumstances of his conviction, he was annoyed that his name hadn't been mentioned, although John Grant, one of the other death-row prisoners, had been discussed briefly. Grant had murdered someone in prison; his guilt wasn't in doubt. In Glossip's mind, their cases were different.

He was also upset that several of the justices seemed to have decided in advance how they felt about the issue. 'It's a problem when we have justices at the Supreme Court who are already going in with the opinion that they're for the death penalty, and therefore they're not going to hear anything that's going to change their mind.' And in response to the state's argument that midazolam was a suitable drug, and the process was humane, he told me, 'If it's so humane then you have to explain what happened to the guy in Ohio who suffered. You have to explain what happened to the guy in Arizona who suffered for two hours. You have to account for Lockett here in Oklahoma who suffered for forty-five minutes. If it's so humane why did those people suffer for so long?'

But Glossip was also aware that for the first time in his legal fight, he was not just representing himself, he was part of a much wider campaign. This had not been the forum to debate the evidence used to convict him, but he hoped it would lead to more people examining the circumstances of his case. 'I'm not doing this just for myself. I'm not the only innocent man on death row in the United States, that's for sure. I'm never going to give up. I've tried to proclaim my innocence for eighteen straight years and it sure isn't going to change 'cause they're going to stick a needle in my arm. I'm innocent and anyone who reads my case knows I'm innocent.'

I wished him well and told him to give me a call when I got back to England. We would stay in touch in the weeks ahead, even though there was nothing more I could do until the Supreme Court announced its decision. And that wouldn't happen until June.

I hoped that when the announcement came, it would be a big story, but the news agenda again intervened. I was sent to Tunisia to report on a terrorist attack that killed thirty-eight tourists, most of them British. It would dominate the bulletins for a week, leaving little room for the latest developments in the death-penalty debate. When the Supreme Court decision was published, I was in my hotel room editing the latest report about the Tunisian slaughter. I quickly read the details on the official website, but there was only one fact that mattered. Richard Glossip and his fellow petitioners had lost 5–4. Justice Anthony Kennedy had voted with the conservatives.

The rationale for the decision was outlined by Justice Samuel Alito. The principal reason was that the attorneys had 'failed to identify a known and alternative method of execution that entails a lesser risk of pain'. He outlined the history of capital punishment since the US Constitution was first written, and said that none of the methods, including firing squad and electric chair, had been judged to have violated the Eighth Amendment as being cruel and unusual punishment. 'Because some risk of pain is inherent in any method of execution, we have held that the Constitution does not require the avoidance of all risk of pain.' He added that to eliminate all risk of pain would effectively outlaw the death penalty.

Alito dismissed concerns about the use of midazolam, saying that after the botched execution of Clayton Lockett, twelve men were put to death using the drug 'without any significant problems'. He said that the prolonged death of Joe Wood in Arizona was because instead of being given a single 500 mg dose of midazolam, he was given fifteen 50 mg doses over a two-hour period.

The conservative justice concluded with a swipe at those who suggested that 'our decision is tantamount to prisoners being drawn and quartered, slowly tortured to death or burned at the stake. That is simply not true and the principal dissent's resort to this outlandish rhetoric reveals the weakness of its legal arguments.'

That 'principal dissent' came not from Richard Glossip's attorneys, or members of the abolitionist movement. It came from two other Supreme Court justices. Stephen Breyer, with the support of Ruth Ginsburg, had written his own conclusion, explaining why they had voted in favour of the prisoners' appeal. He argued that his twenty years as a Supreme Court justice had led him to the belief that the death penalty was unreliable, arbitrary and involved 'unconscionably long delays'.

Breyer's words were an open revolt against the death penalty. He pointed out that researchers had found convincing evidence that innocent people had been executed. He said that 115 people who had been convicted and sentenced to death had been exonerated before the sentence was carried out. In 2014, six death-row inmates who had served more than thirty years in jail were exonerated and declared to be completely innocent.

Justice Breyer argued that the 'death qualified' rule, whereby jurors in capital murder trials have to be willing to impose the death sentence, meant that juries were more likely to produce guilty verdicts. He also quoted researchers who said that they estimated that 4 per cent of those sentenced to death are innocent. By that measure, around 120 Americans are awaiting execution for murders committed by someone else.

He also drew attention to how a small number of areas sent a disproportionately high number of defendants to death row. He put it down to various factors, including race, a lack of resources for defence attorneys and the power of local prosecutors. He added, 'I see discrepancies for which I can find no rational explanations', including multiple murderers being jailed while single-victim killers went to the death chamber.

A study by Harvard Law School's Fair Punishment Project found that just five prosecutors were responsible for 440 death sentences, 15 per cent of the nation's total. It would come as no surprise to Richard Glossip that 'Cowboy' Bob Macy, who oversaw his trial, was prominent on the list of 'deadliest prosecutors'. If the murder of Barry Van Treese had taken place outside Oklahoma County, Glossip would probably have avoided the death penalty.

When it came to how long inmates were jailed before being killed, Justice Breyer pointed out that in 2014, the thirty-five men who were executed had on average been in prison for almost eighteen years. Nearly all were kept locked up at least twenty-two hours a day. He said it wasn't surprising that some inmates volunteered to be executed, and abandoned their appeals.

Breyer was trying to demonstrate that, under the definition of the US Constitution, the death penalty was not only cruel, but unusual, in that few states carried out executions, and it was becoming increasingly rare. Seven states had abolished the practice in the past decade, and it had been more than two decades since a state without the death penalty had passed legislation to reintroduce it.

Internationally, 95 of the 193 members of the United Nations have formally abolished capital punishment, and a further 42 never execute anyone. In 2013, only 22 countries carried out an execution, and none of them were in Europe or the Americas, with the sole exception of the United States. Only eight countries executed more than ten people: China, Iran, Iraq, Saudi Arabia, Somalia, Sudan, Yemen and the USA.

Breyer asked for a full briefing on the subject so the court could discuss it in its entirety rather than focusing solely on the issue of midazolam. The Supreme Court had not only published a lengthy explanation for rejecting Richard Glossip's appeal, it had also published a detailed case by two of its members for abolishing the death penalty. But that wasn't the end of the legal arguments. Justice Antonin Scalia, backed by Justice Clarence Thomas, had read Breyer's paper, and wrote a rebuttal. 'Welcome to Groundhog Day,' it began. Scalia claimed Breyer's argument was full of 'gobbledy-gook', and said he'd heard it all before.

The judicial killing of an individual by the state is always going to be an emotive issue. And two colleagues who had sat alongside each other on the Supreme Court for two decades were using strong language to denounce each other's arguments.

Less than a year later, Scalia would be dead and the two sides in the death-penalty debate would be eagerly awaiting his replacement and to hear where he or she stood on the issue. If the new recruit to the bench leaned towards Breyer's point of view, the abolitionist movement would finally stand a chance of success. The next presidential election in November 2016 would have huge implications for the death penalty.

When Richard Glossip phoned me two hours after the decision had been made public, I was in the bar of my Tunisian hotel. I needed to find a quiet place to be able to put him on speaker and record his answers. The quietest spot was on the hotel terrace, overlooking the beach and the Mediterranean. It seemed an incongruous place to be talking to a man in a concrete cell about a decision that was likely to cost him his life.

And yet, as he always did, Richard was looking for positives and trying not to be disappointed. 'It's not really a big shock that they didn't rule in our favour. Even if they had, Oklahoma has already made back-up plans so they could carry on executing people if the ruling had gone against them. My fight is still the same. I'm fighting because I'm innocent. It doesn't matter what method you use to execute somebody, you're still trying to execute an innocent man.'

His new focus was trying to get President Obama involved, and he'd written a long letter to the White House. 'I told him, if a member of your family was in this situation, wouldn't you be fighting tooth and nail to get them out of this situation? I was polite. I was nice. But if he chooses not to help me, I hope he has courage to contact my family and explain to them why he let an innocent man be executed.'

I tried to explain that the President had no jurisdiction over Oklahoma's courts. Prosecutions were a matter for the justice system in each state, just as interpreting the law and the US Constitution was the prerogative of the US Supreme Court. A politician can make noise, and highlight what they see as wrong, but a president was very unlikely to comment on a relatively obscure individual case. Although Richard Glossip's name had featured in reports of the midazolam appeal, his personal story had received almost no national press coverage at this stage.

Even so, he still wanted to find a way of getting Mr Obama's attention to highlight what he thought was America's hypocrisy. 'We always go around telling other countries that you can't execute innocent people. It's wrong. We will not tolerate that kind of behaviour, but yet we tolerate that same behaviour in our own country. It's a double standard. We need people to stand up and say enough is enough.'

The day after the Supreme Court decision, one of the Oklahoma City TV stations had paid a visit to Richard's niece Billie Jo Boyiddle, so that they could record him talking on the phone to her and get his reaction to the legal ruling. That evening he was able to watch the report being broadcast on a TV set inside death row. He said other prisoners were cheering and banging on their doors at his success in getting the outside world to pay attention to his case. He was thrilled, but the euphoria didn't last long.

Just over a week later, on 8 July, the Oklahoma Attorney General announced a new execution date. Richard Glossip was now due to die on 16 September. My next task was to find out whether I would be there to witness it.

CHAPTER 13

My Friend the Prisoner

July 2015

Richard and I were becoming friendly, but we weren't yet friends. As a journalist, I have always tried to nurture contacts, and to get on with people I deal with professionally. It's part of my job to build relationships with people who will then give me information and trust me not to misrepresent them. If I was going to watch Richard die, I felt a responsibility to get to know him as well as I could, but I also found that I enjoyed talking to him. He would phone me once or twice a week. I would regularly top up the credit in his phone account so he could ring whenever he liked. Thanks to the six-hour time difference, it was late afternoon or evening in the UK when he would try to call.

Normally if someone phones you and you're busy, you just ignore it and call them back later. Or you text them to say you'll be in touch soon. But this was a one-way phone system. I couldn't return his call. So I would always try to answer it and speak for a few minutes before asking him to phone me again later.

My wife and young son became used to me stopping

whatever we were doing to talk to Richard. He would often call me as I was in the middle of reading Oscar a bedtime story. A fairy tale would be put on hold because 'Daddy's friend in America' was ringing. A couple of times I got Oscar to say hello to Richard before I took the phone to another room to continue the conversation. Richard once called me in the middle of a dinner party at a friend's house. I apologised and went to find a quiet place to talk, which turned out to be their baby's nursery. He talked to me about life on death row while I was staring at stuffed toys and a cot.

We would talk about the latest developments in his case, and sometimes I would record his answers for future broadcasts and reports. Other times he was just ringing up because he wanted someone to talk to, and we would chat about our lives. In the beginning, I felt the situation was surreal. His reality was so disconnected from my own that it was like talking to someone from another world. And it was so unusual that I'd be secretly pleased when he would call while I was with friends or colleagues. 'Excuse me, I need to take this call from my guy on death row.' It became a talking point, and I was eager to share his story, and how I became involved.

I was well aware that this relationship could be ended abruptly in the coming months. I often visualised myself in the viewing room of the death chamber, watching him die. I needed to prepare myself for that possibility, but I could never bring myself to talk about it. That was partly because Kim Van Atta had told me Richard didn't like to dwell on the details. He always tried to be in a positive frame of mind, and it's hard to be upbeat while discussing how prison officials are going to kill you. But I also felt that I should try to develop our relationship before asking more personal questions about how he felt about death.

By early July, I knew I was going to have to ask him a very difficult question. I needed to know for sure whether he was going to invite me to be a witness at the execution. Back in January, it had been too late to add me to the official list. With the latest scheduled execution more than two months away, there was time to complete the formal procedures.

Shortly after the announcement that the date had been set for 16 September, I broached the subject with Kim by email. Just like in January, I knew that the only way I could effectively tell Richard's story to the widest possible audience was by giving a first-hand account of his death. Otherwise he was just another American inmate receiving the ultimate punishment. I apologised to Kim that it was a 'ghoulish thing to have to nail down', but that I needed to know. Kim sent me a reply after speaking to Richard.

> Just got off the phone and I asked that he put you on his witness list, as a personal favour to me, if he otherwise is hesitant. I have not asked him for anything in the past 17 years, so let's see. He's going to 'think real hard' about his list over the weekend. I told him that if the worst happens, he needs his story told. He's committed to leaving a mark, and trying to help those that come after him.

But he warned me that other people who were close to Richard didn't feel the same way. I hadn't spoken to Billie Jo Boyiddle since I'd met her outside the prison in January, when she hadn't taken kindly to my question about some family members having lost touch with Richard. I needed to build bridges.

Richard called on 9 July. We chatted about a few things, and then came the awkward moment I'd been putting off for weeks. 'What I do need to talk to you about, Richard, and it's a subject I hate raising but it's important for us to try to sort this out, is whether you still want me ...' Before I could finish my sentence, he interrupted.

'Are you talking about being one of the witnesses?'

'Yeah ... it's a subject I hate talking about. If you still want me to be there, I need to nail down the details of that so that it doesn't become a last-minute sticking point and the DOC [Department of Corrections] try to block it. And I wanted to talk about your feelings about it.'

'Yeah, you'll be on the list. When I fill the paperwork out, your name will be on the list, and you will be one of the witnesses.'

'Well thanks, Richard, I don't know quite how to feel about that deep down, but thank you for doing that.'

'Oh, no problem. No problem. That's already taken care of. Me and Kim talked about it on Tuesday night, and I talked to him again yesterday when they brought me the phone to call my attorneys, and he told me that he wanted that, and I want it too. I think it's important that internationally, this is told well, and I just want everyone to know. So, you'll be there. You'll be a part of that.'

I was relieved, and pleased that we had become so close. But several weeks later, as the execution date drew nearer, our relationship almost disintegrated and Richard came close to withdrawing the invitation. It was a row for which I was entirely to blame. Sky News had issued a press release about my coverage of Richard's case, and I had contributed a few quotes that appeared in several newspapers and online news sites. One of them angered Kim Van Atta, and I woke up to an angry email.

> The *Guardian* quotes you '... and how Glossip was so happy that someone was taking such an interest that he invited me to witness his death'.
>
> Ian, you don't know how much shit I've been taking from his family and friends, and Richard, about what is perceived as gloating. It's creeping everybody out, and if the quote is accurate, now me.

I was mortified. I had tried to highlight how little attention was being paid to Richard's case back in January, but I realised the comment sounded crass. And to make matters worse, it was inaccurate. When I phoned Kim later in the day, he told me in no uncertain terms that it had been his idea to invite me to be a witness, not Richard's. Now he was taking flak from Richard and his family, who thought a British reporter was gatecrashing an execution, and celebrating the fact that he had done so.

I apologised for my poor choice of words. There was no doubt I had pushed to make sure that I was going to be included on the list of witnesses. It wasn't because I wanted to watch Richard Glossip die. I didn't want to watch anyone die, let alone someone I had befriended. The closer we got to the date of the execution, the more I was dreading it, but I didn't want it to pass unnoticed. Without my first-hand account of what it was like to be there, his death would barely get a mention in the British press.

I genuinely believed I could make an impact on the death-penalty debate with my reporting. I wasn't naïve enough to think that it would shift opinion in the United States. But I wanted people in Britain to be offered a glimpse into the process. I still vividly recalled a documentary I had watched nearly thirty years earlier called *Fourteen Days in May*, made by Paul Hamann. It followed a prisoner called Edward Earl Johnson in the days up to his execution in Mississippi.

I clearly remembered Johnson's attorney Clive Stafford Smith saying goodbye to him as he headed for the gas chamber. It was gut-wrenching. I couldn't hope to produce anything as powerful, because there would be no cameras allowed into Oklahoma State Penitentiary. But I felt compelled to do everything I could to make sure that this wasn't just another execution that would be quickly forgotten. And the only way to do that was to tell everyone what had happened and to let them see Richard Glossip's death through my eyes.

I had met Clive Stafford Smith a few months earlier. He'd founded the human rights group Reprieve, which represents prisoners all over the world and lobbies governments to abolish capital punishment. It also plays a leading role in legal challenges to the use of drugs as a lethal injection. I told him that it was his work with Edward Earl Johnson that had motivated me to delve into the death penalty. I hoped that someone would see my report on Richard Glossip and be similarly inspired.

After more than thirty years in journalism, in which the vast majority of the stories I had covered were now long forgotten, it was invigorating to be doing something that had a chance of being memorable. I wouldn't disagree if someone had accused me of doing this for selfish ends. At my age, it was too late to advance my career, but I did want to do something worthwhile before I shuffled off into retirement. So I could understand if Richard and Kim and others thought I was too enthusiastic or too determined. As a journalist, I needed to push for answers about what was likely to happen. I emailed Kim to tell him all this, and asked him to get Richard to call me so I could explain.

He was still angry when he wrote back. He felt betrayed because he had asked Richard to put me on the witness list as a personal favour to him.

Richard did not invite you, nor ask for you. He has been extremely grateful for what you have done, and it has made a difference, but that's a very different thing from who he wants there if he is killed. The only reason you are on the witness list (at least for now) is that I pleaded with him to do so. I asked him to do it for me, as a favor. He knows that I have never asked anything from him during our entire relationship, so he agreed, with reluctance. Every time you say that he asked you or he invited you or you are going to witness an execution makes him cringe (too mild a word, but I can't think of another).

One of the things I mentioned was that it was going to be very hard for me, and I would be surrounded by women and needed a man there. And that I felt comfortable with you. Richard, as usual, was very kind, understood, and said he would have your name on the final list.

Richard's other friend, Crystal Martinez, was also angry with me, even though I explained that if the execution happened, I would do the journalistic equivalent of shouting from the rooftops about what I had witnessed. She wrote:

If my friend dies, it will be murder. He already has such little control. He deserves to have control over as much of his death as he can. Including who will be there in his final moments. It's crazy to manipulate one's way into that room.

I was told Richard would call me that evening. I knew it would be a difficult conversation. I didn't want to demand or beg. I was determined not to put any pressure on him. I would apologise for not understanding that Kim was the real driving force in the decision to have me as a witness, and I would tell him how sorry I was that he felt I sounded too enthusiastic about the prospect of watching him die.

I didn't feel my journalism was being compromised. We hadn't had an argument about something I had written; I wasn't being told I had to be more supportive of his case to curry favour with him. He was simply upset about what he perceived to be my overzealous attitude. I shouldn't have worried. From the moment he called, and without me saying anything, he made it clear that he was not going to remove me from the witness list. He said he had thought about it, and wanted to make up his own mind, no matter what others said.

'I'm not going to let other people tell me what I should or shouldn't do. Whenever I run into a problem I sit back and think about it and I decide what I want to do. All the things you have done have been positive. For anyone to say you're doing this for your own benefit, I don't believe that. You've done more good for me than you've ever done harm.'

He went on to say that Sister Helen and his attorneys would be benefiting from the publicity of being involved in his case. 'Everybody gains from a situation like this, so I can't hold it against you.' I hadn't thought of it like that before. So many people involved in the death-penalty debate do work that they might consider to be selfless. But it also enhances their reputations. I told him it was never my intention to sound as if I was boasting about my role, but I had to explain my connection to the story. He said he understood that. He said that it was the right thing to do to have me on the witness list. I told him that I agreed with something Crystal Martinez had told me: in his situation, there were very few things that he had any power over.

Choosing his witnesses was one of them. It should be his choice alone. He reiterated that he wanted me there.

I went to bed feeling relaxed that the brief schism in my relationship with Richard had quickly been mended. I planned to visit him in the coming weeks to cement our friendship. But by the time I woke up the following morning, all my diplomatic efforts seemed to have been undone. Crystal Martinez had emailed me, and she was furious. She accused me of being 'horribly selfish' and claimed I was 'wearing [Richard] down' by 'manipulating' him. I was dumbfounded. Richard must have called her after speaking to me. So had he changed his mind? I sent her a reply.

Crystal, I'm really sorry you feel that way, but last night I told Richard to take me off the list if he wanted to. He said he didn't want to do that. I repeated your line that he has very little power of choice in his life any more, and he should do what he wanted. He insisted he wanted to keep me on the list. Maybe his personality trait is to tell people what they want to hear … but what he told me is exactly the opposite of what you are telling me. So with respect, I will follow what he tells me, rather than what you say. He can change his mind any time he wants, before, during or after our meeting and I will respect his decision.

Maybe she was angry because Richard had overruled her. Maybe, having been a supporter of Richard for so long, she was bitter about newcomers getting close. Crystal had been friends with Richard long before the media got involved. I wanted to understand, but I couldn't get past the vitriolic tone of her email. I was deeply upset.

Crystal wrote back to say she was staying out of the argument from now on and it was up to Richard what he did. I was relieved, but I feared that the deeply unpleasant experience of witnessing an execution was going to be even worse if Crystal and I were still at loggerheads over my presence.

Soon after our conversation, Richard was told he was only allowed four witnesses, plus Sister Helen as his spiritual adviser. He chose me, plus Kim Van Atta, Crystal Martinez and Kim Bellware, a reporter from the *Huffington Post* who had written about his case. That meant there was no longer a place for Phil Cross from Fox 25, who had provided so much help to me. I felt very guilty and phoned Phil to tell him so. He was a gentleman. If he was disappointed, he didn't let it show.

Phil said he would prefer to be a journalist on the day of the execution, and report it without the restrictions being imposed on Kim Bellware and myself as witnesses. We were outsiders; Kim was based in Chicago and I was coming from London. Phil was the local reporter who would be at the execution anyway because it was his patch.

The DOC had consistently refused my request to interview Richard on camera, but I told him that I planned to visit him, because 'I don't want the first time that I see you to be in the death chamber.' I had decided I needed to go to Oklahoma the following week, because Sister Helen had told me she would be holding a news conference in Oklahoma

City. It would be a bonus if I could get in to see Richard in prison too.

Richard promised to get his case manager to look into my application to visit. Normal visiting days were Friday, Saturday and Sunday, but I'd heard they occasionally allowed special visits on other days if visitors had travelled a long way. Surely nobody had travelled as far as me to visit Oklahoma State Penitentiary. Richard also told me that once an execution date was announced, the prison tried to be more accommodating when it came to visits.

'Most of them know my case. They know this is the craziest thing they've ever seen. They try to help. Even the warden has tried to help. So I'll push it.'

I flew to Oklahoma City via a connecting flight in Dallas. Sitting next to me on the plane was a woman who revealed she worked in human resources with the state government. Her job involved overseeing all the staff within the prison service. She said some of them found executions hard, and were happy to be off duty when the time came. Richard had already told me that some guards who knew him well didn't want to be involved in his execution.

By 9 a.m. the following day, I was back inside the State Capitol for Sister Helen's news conference. This time she was the warm-up act for a new character in the Richard Glossip story. She had recruited an experienced attorney to work on his case, specifically to try to find any new evidence from the original crime. Without it, there was no chance of a court agreeing to look at a new appeal. In recent years, attorneys who had represented Glossip were more focused on trying to demonstrate errors in the legal process, as a way to stop the execution.

Don Knight, a silver-haired lawyer from Denver, had gone back through the events of January 1997 to look for discrepancies in the evidence. But Sister Helen admitted it was going to be tough to find a new angle: 'We are scrambling now against great odds. I'm trying to hustle for money to pay investigators to get out there and do what was never done.' She said that many witnesses had died, leaving 'meagre pickings' for investigators to find. Don Knight called it 'a deeply flawed investigation from the start'. He said the reason Richard hadn't told the police about the murder was because the motel was frequented by 'unsavoury characters', and 'when the police come around you don't always tell them what you know'.

After the news conference was finished, I walked along the corridor to the offices of the Governor, Mary Fallin. I had emailed her press spokesperson, Alex Weintz, a few days earlier to say I'd like to meet him to discuss an interview with his boss. He welcomed me into his office and I tried to explain why a British journalist was taking such a keen interest in an Oklahoma death-row story.

I made the case for why I thought the Governor should do an interview. I pointed out that the only pro death-penalty voice I had heard from was Senator Ralph Shortey, the lawmaker who told me he had no problem with prisoners being beheaded. Did Fallin really want Shortey representing the state of Oklahoma with his outspoken views? Weintz promised to raise my request with the Governor, but my efforts were to be in vain. The Attorney General, Scott Pruitt, also refused to be interviewed, as did District Attorney David Prater. Gary Ackley, his Assistant DA, who had worked on Glossip's second trial, also declined to discuss the case.

One of my priorities while in Oklahoma was to try to build a more fruitful relationship with the director of communications of the prison service. All my phone conversations and emails with Terri Watkins had been terse and negative. I wasn't expecting that meeting her in person would lead to me getting my much-requested TV interview with Richard Glossip, but I had to try. So I decided to turn up at her office unannounced.

The Department of Corrections administrative base is next to a prison on the outskirts of Oklahoma City, and though security wasn't as tight as at the jail, I still needed to show my ID at reception. After about fifteen minutes, the security door was opened and I was invited inside.

Terri Watkins had been an experienced TV reporter before she became the spokesperson for the DOC. She looked tough enough to have moonlighted as a prison guard. She wasn't going to be sweet-talked by another journalist, even if he did have a British accent and a friendly smile, but I deployed both just in case. She made it clear that the DOC would not allow Richard Glossip to give any more TV interviews, to me or anyone else. Every prisoner was entitled to one 'media day', and he had had his the previous November.

I told her that Richard wanted to include me as one of his official witnesses. I wanted to know if she would try to block that. She said she wouldn't, but insisted that I couldn't be both a witness and a journalist. I would not be allowed to take a notebook into the death chamber, and I would be denied media credentials, meaning I could not attend the post-execution press conference and nor could anyone else from Sky. It seemed petty and excessive. But if I kicked up a fuss, I feared it might lead to the prison removing me from the list of witnesses.

The warden of Oklahoma State Penitentiary was also being unhelpful. I had hoped to visit Richard during my trip, but Anita Trammell turned down my request. My amicable meeting with her outside the death-row unit in January did not seem to have bought me any goodwill.

Back in England a few weeks later, I received confirmation from the Department of Corrections that Richard had named me as one of his witnesses. Soon afterwards, I had a brief email from the warden: 'Mr Woods, you will be allowed a special visit with offender Glossip. Let me know when you would like to visit.'

I told Kim Van Atta the double good news, but warned him that despite his fears about it being 'ghoulish', I needed to interview Richard about the execution and ask why he had chosen me and another journalist to be there. It was an important aspect of the story, but I'd been putting off mentioning it directly during our recorded chats.

Kim asked me to tread lightly. He told me that Richard 'still thinks you're morbid, and care too much about watching him die'. The criticism stung. I was trying to be as sensitive as possible, but apparently I wasn't succeeding. It was a particularly hard time, because Richard was being moved back to the isolation unit where prisoners are taken thirty-five days before their death. He'd spent five weeks there in December and January and he knew what it was like. The lights in his cell were permanently switched on, and he was constantly monitored by guards. Kim said Richard had told him he was scared.

It was desperately awkward interviewing a man who was due to be executed about the details of his impending death, but when he called, Richard gave no hint of irritation at the questions. He said he wanted me to be there because in the wake of the Clayton Lockett fiasco a year earlier, he believed that the process needed to be scrutinised.

By coincidence, he called at the same time as a police expert was in my office carrying out some research for me. Graham Wettone is a former Metropolitan Police inspector, and even though he is now retired, he is still involved in training officers in how to interview suspects. I had asked him to take a look at the full Justin Sneed interview from 1997. I wanted a professional perspective on whether it seemed fair, or whether the detectives were manipulative. He finished watching it while I was still recording my interview with Richard, so I invited him into the studio to give us both his assessment.

According to Wettone, 'It seemed very blinkered. It seemed as if they had already made their minds up. I just found it an astonishing interview to watch, and reading what's happened with the case, I just find it amazing that you're where you are now based on that sort of interview and that sort of testimony. I can't imagine a police officer in the UK would conduct that sort of interview in that way.'

We knew the law was different in Britain and the United States, but Richard was heartened to hear support from a police officer, and told him how much he appreciated his comments. Wettone said he thought a British court would have ruled the interrogation to be inadmissible, but it was a hypothetical argument. Richard had exhausted legal appeals, and only fresh publicity about the case seemed likely to make a difference. A high-profile intervention was needed.

CHAPTER 14

A Helping Hand from Hollywood

August 2015

'The Governor of Oklahoma is just a horrible person. And a woman, so it's even more discouraging.'

Susan Sarandon had waded into the Richard Glossip case and caused ripples around the world, and especially in Governor Mary Fallin's back yard. It was exactly what I hoped would happen, even if the actress later apologised for being so personal in her attack. I had tried for months to arrange an interview with Sarandon, ever since my first meeting with Sister Helen Prejean. I knew that the two women had become friends twenty years earlier during the making of the movie *Dead Man Walking*. Sarandon's portrayal of Sister Helen had won her an Oscar, the only time she had picked up the award for Best Actress after having been nominated four times previously

On the night she collected the Oscar, Sister Helen was the first person she thanked in her speech to the Academy, 'for trusting us with your life and bringing your light and your love into all of our lives'. Sarandon had read the book and encouraged her then partner Tim Robbins to write the screenplay and direct the movie, which gave her such an insight into death-penalty issues.

The contribution of a Hollywood superstar wasn't essential in telling this story, but it would help a lot. It would instantly explain to a British audience who Sister Helen was; viewers might not be familiar with one of America's most dedicated death-row campaigners, but they'd probably have heard of the movie about her life. And the endorsement of a celebrity could also give my story about Glossip more impact. Sister Helen promised to put in a good word, and it worked. Finally a time and date was agreed. Susan Sarandon would record an interview at her New York apartment on 1 August.

I'd hoped that securing an exclusive interview with Sarandon would help convince Sky News that the Glossip story was worthy of a documentary, rather than just a series of news stories. But the idea was vetoed because I was unable to secure my own interview with Richard in prison. I was disappointed, but planned to tell the full story at length in a series of podcasts in the weeks before the scheduled execution. The final episode would be released after 16 September, though we could not know how the story would end. I decided to call the series *Another Dead Man Walking* in a shameless attempt to capitalise on the success of Sister Helen's original.

On the day of the interview, I was in France on a story. I'd arranged for my colleagues in New York to record the interview using questions I'd provided, but I spoke to Susan Sarandon on the phone just before filming began. There was an urgency and determination in her voice. She wanted to know when the interview would be broadcast. I said it would probably air in a few weeks, closer to the scheduled execution date. She told me it needed to go out sooner if it was to have an impact on the case. Having read more about Richard's case, she had decided to do a joint interview with Sister Helen on CNN the following week.

That meant I had to make sure our interview was broadcast as soon as possible. I thanked her and allowed the producer Emily Upton and cameraman Jake Britton to get on with their work. When I watched their video the following day, I realised it was a powerful contribution.

Sarandon began by talking about the making of *Dead Man Walking* and how she had got to know Sister Helen Prejean, who even made a cameo appearance in the movie alongside her, standing in a silent vigil outside a prison while an execution was under way. She described taking the nun to the first screening of the film, and warning her that it might be a traumatic experience for her. Not as traumatic as witnessing a real execution, Sister Helen replied.

Then she moved on to Richard Glossip. 'Richard's case is so typical. Bad representation; two trials that were ridiculous. No physical evidence. He's put there by a snitch who actually did kill the person, and then the snitch has life and this guy is being put to death on the sixteenth. Case after case, once a mistake has been made within a judicial system, people just do not want to admit that a mistake has been made.'

She talked knowledgeably about the way detectives had interviewed Justin Sneed. Sister Helen must have briefed her well. 'At both trials nobody saw the video of the confession where the police are practically spoon-feeding him what he should say and offering him to have a lesser sentence. That was never brought up in the first trial, so they gave [Glossip] a new trial and then they still didn't bring it up. That's how bad poor people's representation is, and that's why rich people don't end up in this situation because they have better lawyers. And so he's a perfect example of what's wrong with the death penalty. And so of course I'm hoping that some kind of exposure will give him the opportunity to maybe get his sentence at least commuted because he's clearly innocent.'

Then she got stuck in to Mary Fallin and other politicians who supported capital punishment. 'The Governor of Oklahoma is just a horrible person, and a woman, so it's even more discouraging in terms of digging in. Being tough on crime means being for the death penalty, somehow that got established, so … you're attempting to protect your political career. So you can't ever look at the complexities if you want to keep your mantra going. And the fact that it doesn't work, nobody even talks about the fact that the death penalty is not a deterrent. It's incredibly expensive; the states that kill the most people have the most murder in those states. You would think they would stop doing it because there have been so many people that have proven to be innocent. In other countries that was a good enough reason to abolish the death penalty, but in America it doesn't seem to be.'

She talked about trying to raise awareness in the weeks ahead. 'It's never because of some consciousness-raising that these things change, it's because of some kind of embarrassment. And so this is where public opinion can make a difference ... that's about the only thing that will save him.'

I phoned Sister Helen to thank her for having helped arrange the interview, and told her what Sarandon had said about the Governor. Helen's voice rose several octaves and many decibels.

'She said what?!'

'No, it's good,' I said. 'It will make a lot of headlines in Oklahoma. Stir things up a bit.'

Over the next couple of days, I scripted and edited the story, using sound bites from the Sarandon interview. I also used some material I had acquired a few months earlier but had not yet had the opportunity to broadcast: the police interview with Justin Sneed from 1997. It was very grainy quality, having been recorded on VHS tape, and the sound was almost inaudible at times. But there was enough to demonstrate clearly how the detectives had cajoled Sneed into implicating Richard Glossip in the murder. The jurors in the two trials had not had the chance to watch it, but now it would be played on TV for the first time because Susan Sarandon had referred to it during her interview.

I made sure that Phil Cross at Fox 25 in Oklahoma City had a copy of the Sarandon interview. We had stayed in regular contact since I first met him in January, and it was only fair to offer him the same help he had given me in recent months. I also wanted to make sure that it was seen on Oklahoma television bulletins by the state officials I'd been pestering with interview requests. I hoped to ruffle a few feathers and force them to react. All I had managed to get so far was a written statement from the Attorney General's office.

> A jury has twice convicted and sentenced Richard Glossip in the murder of Barry Van Treese. Glossip has challenged his conviction all the way to the US Supreme Court, exhausting all appeals, and has been unsuccessful at each challenge. The Attorney General's office will continue its work to protect the state's ability to ensure the sentence handed down by a jury can be carried out so that after nearly 20 years, justice can be served for the family of Barry Van Treese.

I included the comments in my story, which was broadcast on Sky News on Thursday 6 August:

> One of Hollywood's best-known actresses has appealed for public help in stopping the execution of a man she says is 'clearly innocent'.
>
> In an exclusive interview with Sky News, Susan Sarandon said next month's scheduled execution in Oklahoma shows everything that is wrong with the death penalty in America.
>
> She also described the Governor of Oklahoma as a 'horrible person' for refusing to intervene.

It was the most viewed story on the Sky website that day, and my video report ran every hour on TV. It felt very satisfying, having worked so long and so hard on securing the interview. I sent a link to the story and video to the press spokesmen for the Governor and the Attorney General so that they would get it when they woke up several hours later. I again asked for an interview about the Glossip case.

Governor Fallin's communications director, Alex Weintz, replied later that day with a suggestion that 'if I was looking to balance Mrs Sarandon's thoughts on the death penalty with another perspective I should interview Donna Van Treese about the loss of her husband'.

As if I hadn't thought of that. I told him that I had tried many times to talk to her via phone and email. She'd initially agreed, but then stopped responding to my messages. A few weeks earlier, I had driven an hour south of Oklahoma City to visit her, but she wasn't at home. Donna is a private citizen. The Governor and the Attorney General have public jobs and should, in my view, accept responsibility for defending a key policy.

But I did send Donna another email, and this time I mentioned that the Governor's office was rejecting interview requests and suggesting I talk to her as an alternative. To my surprise, I got a reply from her the following day. She said she was willing to talk to me and asked when I would like to meet her. It looked as if I'd finally get to interview her when I returned to Oklahoma for the execution.

As the day wore on, I watched the story get picked up and repeated by other national and international media. Richard's niece Billie Jo emailed me to say there had been hundreds of new signatures on her online petition in the past few hours. I waited by the phone. I'd asked Richard Glossip to call me, because I was planning to do something we hadn't attempted before: to put him on air for a live interview from his prison cell. When I raised it as a suggestion in editorial meetings, there was some concern about the unpredictability of such a move. I reassured producers that in all my time talking to Richard, I had never heard him swear once.

I hoped he would call during the afternoon UK time. But the hours passed and there was no call. I was really disappointed, and at 7.20 p.m. gave my apologies to the producers, who were still standing by for the interview. I was walking out of the building to get into my car and drive home when my phone rang. It was Richard. I ran back into the building and shouted to colleagues to get ready.

I told Richard to stand by; that we would be live on air as soon as possible. I sat down in the studio. Then – disaster. Another call was coming in on my phone. Richard always called me via a Skype app on my mobile. But if a regular phone call came through at the same time, it took precedence and cancelled the Skype call.

I swore. It was my brother phoning. I just hung up rather than waste time explaining to him what was going on, and hoped that Richard would phone back immediately. Moments later, the phone rang. It was my brother trying again. I swore even more loudly and gave his number to a colleague to tell him to stop calling me. A minute later, Richard phoned back and we were able to put him on air.

Richard wanted to publicly thank Susan Sarandon for her intervention. A few days earlier he'd been able to speak to her on the phone for half an hour, and he was ecstatic. 'I'm truly happy that Susan Sarandon is speaking out for me. It's really crazy that it's gotten to this point. She can see for herself that this is truly a case of an innocent man who is going to be executed. And I couldn't ask for a better person to stand up and speak out for me.'

We talked for more than five minutes. Normally the producer in the gallery will tell you via your earpiece to wrap up an interview after two or three minutes, but it was the first time that anyone could recall talking to a prisoner live from death row. When it was over, I could sense that my colleagues were as excited as I was that we had been able to make it happen.

When I got home, I picked up some positive comments on Twitter about the Sarandon report and the interview with Glossip. I then watched as the Governor's spokesman tweeted a series of ten comments about the case. They were familiar points about Glossip having had his day in court, and how the Governor could only grant clemency if there was a recommendation from the Pardon and Parole Board. He ended by saying: 'There are multiple victims here, none of them Glossip. A man beaten to death, wife without a husband, five kids with no dad.'

It was clear that Weintz had been getting a lot of calls about Susan Sarandon's comments, and the Governor's office was being forced to respond. I'd made an impact. A few days later, he issued a statement on behalf of Mary Fallin.

> Richard Glossip was first convicted of murder
> and sentenced to death over 17 years ago. He has
> had over 6,000 days to present new evidence.
> Postponing his execution an additional sixty
> days does nothing but delay justice for the
> family of Mr Van Treese.

Fallin had reaffirmed her unwillingness to intervene in the case, and there was still no prospect of me getting an interview with her. But I had stirred up a debate and others were joining in. Susan Sarandon and Sister Helen Prejean took to Twitter to rebut some of the comments coming from the Governor's office. Sister Helen tackled the 'he's had his day in court' argument: 'Over 150 people have been exonerated from death row. All were convicted by juries. Yet all were completely innocent.'

Susan and Helen stepped up a gear. They both publicised my interview on their social media accounts, and then appeared on CNN and MSNBC to talk about Glossip's conviction and sentence. The story was snowballing. The *Dr Phil* show, syndicated throughout the country, decided to devote a whole episode to the case. Because the 16 September execution date was looming, the producers had to break out of their summer schedule of reruns and rush out a new programme. The Hollywood actress and the Catholic nun would be Dr Phil's studio guests.

A few days after it was recorded, the network made a trailer to promote the show. It was spectacularly dramatic. Pounding music. A ticking clock. And an apology to Governor

Mary Fallin. 'I was wrong to call you a horrible person. I'm sorry.' It also showed Susan Sarandon fighting back tears as she read a letter from Richard. For someone like me who had picked up the story when only a handful of journalists had been interested, and who had been battling against apathy from some colleagues, this was jaw-dropping stuff.

The worlds of news and celebrity were colliding. The US showbiz programme *Entertainment Tonight* did a report on the *Dr Phil* show, including a clip from Sarandon being asked how she would feel if the execution went ahead. 'I'll feel ashamed and sad for us all,' she said. 'It's hard to put an animal down, but to put a man down? It's just not how we should be living our lives.'

The publicity also led to Richard's case making it onto the front page of a British newspaper for the first time. Chris Bucktin of the *Daily Mirror* had visited him in prison. 'DEAD MAN TALKING' was the banner headline. The reporter described his outrage that someone could be executed when there were doubts about his guilt.

With less than a month to go before the 16 September execution, the upsurge in publicity could be life-saving. Not only because public opinion could put pressure on the Governor, but also because it might help uncover new information that Richard's lawyers could use. And sure enough, when the *Dr Phil* show aired, someone with knowledge of Justin Sneed was watching. Attorney Don Knight was about to receive an interesting phone call

CHAPTER 15

The Executioner

September 2015

Two weeks before my scheduled visit to the death chamber to watch Richard Glossip die, I went to meet a man with unparalleled experience of America's execution system. Randall Workman had overseen the executions of thirty-one men and one woman in the death chamber of Oklahoma State Penitentiary when he was the warden. He was now retired and lived on an isolated road a few miles outside McAlester. I had written to him months earlier, but he hadn't responded. When I pulled up outside his home, the place looked deserted. But within a minute a pickup truck pulled into the driveway and a burly middle-aged man and several children got out. He was younger than I'd expected. I introduced myself and asked if he remembered receiving a letter from me. He shrugged and said that letters from reporters went in the bin.

It wasn't a promising start. But I said I'd come from London and would he mind if we had a chat. He invited me into his home. The first thing I noticed inside was a revolver on the dining room table and two semi-automatic rifles propped against the fireplace. He was in the process of selling the handgun to a friend who had also turned up at the house. He made me a coffee while he concluded the sale.

Workman would tell me later that, living in a rural area, and travelling to cities like Tulsa that had a high murder rate, he always had a gun within reach for his own protection. Each of his children was taught to shoot and given their own gun at a very early age. He said he would have no problem using a weapon in self-defence, and would leave it to a jury to decide if he was justified in opening fire. 'I'd rather be judged by twelve than carried by six' was his mantra.

I explained at length why I was keen to interview him and how I'd come to be involved in the Richard Glossip case. I told him I was in danger of presenting a one-sided story as so many in authority were refusing to be interviewed. I admitted that I had formed a relationship with the inmate, and that based on what I knew about the case, I didn't think he should be executed. Workman agreed to allow me to return later with a camera, and to tell me all about the mechanics of putting someone to death.

He told me what he said to prisoners about dying. 'You're going to go to sleep. You're going to start snoring, and then you're going to pass away quietly.' He would also share his belief in Christianity with the condemned men, but if they weren't religious, he'd find other things to talk about in their final thirty minutes on earth.

'They might discuss football or the weather or their families. They might not talk at all. Everyone was different. I had some individuals that were being executed that were very nurturing to us and said, "I'm going to go to heaven, don't worry about me, everything is just fine." I have had some individuals that said, "You're going to go to hell. You are committing murder yourself, and you think that's justice for you to commit the same crime that others commit?"'

The response of witnesses could be unpredictable too. Relatives of the murder victim were understandably kept apart from the family of the man being executed. Some relatives, from both sides, preferred not to be there at all. None of Richard Glossip's family wanted to be there to see him die if all his appeals failed. But some of those who'd lost a loved one in a murder were keen to see justice carried out.

'I had one lady that said, "I'm going to eat popcorn in the viewing room when I watch this execution."' He told her, 'No, this isn't a theatre.' Others wanted to see the prisoner suffer, and felt cheated if they thought it was a painless death. They complained to him that the prisoner just went to sleep and didn't wake up. He recalled how the first time he attended an execution he felt emotional, because he had got to know the prisoner and had become close to him. After that experience, he made sure that he studied the details of the murder the inmate had been convicted of carrying out, including looking at photos of the crime scene. He told me he never became emotionally involved again.

He recalled the only execution of a female prisoner he had ever supervised, and how the warden of the women's prison where she had been incarcerated had become deeply upset while watching her die. I'd been told how some prison staff tried to make sure they were off duty when an execution was scheduled, because they didn't want to be part of the process. And yet Randall Workman said there was never a shortage of volunteers to be involved. He tried to avoid using guards who seemed overenthusiastic about the prospect of taking part.

Workman knows what it's like to have a relative murdered. He told me he'd lost a cousin a few years earlier, and he was asked by other family members whether he thought they should push for a death sentence on the killer. He told them it would be a long-drawn-out process and at the end of it they might not feel any sense of satisfaction. The murderer of his cousin is now serving a life sentence. But he still supports the principle of capital punishment. 'I absolutely would keep the death penalty. The death penalty is not a deterrent to crime? Yes it is. That individual will never commit a crime again.'

But what about judicial mistakes and wrongful convictions? A miscarriage of justice that ends in death cannot be overturned. Workman paused and thought carefully about his answer. 'I hear the stories and I see the shows where the DNA has proven that a person was wrongfully committed. Can I say it's possible? Yes, I can say it's possible. Do I personally feel like I've executed somebody that is innocent? I'd say that it's not for me to say. The courts have decided. And from that standpoint until they decide otherwise, until they say he is innocent, then he's guilty, and I go with it.'

I pointed out that Richard Glossip had always maintained he was innocent. 'I'd say of the thirty-two people that I've executed, I'd say probably twenty per cent of the people would say, "You're executing an innocent man", "I was just at the wrong place at the wrong time" or "I really didn't do nothing wrong."'

I finished the interview by asking him to walk me through the process. I wanted to be prepared for what I was due to see in two weeks. He said that the prisoner was already strapped to the gurney by the time the blinds were raised and witnesses could see into the execution chamber. He would be given two minutes to convey any last words or wishes. Then the warden would announce that the execution should proceed. When the inmate was declared to be dead, the blinds would be closed again.

I now had a clear mental image of Richard Glossip lying on the gurney, looking at me and his friends through the glass that separated us. What I couldn't imagine was the look in his eyes. I couldn't visualise whether the man who always sounded so positive on the phone would be terrified when he finally knew for sure that all hope had gone.

My cameraman Dickon Mager and I drove back to Oklahoma City. The downside of interviewing Randall Workman that morning was that I had to miss a news conference with Sister Helen Prejean and attorney Don Knight, who were addressing reporters and taking questions at the State Capitol. I wasn't too concerned, because I had arranged to interview them both later in the afternoon.

In their news conference, they had been pushing a document compiled by Don's legal team called 'When Eight Is Enough', detailing the different stories told by Justin Sneed from his arrest to what he had said in court during both Richard Glossip's trials. Don had emailed me a copy a few days earlier. It was a comprehensive deconstruction of Sneed's often conflicting and evolving version of events, which was useful in engaging public opinion to question whether there really was a justification for Richard's death sentence. But the only way that Oklahoma's appeal court would agree to re-examine the case was if they believed they were being presented with new evidence. This was unlikely to meet the standard required to consider a stay of execution or a retrial.

Don summed up the prosecution's main witness. 'Justin Sneed is a person who has a difficult time with the truth. I know there are people he has talked to … he likes to talk. Maybe he told someone what the actual truth was. The simplest explanation is usually the truth. A guy who had a methamphetamine problem was looking for money, knew Barry Van Treese had the money. He tried to get that money. It didn't work out. As he said in story number three, things got out of control and he beat Barry Van Treese to death, and then tried to cover it up. And when the police closed in on him, he was a scared nineteen-year-old. He thought he was going to get the death penalty; he gave up Richard Glossip because that's what the police wanted.'

Richard's best hope still seemed to be the letter apparently written by Sneed's daughter Justine. If she was prepared to testify that her father had implicated Glossip just to save his own life but was too scared to recant, then surely a court would have to review the case. I knew that Don Knight had hired investigators to track her down, but for weeks he had refused to tell me whether she was cooperating. Finally he admitted to me that she had backtracked and wouldn't swear an affidavit, but that he wasn't yet ready to talk about it publicly in case she changed her mind again.

Instead he was focusing on contacting other potential witnesses, and pleading with the Governor to give him more time to track them down. 'Sixty days would give us the chance to get to those witnesses who should have been contacted ahead of the second trial. Now of course we're not going to get to all of those witnesses because some of them are dead.' Barry Van Treese's friend Cliff Everhart, motel receptionist Billye Hooper, Richard Glossip's drug-dealer brother Bobby, Sneed's boss in the roofing team that he rejoined after the murder; all of them had died during the past eighteen years.

Don Knight lambasted some of the other lawyers who had worked for Glossip during that time. 'I haven't had eighteen years to do the work that I would do as Mr Glossip's lawyer. I saw the work that other lawyers have done in this case and frankly I think they should be ashamed of themselves. There wasn't any work done. There wasn't any investigation done. This was a one-sided fight that the government waged against Mr Glossip and they got what they wanted.'

Sister Helen was willing to tell me a little about her own attempt at a breakthrough. She had asked Justin Sneed if he would allow her to visit him in jail. He had agreed. 'I wrote Justin a letter and I met with him yesterday. The nature of what we talked about was confidential because I went in the capacity of spiritual adviser, and just understanding he was a nineteen-year-old kid under a lot of pressure, and I've actually gotten him a lawyer to help him through whatever steps he's going to take. He didn't see a lawyer for six months [after the murder]. Justice wasn't done for Justin Sneed either.'

It didn't sound to me like Sneed was cooperating or willing to speak out now on Richard Glossip's behalf. If he was, I was sure Sister Helen would have hinted or told me in confidence. But she remained publicly confident about Richard's chances of avoiding execution. 'Every time we talk he says to me, "What do you think's going to happen?" And every time I tell him, "Richard, you are not going to die! Look at all the forces that God has summoned on your side. You are not going to die!"'

She was encouraged by the response to her appearance alongside Susan Sarandon on TV. '*Dr Phil*'s audience doesn't get too much into legal issues or criminal justice issues, but when they got feedback from the audience they were shocked. "Do you really mean a man can go to execution on the word of a nineteen-year-old kid who was under pressure himself? How can this really be happening in the United States?"'

The following morning I drove towards Oklahoma State Penitentiary. Dickon filmed me as I drove, and I talked to the camera about visiting Richard for the first time. I described how strange it was to meet a man I felt I knew so well, but who had never seen my reports about him, or even knew what I looked like. And yet now he was choosing me to be one of a handful of witnesses to see him die. I described how I felt a sense of responsibility that we should get to know each other better.

I drove through the arched gateway of the prison. Just like in January, on my first visit, there were no guards to check my ID. I carried on along the half-mile road that skirted the fence and the walls of the main prison, round to Unit H, where death-row prisoners were incarcerated. It had its own parking lot for visitors and its own reception. I left my personal belongings in the car as I had been instructed, bringing only my driver's licence to prove my identity.

Immediately inside the door was a female prison guard sitting at a desk alongside a metal detector arch. I gave her my name and handed over my licence. She scanned a list on a page and didn't find what she was looking for. She picked up a phone and called someone. I was told to wait. After a few minutes a male guard came along who appeared to be expecting me, and after a brief search he took me through a door and pointed up a long, gradually elevating corridor. 'Do you know where to go?' he asked.

He didn't realise it was my first time inside the death-row unit. When I told him I hadn't been here before, he walked a few paces with me along the grey corridor and told me to keep going until I came to the visiting area. After around forty yards, the corridor opened up to a rectangular area with four seats bolted to the floor on each side. Each seat was in front of a window with thick glass and metal bars. Behind one window was a prisoner engaged in conversation with his visitor.

I'd been told to take a seat on the right at the window furthest away. I sat down and waited. I glanced over my shoulder at the other visitor, a woman, but I couldn't hear her conversation. The roar of a huge air-conditioning unit drowned out all other sounds. There were two windows in the ceiling, which allowed sunlight to stream down, creating golden squares on the grey floor. But because the windows had bars, they cast shadows on the ground, like a prison logo reminding everyone where they were.

I looked around, but there was nothing to catch my eye apart from one notice on the wall: an official proclamation that there was zero toleration of rape in Oklahoma prisons. I wondered if it reassured any of the inmates who read it. It was my first time on death row, but not my first visit to a prison. And each time I'd been inside a jail I'd tried to imagine what it must be like to be locked up for hours on end. I also wondered what it was like for the men and women who guarded the prisoners but who could walk outside and smell freedom at the end of every shift.

The seat on the other side of my window remained unoccupied. I had been waiting for around fifteen minutes. Behind the seat was a door with a window through which I could see guards coming. After a few more minutes, Richard was led up to the door by a guard. It opened and he walked into the cubicle. His hands were handcuffed behind his back. The guard didn't come in. He closed the door and locked it, then reached his hands through a hatch to undo the prisoner's handcuffs. Richard squatted slightly to make it easier for him to reach. He must have done this hundreds of times over the past eighteen years. Only when the handcuffs were off did he look at me. He smiled broadly. My natural instinct was to reach out my hand to shake his, but with glass between us, all I could do was raise it in greeting.

We talked for more than two hours, but I can offer only a few direct quotes because I wasn't allowed a pen and paper to make notes, and I could only commit certain phrases to my memory. I'd already decided that the best thing to do was to simply relax and talk, and I'd try to repeat key parts of our conversation later on the phone, which I could then record. What I remember most is the laughter, because that was the most unexpected part of the visit. Richard Glossip was twelve days away from his execution, but an uninformed observer would never have known that. He looked and sounded relaxed, and had a smile on his face for most of the time, though he looked a lot thinner than when Phil Cross had interviewed him on camera in November 2014.

Naturally we talked about the latest legal challenges to his execution, and what was happening in the outside world in terms of public support. I talked about who I had been interviewing, including my discussion with the former warden Randall Workman. We discussed my podcasts. Kim had played them down the phone to him.

When I asked him about how he would feel if there was no stay of execution, he said he 'would dance into the death chamber'. It was an extraordinary phrase to use and I asked him what he meant. He said it would be 'the happiest execution anyone had ever seen' because he felt that even though he had lost in the courts, he believed he was winning his argument in the court of public opinion. The publicity in recent weeks had led to more and more letters of support, and more than a quarter of a million people had signed online petitions trying to stop the execution.

Naturally he didn't want to die. But he felt he had made an impact, because after years of nobody believing his story, people all over the world were now writing supportive letters. He was elated. The laughter continued as we discussed his love of British comedy. I already knew about his favourite show being *Last of the Summer Wine*, but he revealed he also liked more recent UK exports to America including *Doc Martin* and *The Great British Bake Off*. When he said he liked Piers Morgan and Simon Cowell I pretended to get up and walk out in disgust. Without a hint of irony he told me that his other favourite British comedy was *One Foot in the Grave*.

We also talked about what was in the news, including Donald Trump's recent announcement that he was running for president. I joked that Oklahoma Governor Mary Fallin might be his running mate, and if the pair were elected, being executed might not be a bad option. Looking back, it seems incredible that such black humour could find its way into our conversation, but the two of us were genuinely having fun.

However, I found our face-to-face meeting more difficult than our frequent chats on the phone. The noisy air-conditioning system meant I struggled to hear everything Richard was saying. There was a metal grille at the bottom of the window that was supposed to assist in carrying words back and forth, but to properly hear him I had to keep tilting my head to the side and moving my ear closer to the grille, and in doing so, I lost eye contact.

I looked at my watch a few times and was amazed how quickly time was passing. Richard had said that he was expecting other visitors, including his daughters and niece. But after more than two hours, it was still just us. Then a woman and a man whose face seemed vaguely familiar arrived. We had never met before, but the reason I seemed to recognise him was because he was an older brother of Richard's. They hadn't seen each other for many years, and Richard had never met his wife, who was accompanying him.

As I left them to chat alone, a woman who was visiting another inmate came up to me. She knew all about Richard and his scheduled execution, and had even listened to my podcasts about his case. She told me how much she appreciated my work, and went on to say that Richard was liked and respected by other inmates. She urged me to keep reporting. 'He does not deserve to die,' she said. 'Richard is innocent. This whole thing is crazy.'

Richard was still talking to his brother and sister-in-law, so I told him it was time for me to go. I looked him in the eyes and told him how much I'd enjoyed the visit, and asked him to call me the following evening to record an interview on the phone. He smiled and thanked me for coming. He said he'd had fun too.

I walked back down the long grey corridor more convinced than ever that this was a man who did not deserve to be executed. I know it's illogical and irrational to say that someone could not be guilty of murder just because I was laughing and joking with him seventeen years after he was first convicted. But my gut instinct was that Richard was a decent guy who had been caught up in terrible events and was paying a very heavy price. I was so lost in my thoughts that I forgot to stop at the entrance and collect my driver's licence, which I'd used to prove my identity. It would spend two weeks locked up on death row before I returned to liberate it.

The following evening, Richard phoned me while I was in my hotel room. He immediately started reading a letter he had just received from a British woman living in America, who was writing to him for the first time. She told him that she'd gone on the internet to find some guidelines on what to say to a death-row prisoner.

'That stumped me for a start,' he said. 'I mean, who's giving her guidelines?!'

We laughed, and he continued to read what she'd written about her hobbies and her favourite TV shows, *Blackadder*, *Dad's Army*, *Monty Python*, *The Office*. Richard had never seen *Blackadder*, and he'd only watched the American version of *The Office*. I made a mental note to buy him some DVDs if he was ever released.

He suddenly asked me if it rained a lot in England. I gave him a brief explanation of our temperate climate. He said it didn't seem to rain much in *Last of the Summer Wine*. The reason for his sudden interest in British weather was because his latest pen pal had expressed the hope that one day he would be able to 'eat fish and chips out of a newspaper from a greasy chip shop at the seaside in Great Britain'.

'I'd love to do that myself, because I'm always seeing those guys on *Last of the Summer Wine* eating fish and chips, and I'd like to try that.'

'Okay,' I replied. 'If you get out of prison, I'll take you.'

He thought that would be cool. He was more talkative and happy than I had ever heard him. He talked about all the coverage in newspapers, radio and TV. And for the first time, he opened up about how he felt about me, now that we had met.

'I was definitely surprised. When I heard Crystal talk about you when they were trying to feed that baloney in my ear, I didn't know what to expect, I'll be honest. I don't get where they're coming from. You were polite, you were respectful. I just don't get what that was all about.'

I told him I didn't think it was my personality Crystal was complaining about. I said I thought it was my job. Richard defended me. 'I said I judge people for myself. They tried to tell me don't waste your time with a visit from him. I'm a fair person. That was a wonderful visit and I owe you for that because you sat there and we laughed a lot. I'm glad I got to meet you and talk to you because I got to learn for myself. I told them flat out it was one of the best visits I ever had and so I just want to thank you for that.'

This was exactly what I wanted to hear. Not because it justified my determination to get a place on the witness list, but because I really wanted to have a friendship rather than just a professional connection to this man. I told him I had enjoyed it enormously. I said I couldn't believe how happy he seemed, both now on the phone, and when I had visited him. 'It makes it easier for me to deal with the situation' was his reply. 'I want to enjoy the time I have left, whether it be a few days or thirty years. That's why when you came to visit me you saw that I smile a lot. I laugh a lot. That's me.'

I reminded him that he'd said it was going to be the 'happiest execution they'd ever seen' and how he was going to 'dance into the death chamber'. 'Well, I kind of said it in a way I shouldn't have said it. I didn't mean it in a crazy, sadistic kind of way. It's not that it's an enjoyable situation. I just want them to see that they're never going to break my spirit no matter what they do. I'm not going to be one of the guys that fights them all the way into that chamber. It doesn't benefit anybody and it sure isn't going to benefit me. With other people they have to drag them in there because they don't want to go. If I have to, I'll dance in there for them. I believe in God. Other people don't and are afraid of what's on the other side. It can't be no worse than this life, that's for sure.'

He told me he wanted to donate his organs after his death, but that the law didn't allow it. He thought it was the moral thing to do and could turn a horrible situation into a positive one. The lethal injection would poison his organs, but he said he would be willing to donate a kidney prior to his execution.

We talked for an hour. It was the longest telephone conversation we'd ever had. It seemed that my visit to him in prison had moved our relationship to a new level. It was no longer a reporter interviewing an inmate. We were talking like friends. That was what I had hoped for. It was good for my story, but I also felt I needed it as a human being. I couldn't go through with this experience as a casual observer. I needed an emotional connection to justify my presence in the chamber, to myself and to Richard.

I felt closer to his family, too. I had visited his daughters Ericka and Christina, and his niece Billie Jo, and we had filmed them looking through the latest letters from well-wishers. One of them was a card from England depicting the *Last of the Summer Wine* characters. The message inside said: 'These guys would be on your side.' When I asked his niece what she would do if the execution went ahead, she replied, 'Pray that it's quick. And painless.'

However, my hopes of interviewing the family of the murder victim ended unexpectedly, in a brief email from Donna Van Treese.

Ian,

I have changed my mind on our interview. I respectfully decline.

Sorry for any inconvenience.

Thanks,

Donna

That was the last time I ever heard from her. I asked her why she had changed her mind, but she didn't respond. Maybe she had heard that Richard had asked me to be one of his witnesses. I was very disappointed. Whatever my feelings about the strength of the case against Richard Glossip, I had every sympathy for the terrible loss of her husband, and I genuinely thought I could convey that to her if I met her.

I was also making no progress in getting an interview with a state representative. The Governor's spokesman Alex Weintz had spoken on camera about Richard Glossip's case, reaffirming that Mary Fallin would not grant a sixty-day stay of execution. I knew I could obtain the footage from Phil Cross, but I still wanted to pursue my own interview, so emailed Weintz again.

When he continued to refuse, I made an implicit threat to doorstep the Governor by turning up unannounced at one of her events. The prospect of an embarrassing public encounter prompted a rapid series of rude emails between us, before Weintz finally agreed to talk to me on camera. I phoned him to make the arrangements. The earliest I could see him was the following Monday, just two days before the scheduled execution.

Immediately the tone of our conversation became much more civil. I thanked him and tried to explain why I felt so strongly about this story. I urged him to listen to my podcasts so he would understand where I was coming from. And I had a suggestion. Even if Governor Fallin was still refusing to grant me an interview, I asked him if she would agree to meet me for an off-the-record conversation. He said he'd put it to her.

As we drove back from McAlester, I reflected on the position I might be putting myself in. If I did get the chance to meet the Governor face to face, I wouldn't just be trying to persuade her to do an interview. I would be telling her why I believed Richard Glossip should not be executed. I could be lobbying her to grant a stay of execution just forty-eight hours before Glossip was due to be put to death.

I had ceased to be simply a reporter. I was fully prepared to take the step to being an active participant in the campaign to save Richard Glossip. Even if the Governor refused to meet me and I didn't get the chance to make my case to her, in my own mind I was no longer a neutral observer. I was now fighting to stop an execution that I had successfully lobbied to attend.

CHAPTER 16

Preparing for the End

September 2015

'The letter's arrived. Shall I open it?'

Cherry, my wife, had phoned me from London. Even though I'd given the Oklahoma prison authorities the address of the Sky News office in Washington DC, I'd suspected they would send their invitation to my home address. Cherry read it out to me

> *Offender Richard E. Glossip #267303 is scheduled to die by lethal injection at the Oklahoma State Penitentiary on September 16, 2015 at 3.00 p.m. This execution is in accordance with Oklahoma State Statute 22 Section 1015.*
>
> *Offender Glossip has requested you as a witness to the execution.*

The remainder of the letter was about who to contact and where to go on the day. It contained no advice about what I could expect to see, or how to behave. But when Cherry scanned it and emailed it to me, this hypothetical event that I had been preparing for over the past nine months suddenly became very real. As a reporter, I should have felt a tinge of excitement or relief that the arrangements had been confirmed. Instead, I just felt sick. The formal tone giving the time to arrive read like the confirmation of a hospital appointment, except that here, the medical staff on duty would kill their patient rather than cure him.

The campaign to stop that happening was about to step up a level. Two days before the execution, Richard's lawyers were ready to unveil new information that raised more questions about his conviction. All it needed was for the Oklahoma Court of Criminal Appeals to recognise that it was indeed fresh testimony and agree to delay the execution while it was evaluated.

Don Knight called a news conference at the State Capitol, but interest in the Richard Glossip case meant that the venue had to be moved from the small room that had hosted similar events earlier in the year. This time a lectern and microphone had been set up in the main body of the building, immediately in front of the entrance to what used to be the state's Supreme Court offices.

Knight and his team had traced a man called Richard Barrett, who had been a drug dealer at the Best Budget Inn in the months leading up to the Van Treese murder. He swore an affidavit saying that he sold methamphetamine to Justin Sneed on many occasions, and that Sneed would pay for the drugs with cash he'd stolen from motel rooms or cars belonging to guests. Barrett said that he often saw Sneed 'tweaking', by which he meant that his mouth would twitch and he would chew his lips, a sure sign of a meth addict. In his statement he said that in his experience, 90 per cent of meth addicts would steal to fund their habit: 'People with this addiction will stay awake for days or weeks and will do anything to get more of the drug, even kill.'

Barrett's drug-dealing partner was Bobby Glossip, Richard's brother. He and Richard had been close when they were kids growing up in Illinois, but Richard says that changed when Bobby got involved with drugs. They no longer talked much, but Bobby took advantage of Richard's position to deal drugs at the motel. However, Barrett said that Richard was 'a good-hearted guy' and he didn't believe he was involved in the drug dealing; the only time he saw him, Richard was telling his brother to keep the noise down. Barrett also said he didn't believe Sneed was under Richard Glossip's control, as the prosecution had claimed at his trial.

Barrett was in jail on drugs charges soon after the murder of Barry Van Treese when he was contacted as a potential witness. He said he was scared that his fingerprints would be found in room 102 because he'd often used that room to sell drugs to Sneed and other customers. He didn't want to get involved in a murder investigation. As a result, he had never testified at Richard Glossip's trials, though if he had, the prosecution would undoubtedly have tried to undermine his credibility because he was a drug dealer. On the other hand, the state's main witness was a self-confessed killer.

The news conference highlighted the different requirements of journalists and attorneys when it came to these events. As a reporter, I wanted to hear something punchy; a succinct argument with a couple of good sound bites. It's what you need to tell a story in a TV report. But Don Knight was talking to journalists like we were jurors, slowly building a narrative to its conclusion. I was impatient.

To be fair to Don, it wasn't the media that had the power to grant a stay of execution; it was the appeal court judges who would read and digest the dossier at length. However, public opinion was still important; if there were more stories about a possible miscarriage of justice, particularly in Oklahoma newspapers and on local TV news, there would be more pressure on Governor Mary Fallin to intervene. She didn't have the power to stop the execution indefinitely, but she could delay it by sixty days. That in itself would give Don and his team more time to prepare their legal challenge.

Finally, after three quarters of an hour, Don began to talk about the new evidence that had come to light as a result of the *Dr Phil* show. A man called Michael Scott had been watching the programme, and after hearing about the upcoming execution, he decided to contact Don Knight with information he knew could be important. Nine years earlier, Scott had been in the same prison block as Justin Sneed in the Joseph Harp Correctional Facility. In his affidavit, he said that Sneed often boasted that 'he had set Richard Glossip up and Richard Glossip didn't do anything'. He said it was common knowledge among inmates that 'Justin Sneed lied and sold Richard Glossip up the river'.

Scott said that Sneed had made things up to save his own life. That evidence, together with Barrett's affidavit about Sneed stealing to feed his drug addiction, was surely enough to force the appeal court to examine the new information in detail. Former associates of Justin Sneed were prepared to testify that he was a liar and a drug addict, someone even fellow criminals wouldn't trust. So why had jurors put their faith in his version of events?

But Don was about to lose his monopoly on the story. As well as the reporters and cameramen who had gathered to watch the news conference, another interested spectator was standing at the back. David Prater was the District Attorney of Oklahoma County. Even though he wasn't DA at the time of Richard Glossip's trials, he was now in charge of the office that had successfully prosecuted Glossip for murder and pushed for a death sentence.

Prater had reviewed the evidence in the Glossip case, and had decided the conviction was safe. He didn't take kindly to attacks on the reputation of his attorneys, and he certainly didn't like how Don Knight was handling Richard's defence. As the news conference wrapped up, he walked straight towards the media, bristling with anger, and began sounding off about what he called 'a bullshit PR campaign'.

He told reporters that he had agreed to a meeting with Don Knight to discuss the evidence, but had then been informed that the attorney had cancelled the meeting because he was busy. When he found out that Don was holding a news conference rather than spending his time arguing the merits of the case with the District Attorney, Prater decided to intervene.

'I was supposed to have a ten o'clock meeting with the defence team and I find out late last night that no, there's going to be a press conference here,' he said. 'If they're so interested in their client's innocence, why are they not in my office or in the Governor's office? This is not a legal process. This is a PR campaign. All they're doing is trying to abolish the death penalty in the state of Oklahoma and in this country by spreading a bunch of garbage.'

Prater isn't a tall man and his voice is a little more high-pitched than average. But he knows how to deliver rapid-fire sound bites to the media. Reporters and cameras formed a huddle round him. It was quite a contrast to how Don Knight had outlined his key messages, and Don's forensic analysis was now being washed away in a wave of pithy put-downs from Prater.

'If in fact these are credible pieces of evidence, these affidavits, then those lawyers are committing malpractice. If you're a lawyer, file documents, go to the courthouse, go to the Court of Criminal Appeals, that's what lawyers do. They don't hold press conferences!'

Prater had turned down an interview request from me several months earlier. This was the first time that the office responsible for prosecuting Richard had fought back against allegations that this was a miscarriage of justice. 'Two years ago I went through those boxes and tried to determine in my mind to a moral certainty if Mr Glossip was guilty because that's what lawyers on the other side of this case had asked me to do at the time. And I did so. And I didn't have any question about it.'

I asked him why it mattered if the state executed Richard Glossip in two days as planned, or in sixty-two days. What was the harm in a short delay?

'Why don't you ask the Van Treese family about that? The continuous delays. Why don't you talk about that? We work in the rule of law here, okay?'

Prater put his thumb and forefinger together and held them up to the camera for effect. He'd left a tiny gap. 'And let me tell you what ... personally it really wouldn't matter to me if I had that much, that much, of a question about Mr Glossip's guilt. But I do not, sir. And at some point this process has to stop, especially when the defence team has begun playing games with the process, and with you.'

It was a dramatic intervention. When Prater finished what he had to say, I walked a few yards to where Don Knight was watching and listening, and asked him for his reaction. He defended his decision to present the evidence to the media before submitting it to the court for consideration, saying that new information was coming in all the time and he didn't want to go to court until he was sure his team had pieced together everything possible. He would be taking it to court later in the day. Once court officials had read the documents, he was hopeful that the execution would be delayed while judges took time to decide whether the evidence was worthy of consideration. In response to the arguments between himself and Prater, he tried to shift the focus, saying, 'When this execution is done, Sneed is going to be laughing. He'll soon be laughing at everybody.'

I walked the short distance to the Governor's office. I had hoped to meet her in person for the first time, either for an on-camera interview or an off-the-record chat. I was hoping to explain to her why I had become involved in the story and why I believed the case against Richard Glossip was so weak. I wasn't naïve or egotistical enough to believe that I could persuade her to grant a stay of execution, but it would certainly make me feel a hell of a lot better if I had at least tried.

The Governor wasn't in her office. She didn't want to meet me. I would have to make do with an interview with her spokesman. As Dickon set up his camera, tripod and lighting, I chatted with Alex Weintz and two other advisers to the Governor. I got the impression that they accepted that the evidence against Richard Glossip wasn't as strong as other death-row cases, but they were still convinced that there was no reason for a politician to interfere with a verdict delivered by a jury, and upheld by several branches of the judiciary.

David Prater also walked into the office as we were getting ready for the interview. I introduced myself properly; during the press conference I had simply jumped in with the other reporters asking questions. He apologised for not granting my earlier interview request, but as he talked about the Richard Glossip case, I could tell he was sincere in his view that justice was being served. That didn't surprise me. Those closely involved in the process rarely want to admit mistakes are possible. More than 150 American death-row prisoners have been exonerated, and they had all been told their conviction was safe ... until evidence was found that proved it to be unsafe.

And for some inmates, it was too late to right the wrong. The Death Penalty Information Center lists more than a dozen cases of men who were executed only for subsequent investigations to suggest they were probably innocent. Several states have issued pardons decades after inmates were put to death, based on evidence that was either ignored or unavailable at the time.

I sat down opposite Alex Weintz and began the interview. Because of the silence of other more senior government officials, he'd become the face and voice of Oklahoma's death penalty in recent weeks. He echoed the complaints made by the District Attorney that Don Knight's team were fighting a media campaign because they were losing the legal arguments.

'Usually when you have inmates on death row their attorneys are very keen to meet with the Governor's legal representatives and argue their case and ask for a stay, and that didn't happen. They aren't confident in the information they have and that's why they're fighting this battle through the media, and spending more time collecting signatures and asking celebrities to join their PR campaign.'

But even if Governor Fallin's office was given new information, Weintz didn't hold out much hope that it would lead to a change of heart. 'We have a moral obligation to look at these cases and make sure we are satisfied. We have decided, as the jury did, that Glossip is guilty. He's had ample time to argue his case in court. Everyone has looked at this case, the evidence on both sides. He had a fair trial. The Governor would only get involved if it was some extraordinary circumstance, if there was evidence that we were convinced was relevant and exculpatory, and nothing like that has been presented to our office.'

I said that I thought it was extraordinary that this was a matter of life and death, and yet the Governor was unwilling to be interviewed and explain her reasons on camera, leaving such an important matter to her spokesman. 'The Governor didn't sentence Richard Glossip to death,' he replied. 'What the Governor is doing is declining to give Richard Glossip a get-out-of-jail-free card after he got convicted and sentenced to death by a jury.'

He told me that unless a court intervened, the execution would go ahead in forty-eight hours as planned. I asked him if he and the Governor would rest easy if that happened. He paused and looked down before answering. 'I have looked at the evidence and I think Richard Glossip is guilty. The system we have set up is that judges and juries make these decisions. The Governor's office very rarely gets involved in death-penalty cases.'

As far as Oklahoma was concerned, this was true. Mary Fallin's predecessors had only revoked four death sentences in recent years, following recommendations from the advisers on the Pardon and Parole Board. But governors of some other states have much greater powers to intervene, and have issued clemency orders to halt executions. In 2003, Illinois Governor George Ryan became so disenchanted with what he felt was a flawed judicial system that he commuted the sentences of all 163 men and four women on death row in his state. There hasn't been an execution in Illinois since.

A couple of hours later, we returned to the Governor's office to film Don Knight handing over his dossier of evidence. Later that afternoon, Alex Weintz wasted no time in forwarding me a copy of a letter the Governor had just received from a juror in Richard's second trial. David Piscitello wrote that he and his fellow jurors had exercised 'extreme due diligence' during the month-long trial and had no doubt of Richard Glossip's guilt.

> *Our decision was not based on popular belief or opinion, 30-second news clips, social media blogs or daytime entertainment shows, but on every word of witness testimony and evidence. We anguished over every single detail and piece of evidence.*

He said they took no pleasure in handing down a death sentence, but that it was 'right and just'. He stood by their decision.

> *As a jury we felt that Justin Sneed would never have killed Barry Van Treese if it had not been for Richard Glossip. We thought Mr Glossip was cold, calculating, manipulative and unremorseful. A coward that bid Mr Sneed do his dirty work and that is why we held him to a higher accountability.*

No other jurors have been willing to comment publicly. None has expressed any doubts about the verdict. But none had watched the video of the police interrogation of Justin Sneed, so they were unable to judge whether the detectives had manipulated the killer when they had him in custody, and got him to implicate Richard Glossip.

There was one final attempt to influence public opinion in Oklahoma. On Tuesday 15 September, several dozen supporters marked the eve of the execution with a rally organised by the Oklahoma Coalition Against the Death Penalty. Speakers gathered to denounce state execution, and to attack the Governor for her refusal to intervene. The speeches were predictable in their content, but with just over twenty-four hours to go, there was a new tone of anger and desperation.

Among the guests was a man who had travelled down the dark road to the death chamber but managed to escape in the nick of time. Nathson Fields was sentenced to death for a double murder in Chicago in 1986. The judge in his trial was later convicted of taking a bribe to deliver a guilty verdict. Fields was found not guilty at a retrial and was finally freed after eighteen years in prison. When he later sued for compensation, his lawyer argued that a million dollars for every year in jail would be appropriate. Instead, the jury awarded him just $80,000 in total damages. Fields had flown to Oklahoma to share his story.

'I came within a month of execution. I'm here to represent all those who care about justice for Richard Glossip. He is an innocent man. I had similar evidence where only one witness was against me. Later this witness recanted. The judicial system is comprised of people who are human beings, and as human beings, we all make mistakes. Any time you take the word of the actual killer over a righteous, fair, law-abiding citizen, I think that's backwards.'

When the speeches were finished, the rally ended with a song called 'Your Eyes Are Innocence' written by a British musician. Richard Wynne plays John Lennon in a Beatles tribute act called Made in Liverpool. His song wasn't quite on a par with 'Give Peace a Chance' as a protest anthem, but as the words echoed around the grounds of the Oklahoma State Capitol, it captured the mood of those who were there.

> I've been wronged, and if fairness should prevail
> Let the balanced scales of justice write my tale
> I've been wronged, deprived of liberty and life
> No moral wrong can make a right.

Several people wiped away tears. I felt dejected. If the protest was about trying to halt the execution, it seemed pointless. Nobody who mattered in the decision-making process would be listening. The rally gave reporters like me more material for our stories, but it wasn't going to save Richard Glossip.

Richard phoned Kim Van Atta just as the rally ended. I asked Kim to pass the phone to me so I could have what I expected would be my final conversation with him. I told him how good the rally had been. I told him I wished he could have been there to see it. I hoped it didn't sound like a crass comment. I thanked him for all the conversations we had had over the past few months. I was fighting to choose the right words and felt I was failing. I wished him luck and said I hoped we'd have another chance to speak. Then I said goodbye. I had little cause for optimism that I would hear his voice again until he uttered his final words in the death chamber.

There was one final inconsequential publicity stunt left. A few dozen people made their way to the Governor's office and staged a sit-in. Or rather, they stood around in the lobby for a while until photographers had exhausted their appetite for pictures. Then they went home feeling helpless and indignant.

There was now a third member of the Sky News team in Oklahoma. I had asked for a producer to help me with the logistics of reporting the execution. While I was inside the prison, I would need someone on the outside interviewing protesters and coordinating our coverage with our colleagues back in London. I would not to be allowed to have my phone inside the prison, so I would be out of contact for at least four hours.

Michael Blair was a good producer and a nice guy, and by coincidence, he'd attended the same school as me in Northern Ireland. It seemed a strange quirk of fate that Belfast Royal Academy should have two former pupils involved in an American death-row case, but it was comforting to have someone with me whom I knew well. I honestly didn't know how I was going to feel in the aftermath of the execution if it went ahead. I needed someone who could take charge and steer me in the right direction if I wasn't thinking clearly.

We drove to McAlester, where Dickon, Michael and I would be spending the night in a comfortable hotel a few miles away from the concrete slab where Richard Glossip would no doubt be lying awake contemplating his final hours. During the journey, I checked my emails and discovered that the Governor had released a press statement saying she would not be issuing a stay of execution. Once again they had portrayed efforts to save Richard as a publicity campaign to attack the death penalty.

> Yesterday, forty-eight hours before Glossip's scheduled execution, his attorneys presented my office with a binder of what they have labeled 'new evidence'. After reviewing it with my legal team, we have determined the vast majority of the limited content they have presented is not new; furthermore, we find none of the material to be credible evidence of Richard Glossip's innocence. After carefully reviewing the facts of this case multiple times, I see no reason to cast doubt on the guilty verdict reached by the jury or to delay Glossip's sentence of death. For that reason I am rejecting his request for a stay of execution.

The statement urged Glossip's attorneys to make their challenge through the courts.

> In the event that a court refuses to issue a stay, Richard Glossip will be executed tomorrow. I hope the execution brings a sense of closure and peace to the Van Treese family, who has suffered greatly because of Glossip's crimes.

My mood darkened further. I phoned Don Knight to get his reaction, and he said he was at the Court of Criminal Appeals filing the dossier. It was now in the hands of five appeal judges. They either had to read it quickly and reject it, or delay the execution to give it further consideration.

Sarah Whitehead, my manager at Sky News, phoned me to say that she had heard that the Governor had refused to grant a temporary stay of execution. She repeated something she had told me a few weeks earlier: that I shouldn't feel obliged to attend the execution. She said people would understand. No one would criticise me for walking away from such a grisly assignment. I could have spent time thinking about it, but I didn't want to create any doubt in my mind. I told her that it was too late to arrange for someone else to take my place. If I backed out, one of the last things Richard would see would be an empty chair where I was supposed to be sitting. After all the time we had spent talking to one another, I owed it to him to be there at the end.

I had arranged to meet Sister Helen Prejean just outside the prison as she was on her way in to offer spiritual help to a man who was now just twenty-two hours from death. He had never been this close before. His previous execution had been postponed with just over twenty-four hours left on the clock. In all my dealings with Sister Helen she had always been upbeat, but no longer. She called the Governor's statement 'antagonistic'. 'Yeah, I'm angry. They're going to kill Richard.'

It was 5 p.m., and the prison authorities had granted Kim Van Atta and Sister Helen four hours for a final visit.

But 5 p.m. was also the time that the guards were due to deliver Richard's final meal, the death-row ritual in which a condemned prisoner can order whatever he likes from local fast-food outlets, up to a value of $25. Richard had requested a pizza, fish and chips, and chicken with mashed potato, plus a strawberry milkshake. A condemned man's final meal is rarely part of a calorie-controlled diet.

The delivery time meant Richard had a choice. He could either eat his meal while it was hot but lose precious time with his closest confidants. Or he could see them, and eat later when the food had gone cold. And their visit would have to end early too, because at 9 p.m. his telephone would be taken away and he wanted to spend the last hour making his final calls to his family. He chose to eat the food when it arrived. Kim and Sister Helen would have to wait. It seemed to me the prison rules were either cruel or stupid or both.

I was now angry as well as apprehensive. If this was how I felt on the eve of the execution, I dreaded to think what state I was going to be in while watching Richard die.

CHAPTER 17

Coffee, Cookies and an Appointment with Death

September 2015

'This is a horrible event, but we're going to make it as pleasant as possible. We have cookies and coffee for you.'

It was a most unexpected way to be welcomed into the prison to be an official witness to an execution. The man from Oklahoma's Department of Corrections did not smile as he checked my name against his list. His close-cropped hair, sharp black suit, white shirt and tie made him look like a Secret Service agent, or any number of American security personnel whose demeanour leaves you in no doubt that you'd be wasting your time arguing with them.

I had engaged in both gentle lobbying and bitter arguments to make sure that I would be there to watch Richard Glossip die. I had been accused of being morbidly obsessed with the execution process when all I wanted was to report what I believed to be a terrible miscarriage of justice. And yet I couldn't deny there was an element of personal ambition to tell what could be one of the most memorable stories of my career.

If this really was just macabre voyeurism in pursuit of a dramatic headline, then I would need Richard Glossip to be dead by the time I left the prison. However, I was in no doubt that I wanted him to live. I was desperately hoping to report on a stay of execution. Over recent weeks I'd been moving ever more decisively into Richard Glossip's camp. Now, I had nailed my colours to the mast by writing an article for the Sky News website on my role as a witness. That morning I came out publicly in my support for the inmate.

> I cannot say with certainty that Richard Glossip is innocent. His actions after the murder of Barry Van Treese would make him guilty of being an accessory after the fact. But I believe there is a strong probability that he is not guilty of murder. I certainly believe that there was not enough evidence to justify a death sentence. I believe his execution is wrong. And it's from this perspective that I will watch him die.
>
> I cannot claim to be truly objective. There will be other reporters you can turn to for that. What you will get from me is what it's like to watch a man I like die an unnecessary death.

It was the most-read page on the Sky News website that morning. Several hundred thousand people had also watched the thirteen-minute special report I had made, and listened to the latest episode of my podcast. My work, together with stories written by other reporters, had already succeeded in generating a huge amount of interest in Glossip's conviction and his punishment. He was no longer an anonymous death-row inmate in Oklahoma. A year earlier, only one journalist had attended the clemency hearing where the Pardon and Parole Board had signed off on his death. Now dozens of newspapers and TV networks were following each development, and millions of people around the world had read or watched his story.

It was important for Richard, but it was also important for me. I rarely measured the success of my work by how many people watched or read my stories. Trivial stories often attract far more interest than weighty issues, and are not necessarily a reflection of how much effort has gone into writing or making a TV report. But in this case I felt vindicated by the response to a story I cared passionately about.

I hadn't slept well. I was very rarely nervous on the eve of a big story, an important interview or even a dangerous assignment. But this was like nothing I had ever experienced. I knew exactly what to expect in terms of the execution protocol, but I had no idea how I was going to react to being there. And that was what worried me. If I switched fully into reporter mode and behaved like a neutral observer, that might alienate my fellow witnesses, who were deeply emotionally involved. But if I gave free rein to my own feelings of anger, sadness and revulsion, I might not be able to do my job, and recount accurately what had happened.

By 4 a.m., I was wide awake and knew I wouldn't get back to sleep. I started reading emails and text messages sent to me by friends, colleagues and even complete strangers who had read or seen my reports. They were intended to offer comfort and support, but had the opposite effect. They made me feel even more apprehensive about what I was going to see. One of the editors in our newsroom wrote: 'It's not often that I wish someone's story to fall through, but I hope your man gets a miracle today.'

I went down to breakfast and met Dickon and Michael. They could tell I was subdued. I just didn't feel like engaging in the normal banter that typically flows between colleagues. My mood didn't improve when I got an email from Kim Van Atta. I had sent him links to both my TV report and my website analysis about why I was attending the execution: 'Your piece was perfect, with the exception of "I don't know if he's guilty or not". That feels cruel. You should know enough by now to be able to say he's innocent.'

I phoned Kim and reminded him that I was a journalist. I could never write that I was certain about something that was disputed unless I had clear evidence to prove it beyond any doubt. I pointed out that I had publicly taken Richard's side in saying there had been a miscarriage of justice. I felt I was going out on a limb and I was annoyed that it didn't seem to be enough for Kim. But in a way I was glad: I was demonstrating that I was still independent and not simply a mouthpiece for the Glossip campaign.

A day earlier, I had got into a spat via both Twitter and email with an Oklahoma journalist who was critical of my role as an official witness. Ziva Branstetter, editor-in-chief of *The Frontier*, had never spoken to me, but when she discovered that I was listed as an official witness, she tweeted: 'Here's the lesson. Tell the inmate's story the way he likes it, get access. Be objective, take your chances.'

I emailed her to ask for an apology, or for evidence to back up her comment, which suggested that I wasn't objective. She replied that she was simply criticising the rules that had reduced the number of media seats at Oklahoma executions from thirteen to five. She thought I was just circumventing the media lottery for seats. But she continued to imply that I was biased.

Generally an inmate is not going to choose to place a reporter on his list of chosen witnesses if the reporter has written a story that the inmate believes is unfavorable to his cause. If you plan to write about the event, it would seem that whole situation would call into question any reporter's objectivity in writing about the case.

I apologise if my Tweet was interpreted as a criticism of your reporting. It was meant to be a criticism of a system that the state of Oklahoma has set up. I probably could have phrased it better.

I was still angry. Yes, I had come to the conclusion that Richard Glossip did not deserve to be executed, but I had first been asked to be a witness before I'd written a single word about his case. And I had not ignored alternative points of view about his conviction. However, the argument made me realise that I now needed to be completely transparent about my reporting. It was one of the reasons I wrote a blog outlining why I was a witness.

I wasn't the only journalist taking sides. On the morning of 16 September, the *New York Times* devoted its editorial to Richard Glossip's case. 'Countdown to an Execution in Oklahoma' outlined some of the background to his conviction, and came to this conclusion:

This case pretty well sums up the state of the death penalty in America. Supporters like to say it is reserved for the 'worst of the worst', but that is demonstrably untrue. It is more accurate to say that capital punishment is arbitrary, racist and meted out to those without the resources to defend themselves.

The Oklahoma County prosecutor, David Prater, has called the efforts to exonerate Mr Glossip a PR campaign. That's a remarkably dismissive thing to say when a man's life is at stake. This case is yet another reminder that the death penalty – in addition to being immoral and ineffective – has already taken innocent lives and as long as it exists it is likely to take more.

Richard Glossip, his lawyers and supporters, and those campaigning for the abolition of the death penalty, could not have wished for a more high-profile media endorsement than the editorial column of America's foremost newspaper. But it felt as if the PR campaign of which the Oklahoma authorities were so critical had reached its climax too late.

And of course support was not universal. The Van Treese family had declined interviews, but released a statement ahead of the execution.

> Over these many years our family has endured all manner of pain as a result of the death of Barry. The Van Treese family knows with absolute certainty the state of Oklahoma has provided the opportunity for justice to be served in this case.
>
> The death penalty in Oklahoma is reserved for the most heinous crimes. Two juries who heard all of the testimony agreed this case warranted the death penalty for Richard Glossip. Numerous courts have reviewed the facts of this case and have determined Richard Glossip's case warrants the death penalty. To ensure Richard Glossip received a fair judgment, he was given a second trial where he was represented by a legal team with decades of experience.
>
> The facts and testimony of the case have been proven in two trials and reviewed by every possible court all the way to include the US Supreme Court. And, finally, as the law provides in these types of cases, the Pardon and Parole Board extensively reviewed the case, talked with and questioned Glossip, and voted unanimously against clemency.
>
> Execution of Richard Glossip will not bring Barry back or lessen the empty hole left in the

lives of those who loved Barry. What it does provide is a sense that justice has been served.

We have a right as a family and as citizens of the United States of America to expect justice to be served. Would not you feel the same if this was your loved one?

It was hard for me to take an opposing point of view to a family whose loved one had been murdered, but by supporting Richard Glossip's right to live, I was not being unsympathetic about the way Barry Van Treese had died. I tried to put myself in their position. What if my wife, brother or son had been murdered? In truth, I don't know whether my opposition to the death penalty would survive such a traumatic ordeal. My view of the Glossip case was influenced by how well I had got to know Richard. The Van Treese family had denied me the opportunity to get to know them. It would certainly have forced me to justify my view of the death penalty to them face to face.

It wasn't just that I didn't like capital punishment, or that I had befriended the inmate; I simply didn't feel that the weak evidence in the case justified an execution. The authorities had acknowledged that when they were prepared to accept a plea deal from Glossip a decade earlier. Would the Van Treese family have felt that justice was served if he had accepted that deal?

Seven hours before the execution, I arrived outside the prison and began doing updates on Sky News about what was expected to happen. I had arranged to conduct a live interview with Kim Van Atta just before we went into the prison at 11.30. I asked Kim why he was so convinced Richard Glossip was innocent. He tried to cram eighteen years of legal arguments into one answer, which he did eloquently and with some wit, trying to make viewers understand the bizarre situation in which he now found himself: a New York psychologist who had befriended a death-row inmate in 1999 and was now about to enter an Oklahoma jail to watch his friend die for a murder he didn't commit. I asked him about his final visit the previous evening. He contradicted me.

'First of all, it's not the final time. Where there's life there's hope. Do I have any illusions? No. You know Richard. He is extraordinary. He's upbeat. He feels some peace because his voice has been heard and that's incredible. He gets thousands of letters and thousands of emails. It's been a very lonely sixteen years until about a year ago when Sister Helen got involved, you got involved, then everybody got involved. So he's in a good place. He's in a better place than I am right now.'

I wrapped up the interview; it was time to go inside the jail. I ended by saying that it was the most extraordinary experience of my journalistic career, but it was an assignment I'd rather not be doing. I could feel a lump in my throat and hoped there wouldn't be a follow-up question from Jeremy Thompson, the presenter in the studio, because I might struggle to answer it without choking up.

We climbed into Kim's rental car and travelled all of twenty yards to the entrance gate. It would have been a lot easier to simply walk across the road, but we'd been told to arrive by car. We were soon joined by our fellow witnesses Sister Helen Prejean, Crystal Martinez and Kim Bellware of the *Huffington Post*. After the unorthodox promise of coffee and cookies, we were directed to a parking space and transferred into a minibus for another very short journey of around a hundred yards to the room where we would wait until it was execution time. We were each given a numbered badge to wear, saying *Execution Witness*.

We'd been put in what seemed to be a social club for prison staff. There was a pool table, which had been covered and pushed up against a wall. There was coffee and bottled water, but so far, no cookies. There were a couple of sofas and a table and chairs. We sat down and began to make small talk. Sister Helen tried to engage in conversation with the prison guards who were watching us, but they were unwilling to say anything that might be regarded as vital information.

It was the first occasion I had spent time with Crystal Martinez since our arguments via phone and email, but neither of us raised the subject of Richard's decision to include me on his list of witnesses. This was too important a moment to allow our row to overshadow it.

I chatted to Kim Bellware, the only other journalist who had been invited. Although we had spoken on the phone a couple of times, I didn't think we had met before. Suddenly I realised we had. Kim had been with the family and friends who had visited Richard in prison on the eve of his January execution date. Sister Helen had smuggled her in as if she was a colleague, without telling the warden that she was actually a reporter. It had led to a row with the prison authorities, after which nuns were classified like journalists: not to be trusted. Kim had written a couple of lengthy stories for the *Huffington Post* about Richard, but I sensed that her presence today wasn't just to do with her excellent reporting. She and Richard shared similar taste in music and he enjoyed chatting to her on the phone.

We'd only been in the room for around ten minutes when the door opened and half a dozen men in suits walked in. I recognised one of them immediately as Robert Patton, the director of the Department of Correction. The big boss. He didn't smile but shook everyone by the hand, introducing himself and asking our names. He checked that all Richard's witnesses were in the room. We weren't. Sister Helen had gone to the bathroom a few moments earlier. Patton said he would wait so he could talk to us all together. I assumed he had to give us an official briefing about death-chamber procedures. I didn't want to be told how I should behave, as if I could possibly stay in complete control of my emotions.

But when Sister Helen walked back into the room, and without any verbal fanfare to precede his remarks, Patton said simply, 'There's been a stay.' There were a few moments of silence, because we weren't sure we had heard him right. He was asked to repeat it. He said there had been a two-week stay of execution. We asked more questions, but Patton said he couldn't give any more details.

I was utterly dumbfounded. I hadn't wanted to get my hopes up because it would have been even more heartbreaking if the execution had gone ahead. I was so relieved, and began to hug my fellow witnesses. We were laughing but had tears in our eyes. Kim Van Atta looked stunned, and after the initial elation, he needed a moment alone to compose himself. He told me later that he wasn't used to showing his feelings publicly.

Sister Helen seemed the least surprised of all of us. Even as we were entering the prison she had told me she was optimistic because Richard had 'good lawyers'. She was right. The Oklahoma Court of Criminal Appeals had ordered the stay because the judges wanted to spend more time looking at the latest affidavits filed by Don Knight, Kathleen Lord and Mark Olive, another attorney who'd joined the team, though we knew nothing of these details yet.

Patton and his men walked out of the room. I realised he would have to give the same briefing to the members of the Van Treese family who were due to witness the execution. They were waiting in another room inside the prison. It would only be fair if he had told them first. Their reaction would have been very different to ours. They had already experienced a delayed execution in January, but on that occasion it was postponed with twenty-four hours to go and they had not been at the prison.

We were escorted back to our cars and Kim drove us out of the gates, where I rendezvoused with my colleagues. I talked to the camera and interviewed Kim and Sister Helen about what had happened. I jokingly berated Sister Helen for going to the bathroom and unwittingly delaying news of the stay of execution by a couple of minutes. And I confessed to her that I had dismissed her optimism of just an hour earlier. 'I didn't believe a nun. Shame on me!'

When someone pointed out that the stay was only until 30 September, Sister Helen replied, 'He's not dead, and he's not going to be dead tonight. That gives the lawyers time.'

Kim Van Atta told me that when the men in suits had walked into the room, he thought we were all being arrested. He hadn't recognised Patton. I asked him if he was worried that we were going to have to go through it all again in two weeks. I certainly was. He said that Sister Helen had taught him to take one day at a time, but he thought this was a real breakthrough moment in Richard's case. 'I hope never to have to come back to Oklahoma in my lifetime. I think this is the beginning of something very good. I don't think I'll be here on September thirtieth. I'm convinced of that because they've now laid a legal framework to go higher. I don't think I'll have to come back. I'll only have to come back for his exoneration. I think that's where we're headed.'

A few moments later, I spotted him in a long, silent embrace with his wife Mary, who had been waiting for us outside the prison. The past few weeks had been emotionally draining for them, and despite Kim's optimism, I had a feeling that it wasn't going to get any easier.

There were a few reporters outside the prison to witness our elation, but most of the media were in the press facility inside the complex, where Robert Patton had made a short statement about the postponement. After several minutes they made their way outside and joined in the chaotic celebrations Phil Cross from Fox 25 was there. Sister Helen immediately went up to him to praise him for his work in recent weeks.

Phil is an investigative journalist who phones and visits sources, extracts documents from officials who are reluctant to hand them over, and patiently pores through the records trying to find a new angle to the story. While I'm an international reporter who was interested in telling the Glossip story in broad brushstrokes, Phil wanted to reveal every new detail as it emerged, and present it as an exclusive on the local Oklahoma evening news. He had managed to contact a juror from Richard's first trial who now regretted the guilty verdict and said there should be a stay of execution to consider the evidence. The juror had asked not to be identified. And only a day earlier, Phil had discovered that physical evidence from the murder scene, including the shower curtain from room 102, had been destroyed long before Richard's second trial. It suggested either official incompetence or a deliberate cover-up.

He had also found that the testimony given by the state pathologist at both trials had been inconsistent with her original autopsy report. Chai Choi had told jurors that Barry Van Treese had bled to death and could have been saved if there had been prompt medical attention. This was crucial in pinning blame on Richard Glossip for failing to call an ambulance. Yet her autopsy report said that the cause of death was 'traumatic injuries of head, blunt force' and made no reference to blood loss. The jurors were misled.

Sister Helen Prejean told Phil: 'You played a real role in this … you are a true investigative journalist who believed and found the facts. I think you're one of the real heroes today.' Phil looked slightly embarrassed. Unlike me, he was trying to maintain a neutral tone in his stories, and excessive public praise from America's most famous abolitionist might not help his credibility.

Don Knight had been inside the prison along with fellow attorney Kathleen Lord when the news came through from the Court of Appeals. They hugged Sister Helen and were still embracing as Don filled her in on Richard's reaction. 'He became ecstatic … he said YES! And he pounded on the window. He was just so happy. He said thank you so many times … to everybody. He is thrilled.'

'He is very grateful and very happy. What a relief,' added Kathleen. 'It's only two weeks and we hope we can get as much evidence as we can possibly get, but we are very grateful and very pleased.'

The attorneys didn't know any details of why the court had acted. Reporters who'd received copies of the ruling brought them up to speed. It was the fact that Don had filed the appeal so late that had forced the court to grant them more time. He denied it was a deliberate tactic, and said it was because they were adding new details right up until the last minute.

Richard's relatives were not at the prison to give interviews. They had all been on the road between Oklahoma City and McAlester when the news came through, so turned round and headed home. Billie Jo phoned me to invite me to a celebration at their home; I would have liked to have driven there to film the party, but I had a deadline and a lot of work to do. And I still needed to talk to Richard

He called later that evening while I was at a restaurant with his friends. Everyone took turns to chat to him, and when the phone was passed to me, I went into another room where it was quiet so I could record our conversation. I told him he had given me one of the best days of my life. 'That's good. It's been one of mine too,' he replied. Some understatement.

I meant what I had said. I was heading for a dark place at noon that day. Minutes later, I was outside in the sunshine celebrating a victory, albeit a temporary one. Joy seems more real when it emerges from the depths of despair.

One of the prison guards had asked Richard during his pre-execution medical check-up if there was hope. 'Hell yeah, there's hope, plenty of hope,' Richard replied. He told me the guard had wished him well, said his fingers were crossed and that he hoped for the best. 'You should know me by now, I never ever give up hope. I've been here before. In January I was one day away from execution. It is easy to give up hope. You hear the chances are slim. But Kathleen said I've got a pretty good chance.'

And he continued to be hopeful about what the next two weeks would bring. Today had been a very good day, but there had been many more bad days than good in his previous eighteen years. And there would be more setbacks in the coming month.

CHAPTER 18

Inspiration and Indecision

September 2015

I woke earlier than I would have liked considering I'd been working until 1 a.m. I was exhausted, physically and emotionally. I'd been awake for twenty-one hours the previous day, though I never mind fatigue or long hours if the story is good and my adrenalin is pumping. It had been non-stop work, and I hadn't had time to read the dozens of messages I'd been sent. Because of the time difference, many more had arrived while I was sleeping.

I'd never experienced such a huge public response to my work, and it was all positive. I'd half expected some criticism, but several people complimented me on my 'honesty', for describing how I felt rather than simply reporting the facts. Some went too far in their praise, suggesting I'd helped save Richard's life. No, it was his attorneys, not the media, who influenced the appeal court judges.

All I had set out to do nine months earlier was to tell a story. Now people I didn't know were telling me how much they appreciated my work. One person who'd listened to my podcasts wrote to say they felt they were walking the streets of Oklahoma with me. That made me realise how I'd brought the story alive, which was as much as I could do.

I hadn't expected to get so close to Richard Glossip, or come so near to watching him die. The roller coaster of emotions I had experienced was nothing compared to what he had lived through, but it had been hard work. And making an impact was the reward.

A colleague emailed me to say that the actor David Morrissey had referenced the Glossip reprieve while being interviewed on BBC Radio 4. He was talking about his latest stage role, in which he played a hangman when capital punishment was abolished in Britain in 1965. Then I clicked on an email from my wife. There was a video attached. She wrote, 'I promise you I did not coach him … he just said that's what he wants to do as we were walking to school … so I said I would video him saying it.'

I played the video. My five-year-old son Oscar was talking to camera: 'When I'm grown up, I want to be a journalist like my daddy.'

I laughed out loud and could feel my eyes filling with tears. Then I started to sob. All the pent-up tension and emotion of the past few days came tumbling out. I was happy and relieved, and thrilled that I had done something that had made my little boy proud. Up to that point, he had never expressed interest in my job. He just complained when I was away from home a lot. He didn't think his dad had a cool job. I'm absolutely sure he had not been following the key developments in the Richard Glossip case, but he must have picked up on other people's comments that made him realise I was doing something important. It didn't last. By the time I came home, he'd decided he wanted to be a policeman.

Maybe if that's still his ambition when he leaves school, I'll have to warn him of the dangers of manipulating suspects in police interrogations. A few days after I returned from Oklahoma, Kim Van Atta sent me a copy of a message that had been posted on the Richard Glossip website. Philip Kedge, a former chief inspector with a British police force, had looked into the case and concluded that Richard was a victim of 'corrupt interview techniques', and that his interrogation by detectives Bemo and Cook was 'tainted and fully discredited'. He compared it to the Guildford Four, who were wrongly convicted of IRA activity during the mid seventies.

Such comments helped convince me I had done the right thing in declaring my support for Richard Glossip, even though it still felt a little uncomfortable to be abandoning my traditional role as an impartial observer. When I contacted Kedge to find out why he had taken an interest in the case, he told me it was because he had heard me saying on Sky News that Richard had become my friend. He thought it was so unusual to hear a journalist speaking in such a personal way that it encouraged him to delve deeper into the story. And he was appalled at what he found when he read the transcript of Sneed's interview.

I was interested to hear what fellow journalists thought of me abandoning my impartiality. Some of Sky's senior editors were concerned, but decided that even though I'd crossed a line, I hadn't overstepped the mark to the point where I was overly biased. The consensus seemed to be that it was fine to voice my opinion so long as I was not ignoring and failing to report contrary arguments. I was satisfied I was being even-handed by interviewing Oklahoma officials who were in favour of the death penalty.

A few days later, I picked up more good news about Richard's case. A document had been made public as part of the evidence being submitted to the Oklahoma Court of Criminal Appeals. Dated 1 July 1997, it was a letter from Edith King, Oklahoma's Director of Forensic Psychology, who had conducted a psychiatric analysis of Justin Sneed in prison.

She wrote that Sneed had told her he was in prison for 'killing somebody', and she added, 'He indicated that the alleged crime was in connection with a burglary.' He didn't mention being paid to commit murder. The document wasn't a silver bullet that would destroy Sneed's credibility, but it did add more doubt about his version of events, and why he had killed Barry Van Treese.

Three days later, there was another revelation, which shocked many observers. The District Attorney, David Prater, had tried to intimidate one of the new witnesses who had come forward to support Richard Glossip. Michael Scott, the man who had said that Sneed had boasted to fellow inmates how he had implicated Glossip in the murder, had been arrested.

Prater had phoned Scott's home wanting to speak to him. When Scott didn't respond to the messages, around a dozen police turned up to arrest him, and drew their weapons as he walked out of his house. They said they were taking him into custody because of a drug conviction the year before. Scott had been fined and given community service for driving while under the influence of marijuana. He still owed $200. Only after he went public with his allegations about Sneed was a warrant issued for his arrest.

He was taken to a police station and put in an interrogation room. A file on the table was labelled 'Richard Glossip'. Then David Prater himself walked into the room to question him about his affidavit. Scott later told lawyers he felt scared. He was denied access to an attorney and felt he had no choice but to answer the questions. When they learned what had happened, Richard's attorneys filed a complaint with the Court of Appeal, saying, 'Michael Scott felt that in the circumstances that exist today, where people are often killed in police custody, that he was in very real danger of being harmed, just for having stood up and told the truth.'

Don Knight said he and his colleagues had never encountered such 'outrageous' behaviour and demanded that the state stop intimidating witnesses. It was an extraordinary development. That the District Attorney, who had demanded that Richard's attorneys should take their evidence to court, could then take personal charge of arresting and questioning a witness seemed to me to be a sign of how worried the state was that the execution could face a further postponement. David Prater wouldn't respond to the allegations other than to accuse the defence team of 'dishonesty'.

Some of the worst moments in journalism are when you realise you've been 'scooped' and another reporter has an interview or information that you desperately wish you'd obtained yourself. A week after returning from Oklahoma, I experienced that sinking feeling when I discovered that Justin Sneed had given his first interview to Cary Aspinwall from *The Frontier* website. She had exchanged letters with Sneed, and then gone to visit him in prison.

I had never written to Sneed because I'd been told by several reporters that he didn't respond to letters from journalists. They had tried and failed to get written comments from him, and I had already run into a brick wall trying to get the Department of Corrections to allow me to interview Richard Glossip on camera. So I pursued other interviewees. It was a mistake. I should have tried harder, even if it ultimately ended in failure.

Sneed's comments weren't particularly revelatory. In fact Aspinwall wrote in her article that 'Sneed is not a smooth talker like Glossip', and that he had come across as meek and quiet. 'I stood on my truth. I'm just trying to be an honest person,' he told her, adding that his initial reluctance to tell the police what had happened wasn't because he was lying, but because he knew the state was seeking the death penalty for Glossip and he didn't want to be a part of that. But now, he said, he'd taken responsibility for his role in the murder and doesn't want to cause the Van Treese family more pain.

He denied that he had told his daughter he was willing to recant. He said she didn't know the details of the murder. The optimism from a few months earlier that Justine Sneed's letter could help save Richard Glossip's life had already evaporated when she had refused to cooperate with Richard's attorneys.

Two weeks after interviewing Sneed, Aspinwall returned to the prison; she had persuaded him to do a second interview, but this time on camera. The Department of Corrections gave permission for the filming, and the video was uploaded to YouTube.

It showed Sneed sitting across a table from the reporter and cameraman. This was a medium-security facility, so there were few restrictions. Richard Glossip's interview had been filmed through bars and a thick glass window. Sneed wasn't handcuffed and spent much of the twenty-six-minute interview tapping a pen on the table. He was wearing a plain grey baseball cap worn back to front, and a grey sweatshirt.

'Mr Glossip coerced me and pleaded with me for over three months, and the numerous amounts of money that he was offering me kept changing. I didn't know what his motivation was other than he kept begging and pleading me until the point that he literally pushed me over an edge.'

He claimed that Glossip had made sure he wore gloves while he fixed Plexiglas over the broken window of room 102, to avoid leaving fingerprints. As I watched the video, my immediate reaction was that Sneed had never mentioned that when he testified at either of Richard's trials. Richard's attorneys seized on it too, and included it in filings to the US Supreme Court. They called it 'a lie', and highlighted several other comments Sneed made during the interview that were different from previous testimony.

Sneed agreed that detectives had been manipulative when they interviewed him, but 'Did they get false information from me? Absolutely not.' He agreed he had taken drugs at the motel, but denied he stole from rooms to fund his habit. He was asked about his former fellow inmate Michael Scott's claims that he bragged about putting Richard on death row. He would never boast about such a thing, he replied, in case his own life was threatened by another prisoner for doing so.

It was fascinating to watch Sneed talking. I heard comments from him that I didn't believe or that were inaccurate, and he wasn't as articulate as Richard. He rambled a lot and kept referring to himself in the third person, as 'the nineteen-year-old kid' who had been coerced. Later, Richard's attorneys would accuse Cary Aspinwall of asking 'softball' questions and not challenging some of Sneed's comments. She defended herself by pointing out that she wasn't a TV reporter. But it was undeniably a scoop.

After watching the interview, I noticed something else that *The Frontier* had posted on YouTube. On the right of the screen was a link to the video of Richard Glossip's second police interrogation in 1997, when he finally admitted that Sneed had told him he had murdered Barry Van Treese. I had seen the transcript of the interview, but somehow hearing the words he had spoken was more shocking. And perhaps it was more shocking because I now considered Richard my friend.

Even though he had told me months earlier that he would have pleaded guilty to being an accessory after the fact, it was troubling to hear him speak about it. What bothered me most was an exchange about repairing the broken window in room 102 of the motel.

> Detective: Did you ever see Barry's body in the room at all?
> Glossip: No I did not, I swear.
> Detective: But you knew it was in there.
> Glossip: I had … yeah, pretty much.
> Detective: You knew it was in there, that's why you told him to put the glass in.
> Glossip: Well I was just covering the window, but yeah I did. I didn't go in to make sure, but yeah I did.

By acknowledging to detectives that he knew his boss was dead, he confirmed that he had then lied for hours afterwards.

I felt sick as I listened, and it made me wonder again whether I was right to support him. I've since questioned him about telling the police he thought the body was probably in the room. 'I don't remember the interview that much,' he told me. 'I was really going freaking crazy back then. I don't know what I said at that point. I didn't believe he was actually dead.'

It's fresh in my mind because I've watched the video and read the transcripts, but for Richard it was a conversation from eighteen years ago – albeit a crucial event in his life. He now says it was a mistake and he listened to bad advice from his girlfriend, but it was still a terrible, unforgivable thing to do. However, saying nothing about the crime doesn't prove that he was involved in the murder. I've often wondered whether I would panic in similar circumstances and allow my silence about something I knew to turn into an outright lie that got out of control. I hope not.

It was late Friday evening in London. In Oklahoma, it was the end of the working week, and with no announcement from the Oklahoma Court of Criminal Appeals, it would be at least Monday before they issued a ruling, just two days before the rescheduled execution. The five justices who were assessing the appeal were cutting it fine. In one sense it was good that they were taking their time to consider the evidence, but leaving it late was nerve-shredding for Richard Glossip and his supporters.

I had no choice. I would have to get on a flight to Oklahoma City on Monday morning without knowing whether the execution would go ahead. I hoped it would be a wasted trip, but I feared I could be wrong.

CHAPTER 19

Witness to an Execution

September 2015

I was flying to Oklahoma City via Dallas. Normally on long flights I'll watch movies, but I didn't much feel like being entertained. I had a bad feeling about the news that was going to greet me when I arrived in America mid afternoon, even though everyone close to Richard Glossip had been full of optimism in the immediate aftermath of the stay of execution on 16 September. Kim Van Atta had said he didn't think he'd need to come back in two weeks, he was so sure that Richard was heading for exoneration. Now we were both returning to Oklahoma.

As the wheels touched the runway at Dallas/Fort Worth Airport, dozens of emails landed in my inbox. I scrolled through the list and one immediately caught my eye. It was from a colleague and its title was simply 'I'm so sorry'. I'd also been sent a copy of an Associated Press report.

> OKLAHOMA CITY (AP)   An Oklahoma appeals court has narrowly denied a death row inmate's last-minute request for a new hearing

and ordered that his execution may proceed.

In a 3–2 decision on Monday, the Oklahoma Court of Criminal Appeals denied Richard Glossip's request for an evidentiary hearing and an emergency stay of execution. The court ruled the state can proceed with Glossip's execution, which is scheduled for Wednesday.

Glossip was scheduled to be executed on Sept. 16, but the court granted a two-week stay just hours before he was to receive a lethal injection after his attorneys claimed they had new evidence that he was innocent.

But the court ruled the new evidence simply expands on theories that were already raised on his original appeals.

It was another narrow defeat. Judges in Glossip's 2007 appeal against conviction had voted 3–2 against him. The nine justices of the US Supreme Court had split 5–4 in their ruling three months ago. Now he'd lost his latest appeal by the narrowest possible margin.

Plenty of judges have been sympathetic to Richard Glossip, but not enough to save his life. Two of those who had considered his latest appeal had explained why they supported him. Judge Arlene Johnson said his second trial was 'deeply flawed ... he did not have a fair trial'. Judge Clancy Smith believed that 'the tenuous evidence is questionable at best'. He understood that the legal process was dragging on, but 'the state has no interest in executing an actually innocent man'.

The other three judges essentially said the courts had heard it all before, and it was time to wrap this case up. Finality was more important than reconsidering the verdict. My heart was pounding as I read the details while the plane was still taxiing to its stand. This seemed like the final nail in the coffin. I called Kim, who'd managed to speak to Richard briefly. Richard had been told the news by a prison official and hadn't been able to get hold of any of his attorneys on the phone. He was taking the news badly. Even the most upbeat of people have their limits.

I got off the plane and went through the usual immigration and customs checks ahead of catching my short connecting flight to Oklahoma City. I have a journalist's visa for the United States, and I'm used to being asked by officials about the purpose of my visit. So when the border control officer asked me why I was visiting Oklahoma, I replied that I was going to see an execution. He didn't bat an eyelid, and he didn't ask for details. He just waved me through. Welcome to Texas, where executions are so frequent, they're not worth talking about.

Just before boarding the plane, I called Sister Helen Prejean. She was in New York attending a meeting at the United Nations; she had been so confident that the appeal court would rule in Richard's favour that she hadn't been expecting to fly back to Oklahoma. The latest news would change that.

'My heart just dropped,' she told me. Soon after she got the news, Richard had phoned her. 'I told him, "Okay, Richard, you're really going to have to hold tight now. We're going into the white-water rapids."'

But she still wasn't giving up on a Supreme Court intervention. Mark Olive, another member of Richard's legal team, specialises in constitutional law, and would argue that there was too much doubt about the integrity of the conviction. He'd been to see Richard the previous week and told him the abolitionist movement had been waiting for a case like his, because it exemplified how broken the system was. According to Sister Helen, 'He said this may be the case that the Supreme Court takes that could really undo the death penalty in the United States. And if Mark Olive gets to argue this case before the court, it could really make history.'

It was a bold prediction. It was Monday evening. Richard was due to die on Wednesday afternoon. And the US Supreme Court rarely granted eleventh-hour appeals unless justices saw clear evidence of legal error from lower-level courts.

I was eager to hear from Richard, but Kim told me that he could no longer phone me. For some reason, several of the approved phone numbers on his call list had disappeared from the system. Mine was one of them. We didn't know whether it was a glitch, or whether someone had removed them deliberately.

The following morning, I was itching to get to work, but found myself with little to do. Kim Van Atta and Sister Helen weren't due to arrive until late that evening; District Attorney David Prater turned down my interview request because he didn't want to say anything until all legal avenues had been exhausted. Nobody was talking.

I asked *Frontier* reporter Cary Aspinwall where she'd got hold of the video of Richard's police interrogation. She told me all the files in the case were held at the Judicial Center. In the basement where court records are kept, a helpful clerk brought me three cardboard boxes. Inside were transcripts, crime-scene photographs and videotapes. The Glossip case files had been thoroughly examined over the years. One of the cardboard boxes was falling apart.

I pulled out the photographs and found myself looking at colour pictures of the body of Barry Van Treese, and the bloodstains in room 102. I'd spent nine months reading the details of the case, but it was a sobering moment to see images of the murder victim as he'd been found, rather than the family photo of a smiling Barry I'd been using in my reports. Shocking as the images were, staring at them did not change my view about Richard Glossip. Instead, it made me question how the man who had brutally beaten Barry to death could be trusted as the star witness in Richard's trial.

I picked up the videos from the box but had no way of viewing them. Although there was a TV monitor in the records room, there was no VHS player. I called Phil Cross, told him where I was, and asked if they had a VHS player in the Fox 25 offices. Within an hour, he walked into the room with a machine under his arm.

Some of the material I'd seen before, such as the Justin Sneed interrogation; there was also the video of Richard Glossip's second police interrogation, which *The Frontier* had already posted online. The audio was clear, but the picture was poor. You could barely see Richard. But I also found a copy of his first interrogation, which had never been seen publicly. It was better quality. You could clearly make out

Richard's face. We played it on the monitor and filmed him protesting his innocence but failing to tell the truth about what he knew of the murder. I always found it difficult to watch evidence that confirmed his role as an accessory to murder, but I would not shy away from telling the story in full even if it made it harder for people to sympathise with him.

A few hours later, I was talking to Richard himself. He still couldn't phone me, but he could call Kim Van Atta, so I'd met up with Kim in McAlester. He'd just arrived from New York. It was my first chance to ask Richard about having his appeal rejected.

'I've been dealing with the Court of Criminal Appeals for seventeen years, so I didn't expect anything from them anyway. We'll see what happens. We'll keep fighting and keep filing.'

While we were talking, guards delivered his final meal. This was his third final meal of the year. I asked him if he'd taken the chance to order something different. He said he had: 'I ordered a Domino's pizza instead of a Pizza Hut pizza.'

Less than twenty-four hours to execution time and he could still make me laugh.

Kim and I met for dinner later that evening. While we were eating, Richard phoned Kim, who walked outside the restaurant to take the call. When he returned, he was very upset. In his last hour with access to the telephone, Richard had been trying to ring close friends and family, but couldn't reach anyone except Kim. Sister Helen hadn't answered her phone. His daughter Christina was out, and her sister Ericka said she couldn't talk because she was busy.

Kim was angry because he felt people should have been sitting by their phones, waiting for them to ring, knowing this could be Richard's last chance to speak to them. He said it was the worst moment he had experienced throughout his entire friendship with Richard, and it could not have come at a more difficult time. 'Ten minutes before the phone is going to be cut off for good, and I'm the only one he can get a hold of. He felt very alone. He felt he had been abandoned to his fate. He's learned over the years to handle that kind of frustration when people don't pick up. The difference was, he's going to be executed the next day.'

We went back to our separate hotels anticipating a sleepless night with so much on our minds. But perhaps because I'd already been through the experience two weeks earlier, this time I slept reasonably well. I went down to breakfast in the hotel and sat next to Dale Baich, another one of the attorneys working on Richard's case.

Dale had witnessed many executions before and gave me some unusual advice. When the curtain was pulled back to reveal the death chamber, he said, I should smile broadly. Richard would already be terrified, and if he saw fear or apprehension on the faces of his friends, he would feel even worse. If we were smiling, he would feel more relaxed as he faced death. That thought was planted in my head for the next eight hours. It scared me that I might not be able to hide my true feelings when the time came.

There was a sense of déjà vu as I arrived outside the prison. There were two late interventions to report, though neither was likely to have any impact. First, Archbishop Carlo Maria

Vigano, the Pope's representative in the United States, had written to Governor Mary Fallin calling for her to grant a stay of execution.

> *Together with Pope Francis, I believe that a commutation of Mr Glossip's sentence would give clearer witness to the value and dignity of every person's life, and would contribute to a society more cognizant of the mercy that God has bestowed upon us all.*
>
> *Please be assured of my prayers for you as you carry out your honorable office. May God guide your prayerful consideration of this request by Pope Francis for what I believe would be an admirable and just act of clemency.*

A day earlier, the Archbishop had written a similar letter to the Governor of Georgia, pleading for mercy in the case of Kelly Gissendaner. Like Richard Glossip, she had not actually killed anyone. She had been convicted of conspiring with her lover, who had murdered her husband. She admitted her guilt, repented, embraced Christianity, and studied theology in prison. But the papal plea had no effect. Gissendaner sang 'Amazing Grace' as a single dose of pentobarbital ended her life. She became the first woman to be executed in the state for seventy years.

Virgin boss Sir Richard Branson had also tried to persuade Mary Fallin to stop Richard's execution. He'd paid for a full-page advert in that morning's edition of the local newspaper, *The Oklahoman*. As an opponent of capital punishment, he'd written about his support for Richard

Glossip earlier in the year, and I'd tried unsuccessfully to arrange an interview with him. Having seen the advert, I tried again, and this time he agreed. A camera was sent to Dublin, where he was on business, and he was interviewed live on Sky News.

'I believe, and all our team and our lawyers believe, that an innocent man is in danger of being executed in five hours' time. And we're doing everything we can to try to get the Governor of Oklahoma to intervene to stop the execution. Personally I think it's bad enough executing anybody, but executing innocent people, obviously, is completely unacceptable. The bizarre situation in America is that when someone is convicted of a murder, if they point their finger at somebody else they can avoid themselves being executed. That's what happened in this case.'

Talking to Sky News was great, but it wouldn't be seen by many people in Oklahoma, so I asked Virgin's press officer if Sir Richard would also speak to Phil Cross on Fox 25. Soon Phil was interviewing the businessman via Skype on his computer, while standing outside the penitentiary.

Sister Helen Prejean was still clinging to the hope that five Supreme Court judges would uphold Richard's last appeal. That required Justice Kennedy to switch sides and vote with his liberal colleagues. Since the midazolam hearing back in April, Pope Francis had addressed a joint meeting of Congress and talked about his opposition to the death penalty. Sister Helen reminded me that Justice Kennedy had been among those in the chamber listening to the Pope's words. Would it prick his conscience?

At 11.30, we joined our fellow witnesses Kim Van Atta and Kim Bellware and were taken to the same room inside the prison as two weeks earlier. Crystal Martinez was delayed. She'd turned up without any ID and had to return to her hotel to collect her driver's licence. The prison officials seemed even more guarded and formal than on our previous visit. This time there was no offer of coffee and cookies. Bottled water was all we were given. Once again we clipped on our *Execution Witness* badges. Two female staff watched over us. Once again, the execution was set for 3 p.m.

There was a curtain that partially divided the room in two. Sister Helen took over one side of the room, pacing and praying silently. The rest of us sat on the sofa and chairs and chatted. At one point I put my feet up and closed my eyes. I dozed for about ten minutes and woke up when attorney Kathleen Lord came into the room. She'd been with Richard between 11 a.m. and 1 p.m. and said he was still hopeful things would turn out okay.

The clock on the wall was an ever-present reminder of time running out. For a while the hands seemed to be moving relatively quickly. But when it got to 2 p.m., it felt as if it was running in slow motion, probably because I was staring at it so frequently. I didn't feel like talking any more. I walked over to the window and gazed outside at the occasional comings and goings of prison staff.

I began to feel sick. It wasn't the kind of nausea that would have had me rushing to the toilet. It felt more like extreme butterflies in the stomach. A deep sense of unease. This was really going to happen. I no longer believed there might be a reprieve. Although there was always an outside chance that the Supreme Court might order a last-minute stay, the odds didn't feel good. I could only imagine how much worse it must be for Richard.

Every now and then I'd look over at the others in the room. There was some quiet chatter, but mostly people looked like I did. Pensive and worried. We hadn't been told what time we were due to be taken to the death chamber. I'd assumed we would be driven to Unit H, because it was some distance from the room we were waiting in. That meant our journey would begin at around 2.30. But the hands of the clock carried on moving, while we stayed put.

By 2.45, I'd begun to think there must be a hold-up. I walked over to talk to the others and we discussed the possibility of another legal intervention. When it got to 3 p.m., we asked the female guard what was happening. She made a phone call and told us there had been a delay because they were still waiting for the Supreme Court.

With no fixed deadline to fret about, I relaxed. Soon we found ourselves talking about music. Kim Van Atta had lived in London as a teenager during the 1960s and regaled us with tales of Who and Marc Bolan concerts. During my early career I'd presented a rock music programme on radio, and in recent years I'd worked with one of my favourite bands, Status Quo. To my amazement, Kim told me he'd seen them play during their early psychedelic era. I laughed. The execution of our friend still loomed over us, but with the process on hold – however temporarily – the atmosphere in the room had lightened.

Just before 4 p.m., the guard said she had something
to tell us. We could leave the prison. The execution was
off! There was no further explanation. It was thrilling but
baffling news. Last time Robert Patton, the Department of
Corrections director, had broken the news of the stay, and
explained the reason for it. This time we were left in the dark.

We smiled and hugged, but it wasn't like the previous
occasion. We had been inside the prison for four and a half
hours and the tension had been much worse. But with no
explanation for the postponement, we weren't able to fully
celebrate. We were eager to get outside and find out what
had been happening.

Outside the prison's main gate, it was chaotic. A couple
of dozen relatives and supporters of Richard were hugging
each other, and TV crews were filming them. Details were
confused. There was some sort of problem with the drugs. But
it wasn't the Supreme Court that had halted the execution;
it was the Governor. I was astonished. Mary Fallin had always
refused to intervene. What had changed her mind?

I began interviewing Sister Helen and Kim Van Atta on
camera, but they were still struggling to understand exactly
what had happened. Kim wasn't worried that it hadn't been a
court-ordered reprieve. 'Right now, he's alive. Where there's
life there's hope. Yes, I want him to be exonerated and to
walk out that door, but I'll take what I can get.'

Gradually the details began to emerge. There had been an
almost unbelievable blunder. The executioner had the wrong
drug. Potassium chloride was supposed to be administered
to stop Richard's heart after midazolam and rocuronium

bromide had sedated and paralysed him. But the label on the bottle said potassium acetate, not chloride. There were frantic phone calls between the prison and the offices of the Governor and the Attorney General. Eventually Governor Fallin decided to order a halt to the execution.

It was only later in the day, when I watched the video filmed by my cameraman Duncan Sharp along with our Washington news editor Tim Gallagher, that I got the full picture. While we were inside the prison, they had been monitoring developments outside. Around 3 p.m., Don Knight had taken a phone call informing him that the Supreme Court had declined to intervene and the execution would proceed. The final legal challenge had failed. Don was outside the prison and relayed the bad news to relatives. The video showed Richard's daughters wiping away tears while Don comforted them, telling them that Richard wasn't bitter. 'Through the work that we've done, even though we weren't successful in court, the world knows that Richard Glossip is innocent and I think that's a pretty big deal. For him it's a huge deal. He's not the kind of guy who would do it. And now he knows that people believe him. He told me today, if they're going to murder him today, at least the world would know.'

As I watched the video, I was puzzled. A man I didn't recognise was angry and becoming aggressive. Others were trying to restrain him. I discovered later that he was a distant relative of Richard's who had turned up to vent his anger despite never having bothered to visit him in prison over the past eighteen years. Duncan and Tim had continued filming, waiting for confirmation that the execution had happened. But after almost an hour, an entirely different story began to emerge. Suddenly the video was full of people laughing, hugging and praising God.

Billie Jo Boyiddle told Tim, 'The Governor! I love that woman, I really do! I take back all I ever said about her. Until they actually pronounced him dead I had hope. I will never give up on him.'

Billie Jo's husband, Mike Campbell, gathered everyone together and said a prayer. 'Father, in the name of Jesus we thank you, we praise you for this day, God. We praise you for this wonderful news.' The family had brought balloons with them, and released them into the sky amid applause.

The execution was rescheduled for 6 November, a delay of thirty-seven days. It was an odd number. When I asked why, I was told that it was because two more executions were scheduled in the coming weeks. Other dates were ruled out because of clashes in the Governor's diary. She has to be available when one of her inmates is being put to death.

As I interviewed relatives, lawyers and campaigners, the man at the centre of the drama phoned Kim to ask what the hell had just happened. Richard didn't know about the drug issue. Everyone crowded round and yelled at Kim to put the call on speaker so we could hear. But the phone went dead. We had to wait a minute before it was reconnected.

When Richard called back, Kim handed the phone to Phil Cross. If the execution had gone ahead, Phil would have watched Richard die too. Even though he had been removed from Richard's witness list, his name had been drawn in the media ballot and he would have been one of the designated reporters to be allowed to view the scene in the death chamber. Instead, he and the other reporters had been called to a briefing to announce the postponement. Phil was able to tell Richard about the drug mix-up and ask for his response.

'That's just crazy.'

'Yes it is, Richard!' yelled Kim.

You could tell that Richard's mind was in a whirl. Phil told him the Supreme Court had rejected his appeal. I asked him what he'd been told by the guards. Richard said they'd told him the execution was delayed until 6 October. We had to correct that and tell him it was 6 November. He kept asking if we were positive. Finally he laughed and said he was happy he had an extra thirty-seven days.

'Well, that's great, man, can't ask for better. I tell you what, Phil. You know me, I'm a pretty strong person. I can deal with a lot of stuff. But I'm telling you, that was rough in there. That was the most stressful thing in the whole time I've been locked up. I kept asking people, "What's going on, what's going on?" and nobody would tell me what was going on.'

There were others enduring a painful day too. While we were being ushered out of the prison, an embarrassed Department of Corrections director was having to break the news of another postponement to relatives of Barry Van Treese. Afterwards Robert Patton described it as the most difficult fifteen minutes of his life. The family were angry, and issued a statement the following day. They said that seventeen of them had been left sitting in a small room for three hours, and they suspected that the DOC was hoping that the US Supreme Court would order a stay so 'they would be off the hook'. If that had happened, prison officials wouldn't have had to admit to having the wrong drug, and the problem could have been hushed up.

That thought had occurred to me too, but when I put it to the DOC spokesman, Terri Watkins, she denied it. The Van Treese statement said that the 'appeals process ... only further delays final resolution of an 18-year-old case and causes cruel and unusual punishment for the family'.

It had been a shambles. And to add to the surreal situation, the prison staff who had been preparing to kill Richard Glossip were now worried about his health. Despite two calorie-busting final meals, he had lost a lot of weight since being moved to solitary confinement fifty days ago. There was no mirror in his cell. He had no idea how he looked. He told me about a visit from the prison psychologist.

'She said, "We're very concerned about you." She goes, "You look very bad, I can see the bones sticking out of your shirt, I can see the bones sticking out of your neck."'

When he was moved back to his regular cell, he looked in the mirror.

'I truly looked like I had just walked out of a concentration camp. I had lost so much weight. It was like skin being stretched over a skeleton. I was just so shocked by the way I looked. When you're trying to be strong for your family members ... I just wasn't seeing what was happening to me. It just goes to show how much torture is involved in something like this.'

Richard told me he had been warned that if he became so weak that he passed out, he would be force-fed intravenously to keep him alive until his execution date.

'That should scare the hell out of everybody, not just in this country but everybody in the world, that they would keep me alive just so they can kill me. Thanks to you, we've been able to bring it to the whole world. And now the whole world is shocked. I get letters from England all the time, more and more every day, who say they've listened to your podcasts and that you've really opened their eyes to what is really going on in the United States.'

He filled me in on the details of what he called 'the most chaotic day I've ever seen in this place'.

'Nobody would let me talk to my attorneys. Not knowing is probably more torture than anything. For two hours or more I sat and paced the floor in my boxers, wrapped in a sheet, freezing my behind off in that cell, trying to get answers from people that wouldn't give me any answers. It pretty much scared the crap out of me. I don't think anybody should ever have to go through something like that. You should have access to your attorneys. I think that was just as much torture as waiting for them to kill an innocent person.'

A man in a suit came to tell him that he'd got a seven-day stay. But he was taken to a cell with a TV that was broadcasting news of a thirty-seven day stay. Then the warden came to see him. She also told him it was a seven-day postponement, but phoned back later to correct herself. When he learned about the drugs blunder, his relief gave way to terror that he could have died an agonising death like that of Clayton Lockett. He believed that the press and public interest in his case helped to save his life, because the authorities were fearful of how another blunder would be reported.

'I think they thought that you guys wouldn't stop and you guys would figure out what they'd done. Because of the hell I've caused, and through the press and all these people who've got involved, I think they were happy to hurry up and get rid of me. I'm just thankful it didn't happen.'

There was only one thing that gave him strength during those lonely hours waiting to be taken to the death chamber. 'At two fifty, the inmates didn't know that I hadn't been taken in there yet. So they started kicking on the doors and beating on the glass. Man, it was so loud. I've been through a lot of executions down here and I've never heard it that loud before. And even the guards were freaking out because it was the loudest send-off anybody's ever gotten in here.'

A hundred miles away, in Oklahoma City, there had also been spiritual support from an unlikely source. One of the jurors who had convicted him and sentenced him to death was watching the time as intently as I was. Ever since the trial, this juror had continued to follow Richard Glossip's slow progress to the death chamber.

'I would go online and type his name to see what was happening. That day I was looking at the clock. I was very upset. I was praying for Richard. I went into deep prayer. I'm a Catholic and I feel sorry for him. I was praying for his soul. And then I watched the news and saw some jackass ordered the wrong drug. And that was the first time I really felt bad for Richard Glossip. To me, that's inhumane and cruel to get your last meal, to get up to the door and then someone says, "We're stupid, we ordered the wrong drug." That pisses me off.'

The juror wonders whether there should ever be another attempt to pass the sentence they imposed. 'In the old days they hung them with a rope and if the rope broke that's it. That's what happened here. The rope broke.'

The morning after the aborted execution, I had breakfast with Kim and Mary Van Atta. We were expecting a brief pause in the emotional roller coaster, but it was always in our minds that we could be back in Oklahoma in early November. We said our goodbyes and I drove back to the airport in Oklahoma City. As I checked in for the flight, I picked up an email from attorney Dale Baich. There'd been another twist.

Scott Pruitt, the Attorney General, had announced that all executions in Oklahoma had been put on hold indefinitely while an inquiry was held into the fiasco. Richard Glossip would be kept alive for months. I filed an updated report while I waited for my connecting flight to London. In a noisy airport, the quietest place I could find to record my voice was a toilet cubicle. It was a happy inconvenience.

CHAPTER 20

Another Year to Live

October 2015

Sir Richard Branson needed my help. He wanted to speak to Richard Glossip on the phone, but his staff didn't know how to get their boss's number onto the call list of a death-row inmate. I talked them through the process of setting up a Skype account, and a time was set for Richard to phone the number on a Sunday afternoon. He would then phone me afterwards to record an interview.

There was a technical problem. Sir Richard's PA rang up from Necker Island to say they couldn't make the Skype call work. I talked her through a solution, and half an hour later, Richard phoned me from prison, hugely excited that he had just been speaking to one of the world's best-known billionaires.

'Richard Branson is probably one of the most humble people I've ever talked to in my life. I had a really great conversation with him.'

Virgin sent me a recording of the conversation. Branson was full of praise for Richard: 'You're a remarkable individual because what you've been through ... is barbaric. I don't know how any human being can cope with what you've been through. Well done for being brave, I appreciate that. In your case you seem to have been sentenced to death in the interests of finality and not fairness, and your guilt has not been proven at all beyond reasonable doubt. And in fact everything points to your innocence and that's why your case has mobilised so many people worldwide.'

It had been an extraordinary few weeks for Richard Glossip. And for me. We both needed a break from the stress. Events in Oklahoma had dominated my life for months at a time when there were other important matters I should have been dealing with. Builders had been working on an extension to our home and my wife had had to deal with the dirt, the chaos and the inevitable arguments. That in turn would lead to rows between us because I wasn't giving it my full attention.

Much more importantly, my elderly mother was seriously ill in Belfast, requiring frequent trips to see her. In the space of a few weeks she was diagnosed with dementia and had an unsuccessful operation to stop the spread of cancer. Her condition was now terminal. She had been living alone at home, but that was no longer practical. My brother and I persuaded her to move into a care home, but her dementia left her frightened and confused in her new surroundings.

My visits to Northern Ireland were hard for my young son, who was already struggling with the amount of time I was away in America. It was a relief that I wouldn't have to return to Oklahoma for a while, but on the other hand, I didn't want to turn my back on the story, especially as there were still developments to report.

Reporters at *The Oklahoman* were digging into execution procedures, and a week after Richard Glossip's unexpected reprieve, they discovered that the drug confusion had happened before and been ignored. On 15 January, Oklahoma used potassium acetate instead of potassium chloride to execute Charles Warner. The information wasn't made public at the time. It was only when his autopsy details were being reviewed that the truth was uncovered.

The Warner execution would now form part of the inquiry ordered by the Attorney General. The Department of Corrections was digging an ever-deeper hole for itself. Within a few days a grand jury was assembled to investigate; among the witnesses called to testify in secret hearings were the prison warden Anita Trammell and her boss, Robert Patton, as well as legal advisers to Governor Mary Fallin.

The Attorney General had agreed that he would wait 150 days after the grand jury recommendations were finalised before setting new execution dates in the state. The inquiry was expected to take months, meaning Richard was safe until at least late summer 2016.

But other heads began to roll long before that. Just over a week after testifying, Anita Trammell quit her job with immediate effect. The Department of Corrections said that she was retiring. Officially it was nothing to do with the investigations into the handling of executions, but the timing made attempts to deny a link look foolish.

Just over a month later, the DOC director followed her out the door. Robert Patton had been in the job for less than two years, but that period coincided with the Lockett and Warner executions, as well as Richard Glossip's narrow escape from the lethal injection. The reason he gave was one favoured by politicians down the ages: he wanted to spend more time with his family. He moved back to his home in Arizona and took a job with a private prison company.

Two months later, there was another resignation by a top official in the process. Steve Mullins, the senior attorney in the Governor's office, had also given evidence to the grand jury. His public reason for quitting his job was that his doctor had advised him to reduce stress in his life.

There was certainly less stress in Richard's life. In the months after his close call with death, he was able to relax and revel in his near-celebrity status. For a while he was sharing a cell with another inmate, but soon he was given a cell of his own, partly because he was receiving so many letters from supporters and he needed more space.

Some of the women who wrote to him would send photos of themselves. That would lead to phone conversations with those whom Richard liked, and who were open to the idea of chatting to a man who was locked up on death row. His social network was growing.

Kim Van Atta and I would joke that we were like spurned lovers. 'Where's Richard? He never calls any more!' In some ways Kim was happy to be sharing the workload of campaigning. He had a wife and family and a job. The website he had set up and maintained for more than a year was handed over to a PR consultant, paid for by a sympathetic Silicon Valley business consortium that was also helping to fund Richard's legal campaign. The individuals responsible chose to remain anonymous, but their donations meant that attorneys and investigators who had been giving their time free were now being properly paid and could afford to spend more hours on the case.

Richard was also being discouraged from talking to reporters. More and more journalists were asking for interviews, but his attorneys were wary of him making controversial comments or contradicting anything they were putting together in a future appeal. I could understand their caution, but it was the media spotlight that had helped save Richard's life. The attorneys did the hard graft in putting together their legal submissions, but I firmly believed the execution would have gone ahead if reporters had not been scrutinising the process.

Throwing a protective ring around Richard had an impact. He no longer phoned me for chats. It was frustrating to lose regular contact. It would be New Year's Eve before he called me again, a gap of two months. He sounded very happy. I asked what he'd been doing all this time. 'Writing letters!' he replied. He said it was my fault that he was getting so many letters and cards from the UK. In his previous interview for my podcast he had made a point of thanking British supporters for taking an interest in his case, and apologised for not being able to reply to all the letters he had been sent.

I joked about his female admirers, but he was coy with regard to details. However, he did hint that he had met someone he considered special. We talked about Christmas. A year earlier he had been taken from his cell on

Christmas Day and moved to the cells adjacent to death row, ready for a January execution date. There was no drama during this holiday period.

I was able to tell him about a new documentary I had made about his story and that had been broadcast that week. Among the many responses I received from viewers was one from senior British politician Andy Burnham, who tweeted, 'This is outstanding journalism by @IanWoodsSky. Lays bare brutal inhumanity of US criminal justice.' When I thanked him for his praise, he urged me to 'Keep up the fight. Shocking that one person's word against another could provide grounds for death penalty.'

The next chapter in the story would take me in an unexpected direction. To Rome. Sister Helen Prejean had been in touch with me to say that she had been invited to an audience with Pope Francis in the Vatican. She planned to hand him a letter from Richard. It would be a private meeting, with only the official Vatican photographer to record it, but she wanted me to be there to talk to her afterwards.

I met up with Sister Helen in St Peter's Square. It was great to see her again, especially on such a happy occasion. She was almost bursting with excitement at the prospect of meeting Pope Francis early the following morning. I had lunch with her, and a group of nuns from Montana who had travelled with her for the event. When she told them about my connection to the death-penalty issue, I was readily welcomed into their group.

The following morning she emerged from the Pope's private chapel with an even bigger smile on her face than normal. When the official photos were released later in the day, they showed her handing an envelope to the Pontiff along with a photo of Richard. In the letter he thanked the Pope for arranging for his American archbishop to write to Governor Fallin requesting a stay of execution: 'I want you to know how much it means to me that you know my name and you are praying for me. I want to thank you for taking an interest in me.'

The timing of the visit was topical. A few hours earlier, Texas had performed its first execution of 2016, ending the life of Richard Masterson, a convicted murderer whose case Pope Francis was said to have been following closely. Sister Helen said the Pontiff had asked her whether the execution had gone ahead. When she confirmed it had, his face fell. Then she gave him the letter and photo.

'I said, "This is Richard Glossip in Oklahoma, whose life you saved." You could tell he has the interests of death-row inmates close to his heart. He took my hand and he smiled. I gave him my book *Dead Man Walking* in Spanish and he opened the book and he was looking at it. He is in the same quest to end the death penalty. So it was the highlight of my life today!'

In April 2016, my friendship with Richard Glossip deepened when we shared a similar experience. My mother was dying. Slowly. Painfully. Her cancer had spread into her bones, weakening an already frail body. So when she had a fall and injured her hip, I feared the worst. She'd been moved from her care home to hospital, but she was in agony. On one visit to the hospital the curtains were drawn round her bed but I heard her squealing in pain as nurses tried to give her a bed bath. Her pelvis had been fractured in two places and would never heal. She would be bed-bound for the rest of her life. I began to hope that for her sake, that wouldn't be long.

By the time she was sent back to the care home, her condition was deteriorating. She'd choked on some food and was now unable to swallow. It was now a case of controlling her pain and waiting for her to slip away. I flew in from London on a Sunday morning. My Belfast relatives and her friends were already keeping a bedside vigil. Mum was begging for a drink of water, but all we could offer was a tiny sponge on a stick, to moisten her mouth. It was deeply distressing. I wanted her to be kept sedated, preferably unconscious, so that she wasn't suffering.

We had to plead with the staff to provide more diamorphine, but they were having difficulty getting hold of supplies because it was a weekend. I asked what else they were giving her.

Midazolam.

The young nurse must have wondered why I looked stunned when I heard that answer. The drug that I had spent a year writing about, the drug that formed part of the lethal injection, was now being given to my mother to sedate her. Every time her eyes opened and she cried out for water, or begged God to take her, I wanted them to increase the dosage to put her into a deep sleep from which she would never waken.

A specialist palliative nurse told me on Monday morning that she was slipping away and would probably die within hours. But she didn't. On Tuesday morning she was conscious again and I was having to wet her lips and try to explain to her that I couldn't give her a proper drink because she would choke. The diamorphine and midazolam were not doing the job. The dosage needed to be increased again.

Throughout Tuesday and Wednesday, in the brief times that I was alone at her bedside, I contemplated the unthinkable. I imagined myself taking one of her pillows, putting it over her face and ending this pitiful scene. I am sure other people in similar circumstances, watching the suffering of someone they love, have experienced the same dark thoughts. And as I sat there, I pondered the bitter irony that I would be committing a murder, something my friend on death row had never done.

Of course I didn't do it. Cowardice, decency, fear of the consequences; there were many reasons why I didn't even come close. But it was the first time I had even considered what it must be like to end someone's life. I thought of Justin Sneed with a baseball bat in his hands. What made him kill Barry Van Treese? Did he, as he first told police, simply intend to knock him unconscious, and got carried away because the motel owner fought back? Or did he walk into room 102 knowing in advance that he was going to commit a murder?

By Thursday morning, I couldn't bear to watch my mother suffer any longer. I had broken down in front of nursing staff on several occasions that week, and one of them told me that I really shouldn't feel obliged to be there at the very end. My wife and son were in London. I was gently advised that maybe I should be with them. I didn't need to be persuaded. My brother Bryan and his wife Jane were prepared to stay at her bedside. I went into Mum's room at around 6 a.m. and said goodbye. I walked out feeling relieved. Later that afternoon I was on a plane back to London. My mother died while I was in the air, somewhere over the Irish Sea. I got the news when I landed at Heathrow.

For a year I had pushed to be allowed to witness a man being put to death. But when the time came, I was unable or unwilling to watch my own mother die. I still can't quite reconcile that conflict. I was her youngest son. When I gave the eulogy at her funeral, I told the mourners, 'I couldn't bear to be there at the very end. I ran away back home because when it comes down to it, I'm still her little boy.'

If the time does come that I return to McAlester for an execution, I hope I can be braver.

A few weeks later, Richard phoned me. I told him about my mother's death, and he opened up about the death of his mother a few years earlier.

'What you went through is exactly what I went through. The hospital that was looking after my mother called the prison and said, "Get Richard Glossip on the phone right now because she's passing away." So they came and got me, and my mom was in so much pain that I cringed when I was talking to her on the phone. I wanted to do something so badly because I couldn't stand that she was in so much pain, so I know what you're going through. You want to do what's right and not have them suffer any more. I tell you, dude, that was the hardest phone call I ever had to deal with in my life.'

Suddenly my powerlessness as I watched my mother die was put into perspective. At least I could be in the room to say goodbye. I asked Richard how he had felt.

'It was eating me up. They had the chaplain sitting next to me because they were a little worried that I wasn't going to handle this very well, and they were right to do that. When you hear someone suffering that bad and you can't do anything for them, it really sucks. She gave birth to me and she raised me and you get to feel you owe them. And I felt horrible that I wasn't able to be there to help her with what she was going through. She had always been there for me throughout this whole thing that I was going through.'

I asked him if his mother always believed he had been wrongfully convicted.

'Her last breath before she passed away, she told me on the phone, "Don't you dare stop fighting." My mom always knew I was innocent. She always did. She made sure that just before she passed away, the last thing I would remember coming out of her mouth was for me never to stop fighting. I think part of the reason I started fighting so hard was because of what she said. I didn't want to let her down, and I wanted to just give it my all.'

It was the most intimate conversation Richard and I had ever had. Two men in their early fifties, talking about the deaths of their mothers. One in a prison cell in Oklahoma, the other in a car parked in a London street, because he had phoned me while I was driving. Worlds apart, but united by a shared loss, and the trauma of how to deal with it.

CHAPTER 21

Careless, Reckless, Guilty

May 2016

There was a judge and there were jurors. But nobody was on trial. There was testimony from witnesses, though not from the man who could be described as the victim. And even though there was no formal verdict, there was a damning indictment of some of those involved.

The grand jury investigation into the Oklahoma execution system had taken more than six months. For Richard Glossip, the conclusion was worth waiting for. The report said officials had been 'cavalier' in the way they tried and failed to end his life. Donald Deacon, the judge who had overseen the inquiry, thanked the jurors for looking into what he called the 'monkey business at the Department of Corrections', and bemoaned how the state had been ridiculed around the world for the way it handled executions.

Journalists had come to the county court to collect their copies of the 106-page report, and immediately began to trawl through the extensive details in search of the most pointed criticisms of individuals and the system. I was sitting at home in London, reading their initial findings via Twitter, impatiently waiting for the full report to be posted online.

I had desperately wanted to be in Oklahoma for the conclusion of the inquiry, but there was no certainty of the date the report would be published. The grand jury, drawn from citizens across Oklahoma, had been meeting for two or three days each month to hear testimony. Their meetings were held behind closed doors, and there were no updates on their progress.

Finally, in May 2016, a few months later than expected, their conclusions were made public. When the details eventually appeared online, the most important point to be reported was that nobody had been indicted. There had been mistakes; rules had been broken, but nobody would be held criminally responsible. Those guilty of the most serious errors of judgement had already quit their jobs.

The report first examined the execution of Charles Warner in January 2015. In the aftermath of Richard Glossip's failed execution, it was revealed that potassium acetate rather than potassium chloride had been used to kill Warner. Now it was revealed in full detail how the mistake had been made, lifting the lid on a process that had been conducted in utmost secrecy. Even though the report detailed what happened, it still withheld the names of almost all the individuals involved.

In the months leading up to Warner's execution date, staff from the Department of Corrections began calling pharmacies to try to acquire the drugs for the lethal injection. Several said they were unwilling or unable. The first pharmacy that agreed was given the order. A verbal deal was struck, including the amount of each drug required, but there was no written order.

The pharmacist was paid $869.85 in cash to provide enough midazolam, rocuronium bromide and potassium chloride to complete six executions. But when he contacted his wholesale supplier, he ordered potassium acetate. When asked by the grand jury why the mistake had occurred, he told them that in his mind, the two drugs were interchangeable. 'I did not look close enough and look at the acetate or chloride. I was looking at potassium.'

On the day Charles Warner was due to die, the drugs, in a sealed cardboard box, were picked up by an agent, taken to the prison and handed to the warden, Anita Trammell. She opened the box, took out the bottles and they were photographed. She later testified she didn't notice anything wrong, and passed them over to the doctor who had been hired to carry out the execution. The doctor, who was also being paid in cash, didn't spot the discrepancy but now accepts responsibility for the error.

> I should have noticed it. I didn't notice it. And I feel terrible for that. And I feel terrible that if anyone else is, you know, taking any heat for that, because it was my job. It was my role. And if anyone dropped the ball, I dropped the ball. And I don't want to make an excuse. There's no excuse, and I will accept the full weight of responsibility. All I can conjecture is that this was my first foray into this very unusual world

of executions, lethal injections. And as you can
imagine, my anxiety level was significant. The
high stress environment is not new to me, but
this was very unique and very unusual.

The execution proceeded, and although Charles Warner's
final words were 'My body is on fire', the grand jury concluded
that there was 'no evidence the manner of the execution
caused Warner any needless pain'. When his body was taken
away for an autopsy, the empty bottles, including those
labelled as potassium acetate, were placed in the body bag.
The post-mortem report recorded that potassium acetate
had been used, and copies were sent to the prison, and
to the offices of the Attorney General and the Governor.
Nobody spotted the error.

Eight months later, it was Richard Glossip's turn to be
executed, and the same pharmacist supplied the drugs,
including potassium acetate, which were collected and
brought to the prison on the day of the execution. Once
again they were unpacked, photographed and readied for
use. But three hours before the appointed time of death,
the Court of Criminal Appeals ordered a two-week stay of
execution. The drugs were sent back to the pharmacist
unused.

On 30 September, the drugs were returned to Oklahoma
State Penitentiary and once again unpacked by the warden.
This time Anita Trammell spotted the discrepancy between
potassium chloride and acetate, but she didn't tell anyone
else. She told the jury:

> I thought it was the same thing. I didn't know
> who ordered the drugs. That's not part of my
> job duty. I didn't know it hadn't been looked
> at, I assumed it had been. I assumed that what
> the pharmacist provided was what we needed.
> So in my mind, that potassium acetate must
> have been the same thing as potassium chloride.

Even though Oklahoma was already in the national spotlight over its handling of executions, the warden didn't alert anyone. She told the grand jury she wasn't a pharmacist or a doctor and said it wasn't her responsibility. But shortly before midday, the doctor who was preparing the syringes noticed that the bottles were labelled potassium acetate, and raised the issue with prison officials. They asked him if there was any difference, and he told them that in his opinion they were different drugs but were medically interchangeable and would have the same effect.

David Cincotta, the Department of Corrections general counsel, was informed and told the doctor to continue preparations. In the meantime, he phoned the pharmacist, who first told him the drug had been ordered by mistake, then said it was because potassium chloride wasn't available. Then he dropped the bombshell, telling Cincotta that he had also supplied acetate to execute Charles Warner.

The debate about whether the execution could proceed moved rapidly up the chain of Oklahoma government, and reached the offices of the Attorney General and the Governor. To get an insight into what went on that day,

I contacted Alex Weintz, who'd quit his job as Governor Fallin's spokesman a few months previously. He now works in the private sector, and even though it allows him to speak freely, he is still supportive of the Governor's position.

'This definitely counted as high drama. There was a lot of confusion. In fact I still think it's unclear what needed to be done. The consensus was that they needed to delay the execution out of an abundance of caution to make sure they followed the exact letter of the law. After weeks of saying under no circumstances would we grant a stay, you know, I basically had, starting after the time that Richard Glossip was already supposed to be executed, I had to run to my office and write a press release saying his execution was delayed and get it out in ten minutes.'

The advice from the Attorney General, Scott Pruitt, was unequivocal: the execution had to be postponed. But the Governor's chief legal adviser, Steve Mullins, disagreed. He wanted it to proceed, arguing that there was no difference between the two drugs and telling colleagues to 'google it'. He said that a stay of execution 'would look bad for the State of Oklahoma because potassium acetate had already been used in Warner's execution'. Pruitt told him there was no legal ambiguity. It was the wrong drug. Even if it had been effective in killing Warner, it broke the rules. Prisoners and their attorneys have to be informed exactly how the execution will be carried out, and any unauthorised change is a breach of protocol.

There was scathing criticism of Mullins's role from the grand jury:

It is unacceptable for the Governor's General Counsel to so flippantly and recklessly disregard the written Protocol and the rights of Richard Glossip. Given the gravity of the death penalty, as well as the national scrutiny following the Lockett execution, the Governor's Counsel should have been unwilling to take such chances. Regardless of the fact the wrong drug was used to execute Warner, the Governor's Counsel should have resoundingly recommended an immediate stay of execution to allow time to locate potassium chloride.

The warden, Anita Trammell, was also castigated for her inaction, with the jury concluding that she did not do her job:

Although the Department and the State would have suffered embarrassment and criticism had |she| told someone the wrong drug had been received for the Warner execution, potentially years of litigation and this investigation could have been avoided. It is inexcusable for a senior administrator with thirty years as a Department employee to testify that 'there are just some things you ask questions about, and there's some things you don't'. [She] either lacked or failed to exercise the responsibility and leadership expected from an experienced administrator involved in the death penalty.

Mullins and Trammell had already quit their jobs. So too had the DOC director, Robert Patton. If they hadn't resigned, the grand jury might have had even stronger recommendations. Despite the error made by the pharmacist, the jury decided not to recommend a charge of criminal negligence.

Scott Pruitt had been a staunch defender of the death penalty, but as the state's most senior lawyer his unequivocal legal advice had halted the execution. He had ordered the grand jury investigation, and had this to say about its conclusions: 'A number of individuals responsible for carrying out the execution process were careless, cavalier and in some circumstances dismissive of established procedures.'

After the report was published, Richard Glossip phoned me and reflected on how the Attorney General had unexpectedly intervened to save his life. He had already written Pruitt a letter to say thank you. 'I was really blown away when I found out he was actually the one who stopped my execution. Not only did he stop it, he fought for hours against the people who wanted to continue my execution. It's changed my opinion of him a lot because he was the only one with the courage and the integrity enough to stand up and say this isn't right, we're not going to do this.'

Richard said he wished he had been given the opportunity to tell the grand jury about his experience. He particularly wanted to tell them about an incident involving the DOC director. 'The day before my execution, Patton came up to the door after they'd finished their training that day and looked at me and said, "We're ready to execute you," and walked off. He said that to me. To my face.'

I was genuinely shocked. I asked Richard how he'd reacted at the time.

'I just smiled at him. I wasn't going to give in to him and get mad, and hit the door like most people would have. I just looked at him and smiled and went back to my bunk and sat down. I think he enjoyed seeing an inmate suffer.'

Following Patton's resignation, the DOC appointed Joe Albaugh as interim director. Albaugh had no experience of working in prisons, but he was a former head of the federal emergency agency FEMA and a friend of former President George W. Bush. The fact that he was also the only person who applied for the job was another factor in his appointment.

I had requested an interview with him several times, and the bid wasn't rejected outright. I was told he might comment after the report became public. But after the grand jury report came out, I exchanged emails with the DOC press spokesman Terri Watkins, whose final communication read: 'You have listed yourself as a friend for visitation and execution purposes. The director says no, you will not be granted an interview.'

Albaugh did, however, talk to the local ABC affiliate KOCO, saying, 'We are confident that we are on the right track to address every one of the concerns the grand jury had. I can understand their deep concern. When an individual commits a heinous crime and avoids Oklahoma law, there has to be an accounting, so my job is to go forward, take their recommendations under advisement, work those into our protocols and procedure. We practise monthly now on a lot of different scenarios so I think we'll all be prepared when the time comes.'

He was asked about alternative methods of execution. The grand jury had recommended that nitrogen gas should be considered, but Albaugh said, 'Well, I don't know anything about nitrogen hypoxia. It's number two on the list of approved ... number three happens to be a firing squad. I know what would be the quickest, most effective and cheapest to the taxpayer but I'm not sure that society is ready for that. They use firing squads in other states.'

That wasn't strictly accurate. At the time of writing, Utah is the only state apart from Oklahoma that still retains firing squad as an available method, and it hasn't been used since 2010. But the problems with lethal injection are forcing Oklahoma to keep its options open. As Alex Weintz told me, 'It's almost impossible to get these drugs. The protocol is so complicated and difficult to carry out, and the consequences and repercussions for doing anything incorrectly are so great that it probably has a lot of people, even people who support the death penalty, wondering, is this worth it?'

Weintz is relieved that his change of job means he's no longer Oklahoma's unofficial voice of the death penalty. 'I personally hated it. It's not a fun topic to discuss. It's not why I got into public service or politics. It's not an issue, to be honest, that I feel particularly passionate about. The one thing I was passionate about is that I wanted to accurately convey to people why the state and the Governor was doing what it was doing. At times I was a little frustrated that I had to do that, but I did not want people to think that the state of Oklahoma was knowingly executing someone who was innocent. He [Richard Glossip] did get a fair trial and the justice system bent over backwards to give him one.'

The failures at the Department of Corrections had finally sparked a serious debate about the future of the death penalty. A former governor, Brad Henry, agreed to chair an independent commission looking at all aspects of the judicial system. 'The grand jury is currently focused on one small aspect of the capital punishment process ... the execution aspect. But nobody's ever looked at the process from arrest through execution. I think everyone can agree to that, everyone can agree that if we're going to have the death penalty it should be done right and it ought to be done within the confines of both the Oklahoma and the federal constitutions.'

The grand jury report put Richard Glossip back in the news for the first time in months. His attorneys still wanted him to keep a low profile and refuse all interview requests while they put together another legal challenge to his conviction and sentence. It led to several arguments with Don Knight, who hadn't realised that I was still getting regular calls from Richard.

When he found out that Richard had given me a reaction to the grand jury report, he was furious. We exchanged terse emails and he asked me to call him. When I did, he launched into a lecture about how I had 'manipulated Richard just like Bemo and Cook did in his interrogation'. I was shocked at his language. When I defended myself, he talked about the pressure he was under, the burden of having Richard's life in his hands.

There were tensions between Don and Richard too. The attorney was patiently searching for new evidence, while his client was eager for him to rush to court with what had already been gathered. Richard's impatience became particularly acute because he had fallen in love, which made him all the more eager to regain his freedom.

His new girlfriend had been among the many well-wishers who had written to the prison having read about his case. Like a lot of the women who contacted him, she also included a photograph of herself. The letters soon turned to phone calls, and eventually she became a regular visitor. Richard was smitten.

It's not unusual for death-row inmates to attract the attention of female admirers. It's a phenomenon that I can't quite understand, but when I interviewed the woman by phone, she seemed very level-headed. She was also resourceful and determined to play her part in campaigning for Richard. On one occasion she wanted to ensure that Governor Mary Fallin read a letter she had written in support of Richard, so she sent it along with a $300 bouquet of flowers.

But there was a downside to this relationship. They could talk on the phone and they could meet, but thick glass and metal bars separated them. They could not touch, let alone consummate their relationship. Richard told me it was driving him crazy. It made him all the more determined to win his freedom, but it also made him impatient. After nineteen years in which he had become accustomed to the monotony of prison life, he now had the prospect, however remote, of an exoneration and a new life. He could not bear to wait.

I've agreed not to name the woman, because the relationship did not last. She says she was given the impression that Richard could be released from prison within a short period of time. But there was no chance of that happening. Arguments between them became more frequent, and the relationship disintegrated.

Richard's potential path to freedom was long and uncharted and his attorneys still hadn't formally begun a new appeal. Time was a precious commodity when there were only days to go before an execution. Now they were making use of the weeks and months to gather new information. They knew that they probably had only one more shot in court, and they wanted to make it count. They wouldn't do it until they were ready, or until they had no choice because the state named a new execution date. But the Oklahoma authorities were taking their time, unwilling to resume executions until they were confident they had the drugs and detailed new procedures in place to avoid another catastrophic mistake.

CHAPTER 22

Trumped

December 2016

The rain was falling heavily and Unit H of Oklahoma State Penitentiary was looking bleaker than ever. I had returned to visit Richard Glossip for the first time in more than a year. Previous attempts to see him had been thwarted by prison bureaucracy. I'd been told I needed to resubmit an application to visit and had sent the necessary forms in June. But for months, every time I phoned, I was told the paperwork had not been processed. It meant I wasn't able to visit him as planned on 30 September, the anniversary of his closest brush with death. Finally I had to ask the Department of Corrections press officer, Terri Watkins, to intervene, even though it wasn't her job. She got the visit approved.

I handed my ID to the prison guard and explained who I was there to see. He made a phone call while his colleague gave me a half-hearted body search. He then tried to open the locked door giving access to the visiting area, but had the wrong key. It is a low-paid, unskilled job, and the Department of Corrections appeared to be finding it difficult to recruit staff who were fully motivated. No wonder the DOC had been heavily criticised for the way it handled procedures.

After a thirty-minute wait, Richard was finally escorted into one of the four cubicles and I took a seat at the window in front of him. As his handcuffs were removed, I was stunned at how well he looked. He was now fifty-three years old but looked a decade younger, despite having been in prison for coming up to twenty years. When we'd discussed his appearance on the phone in the immediate aftermath of his last execution date, he'd said he looked gaunt through stress and weight loss. Since then he had put on forty pounds and worked out regularly in his cell to keep fit. I told him I was jealous that he looked healthier than I did. He smiled, and kept smiling for much of the next four hours.

Just like on my first visit, it was difficult to hear him because of the noise of the air-conditioning system. I pressed my body so close to the window ledge between us that the following day I discovered that my chest was bruised. It was a relief to re-establish our relationship face to face. Several months earlier, it had almost broken down after a row. He knew that I was writing a book about his case and had been eager to cooperate, but I was on holiday and out of contact when news of the book's publication was announced. Richard was angry and felt he hadn't been kept informed, and threatened to withdraw his cooperation.

It was all a misunderstanding that was resolved when I returned from holiday and was able to speak to him on the phone, but it made me even more anxious to return to Oklahoma to see him in person. Isolation in a cell and being cut off from the outside world can magnify problems out of all proportion until communication is restored.

It had been a difficult few months for those opposed to capital punishment. Abolitionists who thought the death penalty was in terminal decline were given a harsh reality check by voters in Oklahoma, Nebraska and California. While most people were focused on the bitter battle between Donald Trump and Hillary Clinton, election day in the United States isn't just about choosing a president, senators and congressmen. There are dozens of state and local positions to fill, and it's also an opportunity to test opinion on issues such as the legalisation of marijuana.

In Oklahoma, legislators were concerned about the constant attacks on how the death penalty was implemented. They thought the best way to safeguard it was to enshrine it in the state's constitution, specifying that 'Any method of execution shall be allowed, unless prohibited by the United States Constitution.'

Opponents argued that Oklahoma's State Question 776 would make no practical difference because there would still be expensive legal challenges, but the legislation to put it on the ballot paper was carried overwhelmingly, 80–10, in the state's House of Representatives, and unanimously in the Oklahoma Senate. Anthony Sykes, the state senator who introduced the bill, said, 'We have an obligation to the people of Oklahoma to ensure that we can effectively enforce the death penalty. Oklahomans strongly support the death penalty, and it is critical that we protect our ability to enforce it.'

Nebraska's position on the death penalty was also being debated. The state Senate had voted to abolish capital punishment in 2015, but the Republican governor vetoed the bill. The Senate then voted to overturn the veto. So now the issue was being put to the electorate.

Confusingly, California voters were presented with two alternative questions about the same issue on their lengthy ballot paper. Proposition 62 would repeal the death penalty in the state. Proposition 66 would retain it and speed up the appeals process to take inmates more quickly from death row to death chamber. In theory, if voters approved both, they would cancel each other out. In practice, the proposition that received the largest number of votes would be enacted.

California has more than 700 inmates sentenced to death, but hasn't carried out an execution since 2006. In 2012, a previous ballot to abolish the death penalty failed, but the sheer numbers of prisoners waiting to die, the shortage of lethal-injection drugs, and a clogged-up appeals system have effectively brought the process to a standstill. The decade without any executions means that most of those at the top of the list are old men in their sixties and seventies.

On election night, I was in Florida reporting on how the crucial swing state had voted in the presidential election, and was watching the results come in at a party for Republicans in Tampa. As they celebrated a Trump victory, I was also keeping an eye on how the death-penalty ballots were going. It was a bad night for liberals.

Oklahoma voted two-to-one in favour of putting capital punishment in the state constitution. Despite all the problems that had been exposed in recent executions, 942,504 people supported the death penalty, 66 per cent of those who voted. Sixty per cent of Nebraska voters were in favour of bringing back executions; in California, the results were much closer, but similarly disheartening for abolitionists. Five million people in the biggest state in the Union wanted to keep the death penalty. Slightly fewer supported the idea of speeding up the execution process, but Proposition 66 was carried with just under 51 per cent of votes cast.

The election of Donald Trump was also a crushing blow to the optimists who thought that another Democratic president would help shape a Supreme Court that would rule the death penalty unconstitutional. If Hillary Clinton had won, she would have had the chance to choose at least one new liberal justice to tilt the balance of the court. The future of the death penalty was not an election issue. Although the Democratic National Convention had backed abolition, Hillary Clinton was conflicted, saying she still supported it in certain circumstances, but she'd 'breathe a sigh of relief' if it were ruled unconstitutional.

Her husband had previously used the death penalty to his own advantage. When Bill Clinton was running for president in 1992, he travelled back to his home state of Arkansas to oversee an execution. During his time as governor, four men were put to death, and Clinton declined to intervene. He didn't need to be in Arkansas for the execution of Ricky Ray Rector, but it was good politics. It showed he wasn't soft on crime the way other Democrats had been portrayed.

In 2016, his wife tiptoed around the issue. Although no questions were asked about it during her three televised debates with Donald Trump, Mrs Clinton was confronted about her ambivalent stance earlier in the campaign when she was tussling with Senator Bernie Sanders for the Democratic Party's nomination. In a debate in Ohio shown on CNN in March 2016, Ricky Jackson, captioned 'Undecided Voter', rose to explain his background before asking a question.

As a teenager, Jackson had been wrongly convicted of murder and sentenced to death, and had come within two months of his execution date. Ohio abandoned the death penalty, but Jackson served thirty-nine years in jail before he was exonerated. He asked how Hillary Clinton could justify her stance. Clinton criticised the way states had handled murder trials, but said she still wanted the federal government to retain the right to execute terrorists, and highlighted the Oklahoma City bombing and 9/11 as examples.

Donald Trump's support for the death penalty is unequivocal. During the presidential campaign, he advocated mandatory death sentences for police killers, and as far back as 1989 he bought advertising space in New York newspapers in support of executing convicted killers.

After his election, I wrote a story for Sky's website entitled 'Trump a Shot in the Arm for Lethal Injection', and recalled how a year earlier Richard Glossip and I had joked that if Trump was elected, Richard would be better off dead. It seemed preposterous, but it was now reality. The Supreme Court would return to leaning conservative, and Trump could even appoint federal judges who would be more likely to throw out death-penalty appeals.

President Trump also had a direct impact on Richard Glossip's case. Scott Pruitt, Oklahoma's Attorney General, had ensured that Richard's execution was postponed because of the mix-up over the lethal-injection drug. But he would not be the person who would decide when the state's death chamber would reopen for business. Trump appointed him to his Cabinet and he left Oklahoma to become head of the Environmental Protection Agency.

The election of Donald Trump seemed to kill off any remote hopes of abolition. I spoke to Robert Dunham from the Death Penalty Information Center, expecting to find him despondent after the electoral setbacks. But he focused on the positive, pointing out that 2016 had been another year of decline in the number of death sentences and executions.

The first execution of the year had been in Florida, but within days the US Supreme Court ruled the state's system unconstitutional. Currently judges were allowed to have the final say as to whether a convict should be executed, but the court ruled that the decision should rest entirely with juries. Even though the law was later revised, there were further legal challenges and the year ended with Florida executions still on hold. The state of Delaware also ruled its death-penalty law unconstitutional, though it hadn't carried out an execution since 2012.

Georgia bucked the national trend of declining enthusiasm by executing nine men, overtaking Texas as the busiest death chamber. It was the highest number of state killings in Georgia in half a century, and included two men who had waited more than thirty years from the time of their conviction to the time of their death.

Arizona tried to overcome the shortage of lethal-injection drugs by proposing what became dubbed 'do-it-yourself' executions. The authorities said the lawyers of prisoners should be responsible for supplying whatever drugs they found acceptable. Attorneys responded that that was both absurd and illegal.

However, it was Arkansas that stole the headlines for the most controversial use of the death penalty for many years. The state announced plans to kill eight prisoners in eleven days, with four back-to-back executions. Arkansas hadn't put any prisoners to death since 2005, but its Republican governor, Asa Hutchinson, decided to press ahead with what critics dubbed a 'conveyor belt of death'. The reason for the haste was that the state's stock of midazolam had a use-by date of April 2017, so the executions were scheduled to begin immediately after Easter.

There was a flurry of legal challenges, including lawsuits from pharmaceutical companies who were angry that their drugs had been procured using underhand methods and who totally opposed their use in executions. Their complaints were ultimately dismissed, but four of the prisoners received stays of execution for other legal reasons related to their individual cases. The last of the four executions that did go ahead provided more ammunition for those who argued that midazolam was unsuitable. Media witnesses reported that

Kenneth Williams gasped and went into convulsions shortly after the drug flowed into his veins, his body lurched forward on the gurney and he moaned and groaned.

In the middle of the Arkansas controversy, there was encouraging news for those on death row in Oklahoma. The independent commission led by former governor Brad Henry issued its long-awaited report, which recommended that executions in the state should remain on hold until there were significant reforms to the judicial and prison system. It concluded: 'Many of the findings of the commission's investigation were disturbing and led members to question whether the death penalty can be administered in a way that ensures no innocent person is put to death.'

It seemed to me that the commission's report meant there was no way that Oklahoma could set a new execution date for Richard Glossip for the foreseeable future. But within twenty-four hours, the new Attorney General, Mike Hunter, rejected the conclusions and said the state was continuing with its plans to resume executions as soon as it was feasible.

The mixed news across the country demonstrates how the road to abolition is not straightforward. Every few days brings word from a different state of a legal victory or defeat that either advances or diminishes the cause of those who want the practice to be banned permanently. Only a definitive ruling by the US Supreme Court will change that, and Donald Trump's election could postpone that prospect for years.

The occasional setbacks did not seem to depress Richard Glossip. During my visit we talked at length about his reasons for optimism. He was excited about a new documentary being made by a film-maker with a track record of exposing miscarriages of justice. A few years earlier, Joe Berlinger had helped free three men convicted of murder in Arkansas.

When two guards came to the door of his cubicle to tell Richard that visiting time was up, he thanked me for coming and raised his hand to fist-bump me through the glass. Then he squatted down, put his arms behind his back and allowed the guards to reach through the slot in the door to loop handcuffs around his wrists. He smiled as they led him back to his cell.

Killing Richard Glossip was shown on the Investigation Discovery Channel the following April. It brought Richard's case to a new and larger audience. Richard and his attorney Don Knight hoped that it would lead to new witnesses coming forward with information about what had happened at the Best Budget Inn. The documentary featured interviews with Richard, Justin Sneed and retired detective Bob Bemo, who predictably had no regrets about how he had handled the murder investigation. It was a stylish and well-crafted series and I envied the time and resources available to Joe Berlinger to make it.

When I spoke to Joe, he complimented me on the work I had previously done on the case and told me that 'Richard Glossip is the poster child for everything that's wrong with the death penalty and everything that can go wrong in somebody's case.' Yet those who put him on death row remain convinced he is guilty.

During my trip to Oklahoma, I spoke to Connie Smothermon, the Assistant District Attorney who did an effective job in convincing the 2004 jury that Richard Glossip was a murderer who should die. She revealed that she had stayed in touch with the Van Treese family, partly because, by coincidence, she shares a birthday with Barry Van Treese and once a year his relatives send their greetings.

She told me she regarded it as a 'run-of-the-mill murder-for-hire' case that was only worthy of debate because of the death sentence. 'I have never tried a case where I believed there was a doubt about the defendant's guilt. I wouldn't do that.' When I told her about my relationship with the man she'd prosecuted, and said I liked him, she replied, 'He's quite charming. I can see how he pulls people in.'

As a journalist, I am constantly re-examining my view that Richard Glossip has been a victim of a miscarriage of justice. If evidence was presented that conclusively proved he had arranged for Barry Van Treese to be murdered, I would hold my hands up and admit I was wrong.

When people ask me if I think he's innocent, I shake my head. No, I say, he's guilty of being an accessory to murder, by lying and concealing that he either suspected or knew for sure that his boss was dead. I believe his failure to tell the police can be put down to the fact that for months he had turned a blind eye to drug deals and shady characters operating in and around his motel. He didn't benefit; he just panicked and didn't want to be involved. But the murder was a crime he could not and should not have ignored.

I can understand his actions even if I don't agree with them. But I do not believe he paid Justin Sneed to commit murder. The suggested motive is weak. Killing his boss would not have given Richard control of the motel. And if he was indeed a manipulative mastermind as the police suggested, the way the murder was carried out and covered up was anything but smart. Justin Sneed's story is inconsistent. He said initially that he was trying to rob Van Treese, not kill him. I think this is a more likely scenario.

Even if I'm wrong, I believe there is sufficient reasonable doubt to make the death penalty inappropriate. If you believe in capital punishment, at least make absolutely sure the death sentence is reserved for those whose guilt is beyond question. Richard Glossip was not a saint in 1997. But over the past two years he's become my friend, and I am prepared to stand by my verdict.

Not guilty.

EPILOGUE

September 2017

When people asked me 'How's Richard Glossip doing?' I could usually give them a quick and generic answer. 'He's fine, considering…' I would tell them, and update them on the last time we spoke.

Sadly, I cannot do that any longer.

Richard Glossip survived another year on death row but our friendship did not. My messages to him, urging him to call me, went unanswered.

Richard became increasingly irritated by the idea that I was publishing a book about his case. Although he had supported and cooperated fully when I began writing it, in later months he told me he was trying to write and publish his own book. I encouraged him to do so, and tried to reassure him that the story I would be telling had a much wider perspective than his.

I never sought Richard's formal endorsement of this book; I always wanted to retain my independence, free to write whatever I wanted. But I did want to maintain my friendship with him and I tried to resolve our differences.

I asked Kim Van Atta to mediate, and he did so, urging Richard to see my book as a very positive development in telling his story. But Richard then became annoyed that his closest confidante was taking my side, rather than his. He blamed me for damaging their friendship.

All of this information was relayed to me by Richard's new best friend, a young British law graduate who had written a dissertation about his case, and who had come to know his story through my reporting. She later worked pro bono on several death penalty cases in Texas and visited Richard in prison. She became his most trusted ally, and was a useful intermediary for me for more than a year. She has asked not to be identified.

After becoming so close to him in 2015, I was desperately sad that my relationship with Richard Glossip should end in this way. However, to allow him to dictate the style and content of this book would be wrong. I had become an advocate for his case over many months, but I could not give up my editorial independence.

Several friends asked me if our arguments made me re-evaluate my belief that Richard is not guilty of murder. The answer is no. I still believe he was not responsible for the murder of Barry Van Treese. I do believe that the three execution attempts, particularly the last one, have had a profound impact on Richard's mental health. A psychiatrist who has visited him in prison believes he is suffering from post-traumatic stress disorder. I am not surprised given what he has endured. Trivial matters can become major problems in the mind of someone locked up for so long, with so much time on his hands. Problems fester and grow in magnitude, fuelled by isolation.

I sought the advice of Sister Helen Prejean who reassured me that it was not unusual for death row prisoners to react in this way. She called it the 'caged-animal syndrome' and said that many fine lawyers were fired by their clients for no reason, just because the prisoner needed to lash out at someone. Sister Helen told me to take consolation from having played a part in saving Richard's life in 2015.

My final telephone conversation with Richard, like so many others, was slightly surreal. I was standing at the graveside of the Sinn Féin politician and former IRA commander Martin McGuinness, as I was reporting on his funeral. The cortège was making its way through his home city of Derry, and I was awaiting its arrival.

My phone emitted the tell-tale ringtone of a Skype call from Oklahoma State Penitentiary. I moved to find a quiet spot in the cemetery to talk to Richard. We had argued during our previous conversation a few days earlier, but in this call he was calm and friendly, and it felt as if we had put our differences aside. I told him to keep ringing me and we would discuss any problems. He never did.

When the conversation ended, I walked past dozens of headstones marking the graves of IRA members, many of whom had murdered and maimed my fellow citizens during the political and sectarian violence of my youth. How strange that I grew up surrounded by killers, but the convicted murderer I came to know best lives thousands of miles away, and did not kill anyone.

Capital punishment in America continues to survive, despite the obstacles placed in its path by abolitionists. In August 2017 Florida resumed executions after an eighteen month hiatus, using an untried alternative to the anaesthetic midazolam called etomidate. Potassium acetate completed their lethal injection cocktail. That's right, the same drug which was wrongly supplied to kill Richard Glossip, and which caused his execution to be postponed, has now been legitimised in Florida. After all, Oklahoma accidentally proved it was effective when prison officials mistakenly used it on Charles Warner in January 2015.

If Richard Glossip is executed, it's now highly unlikely that I will be there to witness it. I cannot imagine that he will nominate me again as one his chosen friends. In some ways I am relieved that I will not have to watch a man being put to death, but my greatest wish is that neither of us will ever see the inside of the Oklahoma death chamber.

ABOUT THE SOURCES

The vast majority of the interviews in this book were conducted face to face in Oklahoma, Washington DC and New York between January 2015 and December 2016.

The exception of course is Richard Glossip. In our two meetings at Oklahoma State Penitentiary I was not permitted to have a pen and paper to make notes, so all our interviews were conducted over the telephone. I've only quoted from conversations that I recorded.

Interviews with some of the main characters, such as Sister Helen Prejean, Don Knight and Kim Van Atta, were supplemented by later phone interviews. The only other person I interviewed on the phone but did not meet in person is prosecutor Connie Smothermon.

The campaign against the death penalty in the USA is fought on a daily basis in more than a dozen states, and I'm indebted to those campaigners who have drawn my attention to developments reported in their local media. There are too many stories to mention, but when I have quoted articles directly, I have credited the newspaper or TV network concerned.

Some court documents and other important publications are available online in their original form, and I have endeavoured to provide links to those.

The official court transcripts of Richard Glossip's trials were provided by his lawyers. Other evidence from those trials is publicly available for inspection, but not online.

Successful appeal 2001
http://law.justia.com/cases/oklahoma/court-of-appeals-criminal/2001/264135.html

Unsuccessful appeal 2007
http://caselaw.findlaw.com/ok-court-of-criminal-appeals/1466730.html

Unsuccessful federal appeal 2013
https://www.ca10.uscourts.gov/opinions/10/10-6244.pdf

Newspaper report on murder
http://newsok.com/article/2568336

Newspaper report on opening day of Trial 1
http://newsok.com/article/2615465

Newspaper report on conviction in Trial 1
http://newsok.com/article/2616165

Newspaper report on death sentence in Trial 1
http://newsok.com/article/2616268

Newspaper report on death sentence after Trial 2
http://newsok.com/article/1905526

Supreme Court oral argument, Glossip v. Gross
https://www.supremecourt.gov/oral_arguments/argument_transcripts/14-7955_1b72.pdf

Supreme Court opinion, Glossip v. Gross
https://www.supremecourt.gov/opinions/14pdf/14-7955_aplc.pdf

Grand Jury report into Richard Glossip botched execution attempt

https://www.ok.gov/oag/documents/MCGJ%20-%20 Interim%20Report%205-19-16.pdf

Official report into Clayton Lockett botched execution
https://deathpenaltyinfo.org/documents/ LockettInvestigationReport.pdf

Oklahoma Independent Commission on Death Penalty Report
https://drive.google.com/file/d/0B-Vtm7xVJVWONmdNMmM5bzk3Qnc/view

ACKNOWLEDGMENTS

My sincere thanks go to everyone who has contributed to me being able to tell this extraordinary story, including attorneys and state officials in Oklahoma. Sometimes they were helpful and sometimes they were obstructive but they were just doing their jobs.

In particular I would like to thank Phil Cross and Kim Van Atta who, from the moment I first contacted them, were instantly keen to help a British guy they'd never heard of.

Sister Helen Prejean encouraged my reporting every step of the way, and persuaded Susan Sarandon to give my story some much-needed publicity.

John Ryley and Sarah Whitehead at Sky News were fascinated by the story and gave me the time and resources I needed to travel to Oklahoma. Sarah came up with the idea of telling the story through a series of podcasts, which were brilliantly put together by Dave Terris and Matt Steele.

Cameramen Dickon Mager, Duncan Sharpe and Jake Britton, plus Sky's Washington bureau chief Tim Gallagher, all helped turn a tale with few pictures into a dramatic television story.

My family patiently put up with me regularly disappearing to America, or to my study to write.

My literary agent Kate Shaw, and Mike Harpley from Atlantic Books believed this was a story which demanded to be told. Thanks also to Margaret Stead, Susannah Hamilton and Jane Selley for helping the book take shape. My lifelong friend Steve Bailie was the first to realise that sometimes the truth is more powerful than fiction, and turned my words into a screenplay.

And finally to Richard Glossip, who trusted me with his story. I've always tried to be objective while telling his story. It led to some disagreements between us. But if I was locked up in a concrete cell for twenty years, spending most of the day alone, waiting to be exonerated for a crime I did not commit, fearing death at the hands of the state, then I'd get angry too, and struggle to trust anyone. I find it incredible that Richard Glossip still smiles and tries to be positive every day. I hope one day he is vindicated.

Index